T0330171

Divergences in Productivity Between Europe and the United States

IFO ECONOMIC POLICY

The Ifo Institute for Economic Research at the University of Munich is one of the leading economic research institutes in Germany. Its legal form is that of a private, independent non-profit association. It closely co-operates with the Center for Economic Studies (CES) at the University of Munich, and members of the international CESifo Research Network. Together, the CESifo group forms a research group unique in Europe in the area of economic research.

The *Ifo Economic Policy* series provides a platform for publishing studies of the Ifo Institute and its collaborators that are of interest for an international audience and deal with issues in economic policy which are topical not only in Germany but in the whole of Europe or even on a global level. The series addresses students, scholars in the economics discipline and related fields as well as policymakers and consultants.

Titles in the series include:

Divergences in Productivity Between Europe and the United States

Measuring and Explaining Productivity Gaps Between Developed Countries

Edited by

Gilbert Cette

Director of Macroeconomic Analysis and Forecasting, Banque de France and Professor of Economics at the University of Aix-Marseille II, France

Michel Fouquin

Deputy Director, Centre d'Etudes Prospectives et d'Informations Internationales (CEPII), France

Hans-Werner Sinn

President, Ifo Institute for Economic Research, Professor of Economics and Public Finance and Director, Center for Economic Studies, University of Munich, Germany

IFO ECONOMIC POLICY

Edward Elgar
Cheltenham, UK • Northampton, MA, USA

Published by
Edward Elgar Publishing Limited
Glensanda House
Montpellier Parade
Cheltenham
Glos GL50 1UA
UK

Edward Elgar Publishing, Inc.
William Pratt House
9 Dewey Court
Northampton
Massachusetts 01060
USA

A catalogue record for this book is available from the British Library

Library of Congress Cataloguing in Publication Data

Divergences in productivity between Europe and the United States : measuring and explaining productivity gaps between developed countries / edited by Gilbert Cette, Michel Fouquin, Hans-Werner Sinn.
    p. cm.
  Papers from a seminar held at the Royaumont Abbey on 22 and 23 March 2004, and organized by the Banque de France, CEPII, and the Ifo Institute for Economic Research at the University of Munich.
  Includes bibliographical references and index.
  1. Industrial productivity–Europe–Congresses. 2. Industrial productivity–United States–Congresses. 3. Industrial productivity–Japan–Congresses. 4. Industrial productivity–Measurement–Statistical methods–Congresses. 5. Information technology–Economic aspects–Congresses. I. Cette, Gilbert. II. Fouquin, Michel. III. Sinn, Hans-Werner.
  HC400.I52D58 2007
  338'.06–dc22

2007030273

ISBN 978 1 84720 641 1
Printed and bound in Great Britain by MPG Books Ltd, Bodmin, Cornwall

Contents

Figures

Tables

Contributors

Nadim Ahmad, OECD

Bart van Ark, University of Groningen

Nicolas Belorgey, Banque de France

Gilbert Cette, Macroeconomic Analysis and Forecasting, Banque de France

Theo Eicher, University of Washington

Michel Fouquin, Deputy Director, CEPII

Thomas Fuchs, Human Capital and Innovation, Ifo Institute

Robert Inklaar, University of Groningen

Dale W. Jorgenson, Harvard University

Yusuf Kocogluc, University of Aix-Marseille II

Rémy Lecat, Banque de France

François Lequiller, OECD

Jacques Mairesse, CREST-INSEE

Pascal Marianna, OECD

Tristan-Pierre Maury, Banque de France

Johanna Melka, CEPII

Kazuyuki Motohashi, University of Tokyo

Laurence Nayman, CEPII

Marcin Piatkowski, Transformation, Integration and Globalization
    Economic Research (TIGER), IMF

Dirk Pilat, OECD

Paul Schreyer, OECD

Bertrand Pluyaud, Banque de France

Hans-Werner Sinn, President, Ifo Institute

Marcel P. Timmer, University of Groningen

Hans-Günther Vieweg, Industry Branch Research, Ifo Institute

Anita Wölfl, OECD

Series Foreword

The Ifo Institute for Economic Research was established in 1949 and is now one of the leading economic research institutes in Germany. It is a private, independent, non-profit institution that is financed, according to Article 91b of the German Constitution, by the German federal government and the German states as well as by project-related funding from various sources. Its mission is to act as an internationally oriented centre of empirical economic research and as a provider of services for the research community, private businesses, the public administration and the general public by generating data and information regarding economic development at the national and international level, thus stimulating the debate on economic policy in Germany and Europe. Based on close linkages and a lively co-operation, the Ifo Institute was officially proclaimed an institute at the University of Munich in 2002. In many other ways, the institute has established an exchange of ideas and persons with research institutions, universities and researchers throughout the world.

The 'Ifo Economic Policy' series published with Edward Elgar Publishing Ltd is meant to bring work emerging from Ifo research and from our research co-operations to the attention of an international audience of policy-makers, academics and business people. The studies included in this series are either international in their themes, dealing with important aspects of economic development and institutional design that are looked at in a comparative fashion, or are of relevance at a supra-national level. Or, alternatively, even if the contributions are to some extent focused on the economic situation and economic policy in Germany or Europe, they are considered to be of broader interest, for instance, because the set of problems to be dealt with as well as potential solutions for these problems are basically similar elsewhere. In any case, with the initiation of this book series, we want to contribute to establishing a joint, international forum for the discussion of results of applied research on economic policy issues that are topical around the world.

Hans-Werner Sinn, President, Ifo Institute

Introduction: Measuring and Explaining Productivity Gaps Between Developed Countries

Gilbert Cette, Michel Fouquin and Hans-Werner Sinn

In the 1990s, labour productivity growth has accelerated in the United States while it has slowed in the other industrialised countries, reversing a three decade long tendency of convergence. The Banque de France, CEPII and the Ifo Institute for Economic Research at the University of Munich joined their efforts to organise a seminar at the Royaumont Abbey on 22 and 23 March 2004, with the purpose to compare explanations of the gaps in productivity growth rates between the United States and other industrialised countries.

At this seminar, some forty economists from Europe, the US, and Japan made presentations and discussed the papers collected in this volume. The discussions mainly focused on four themes. The first theme, changes in productivity trends over time, enabled participants to identify the methodological and statistical problems involved in measuring productivity and making comparisons between countries. The other three themes were discussed with due consideration for the resulting uncertainties. These three themes were: the role of factors of production in changing trends, with particular emphasis on information and communication technology (ICT); international comparisons and identifying the sources of gaps between countries; and, last, seeking the determining factors of productivity gains.

MEASUREMENT ISSUES

Comparing Labour Productivity Growth in the OECD Area

The paper presented by François Lequiller (chapter 1) dealt with the uncertainties surrounding productivity measurement. The authors point out protracted measurement differences between Europe and the United States, but find that these differences do not affect the conclusion that Europe's productivity level stopped catching up to America's. Some of these differences are now being addressed. They include GDP measurements that make different splits between intermediate and final consumption with regard to military expenditure, financial services and software expenditure. These three differences tend to increase American GDP compared to European Union GDP; however, the impact in terms of productivity growth is less significant and works in different directions. Another problem currently being solved relates to the methods for calculating GDP deflators, which rely to varying degrees on hedonic pricing in Europe, whereas chained price indices are used more systematically in the United States. This measurement difference has a limited impact on productivity growth. The differences concern the measurement of financial services and non-market services. Measurement of labour input preferably uses the aggregate number of hours worked, with some adjustment for labour quality. This raises problems that relate more to the quality of source data than methodology and give rise to specific bias adjustments for each data source, such as employer surveys, employee surveys and administrative data sources.

Nicholas Oulton (London School of Economics) was the discussant for this paper. He highlighted the impact that software expenditure measurement problems have on productivity estimates in the United Kingdom. He noted that the System of National Accounts underestimates software investment by between 3 and 10 times, which would mean that GDP growth had been understated by at least 0.16 percentage points per annum between 1994 and 1998. He also pointed out that there are still significant differences between European countries. For example, the United Kingdom has been using a measurement method for non-market services output that is based on direct observation of output volumes, in contrast to other countries, where productivity growth is assumed to be zero. The general discussion highlighted the importance of establishing a link between per capita GDP and productivity measurements in order to determine the impact that differences in employment rates have on such measurements.

The Breaks in Per Capita Productivity: Trends

Bertrand Pluyaud presented a paper related to the research of breaks in productivity growth. It offers a reinterpretation of the main stylised developments in productivity per employee in the leading industrialised countries in the twentieth century using the method for sequential estimation of break dates developed by Bai and Perron (1998). The paper upholds the 'one bigwave' description offered by Gordon (1999), which states that the American productivity growth rate increased until the nineteen-sixties and then slowed.

It also confirms that the European and Japanese economies started catching up to America's productivity growth in the second half of the twentieth century and that labour productivity growth slowed down in Europe and Japan in the nineteen-nineties, in contrast to faster productivity growth in the United States during the same period. The discussant was Neale Kennedy (European Central Bank). He pointed out that the paper provides solid statistical evidence for the economic phenomena that have often been observed using somewhat subjective approaches. However, the Bai and Perron method cannot provide a clear-cut statement on productivity growth since the early nineteen-nineties, because most of the breaks shown in more recent years were less significant than earlier breaks. The need for long data series for statistical testing also meant that the choice of data sources was limited. This made it difficult to extend the analysis to total factor productivity series or hourly productivity series. The general discussion focused on the United Kingdom, where only one slightly significant break in the productivity growth trend was observed around the oil shock period. Bertrand Pluyaud said that this finding seems to be in line with those of Card and Freeman (2002) in their work on the United Kingdom.

The Spread of ICT and Potential Output Growth

The emergence and diffusion of information and communication technology (ICT) resulted in lasting productivity gains that were sustained by rapid product improvements. The paper was presented by Gilbert Cette, who shows that this increase is likely to give a lasting boost to the potential output growth rate through ICT capital deepening and gains in total factor productivity. It will also provide a transitory boost as a result of the lag with which wages adjust to productivity gains. Empirical measurements of both types of impact that the diffusion of ICT has on potential output (compared to a theoretical extreme situation in which there is no ICT) are bound to be very tenuous. The orders of magnitude that these methods produce show that the medium-to-long-term impact could be substantial. Potential output growth could rise by some two percentage points in the United States and by one percentage point in France. The empirical evidence does not seem to substantiate the shorter-lived short-to-medium-term effect that is often mentioned in the literature. The discussant was Werner Roeger (European Commission). He said that it would be worthwhile to expand the analysis to a less constrained production function than a Cobb-Douglas function, suggesting, for example, a constant elasticity of substitution function, with a further distinction between skilled and unskilled labour components. With regard to the short-term analysis, the discussant stressed that the inertia effects in price adjustment might explain the apparent overindexation of wages with respect to productivity gains in the United States between 1997 and 2000. In fact, the expected wage adjustment lag frequently commented on in the literature may have been observed in earlier years. During the general discussion, some participants stressed the value of modelling the economy with several sectors, with one sector producing the ICT used by the other sectors.

INTERNATIONAL COMPARISONS

ICT and Europe's Productivity Performance: Industry-Level Growth Account Comparisons with the United States

Growth accounts at the macro-economic level, followed by industry-level growth accounts, help to explain the divergences between four European countries (Germany, France, Netherlands and United Kingdom) and the United States from 1979 to 2000. Marcel Timmer presented the paper, which notes that the differences in hourly productivity growth between Europe and the United States between 1995 and 2000 can mainly be attributed to differences in ICT and non-ICT capital deepening, since there are virtually no differences in the contributions of labour quality and total factor productivity. The growth of ICT capital is equivalent in Europe and in the United States. On the other hand, the share of ICT in aggregate capital compensation, which is used to weight capital services in the decomposition, was much higher in the United States than it was in Europe from 1995 to 2000 in all of the industries considered. This explains the difference in the contributions that ICT makes to hourly productivity growth in Europe and in the United States. However, there are differences between industries. The differences in ICT capital deepening in wholesale and retail trade are minimal, but ICT capital deepening in the banking sector was much more rapid in the United States from 1995 to 2000, and it was much more rapid in business services in Europe in both periods considered (1979–1995 and 1995–2000). One of the most plausible explanations for the differences in capital deepening could be relative factor prices, i.e. the relative unit compensation rates of labour and ICT and non-ICT capital.

The discussant was Michel Fouquin (CEPII). He thanked the authors for having made their database available to the public. However, he questioned the use of industry-level data for calculating total factor productivity. Working with these data requires a series of delicate estimates to decompose the figures by industry and to determine investment and capital stock. The debate also evoked the problem of determining the impact of agency temping labour, which is counted as services employment, and the output of this labour, which is counted as manufacturing output. The discussant pointed out that the authors have not provided much explanation of how productivity levels are calculated at the branch level. They do not explain, for example, if the purchasing power parities that they use in their 'EU-4' are calculated at the industry level or the country level. The discussant also regretted that the link between compensation of labour and labour productivity was not explained in greater detail. In the general discussion, it was mentioned that the picture would be very different if Italy and Spain were included in the EU countries considered.

Growth Patterns in the OECD Area: Evidence from the Aggregate, Industry and Firm Level

Dirk Pilat offered a macro-economic and industry-level analysis of differences in productivity growth between OECD countries. There are still substantial differences between countries. Labour and product markets are structurally less rigid in the United States, which explains the very high level of investment there, and, to a lesser extent in Canada, Australia and the Netherlands. These countries feature lower set-up costs, more flexible and responsive organisational set-ups, more highly qualified personnel, more flexible labour legislation, keener competition and less regulation, which all provide incentives for businesses to invest in new technology. Dirk Pilat also explained differences in total factor productivity growth in terms of competition between firms in the same market, as measured by entries and exits of firms from the market. Business demographics seem to show that the American market is much more dynamic than the European market. This means that total factor productivity growth in the United States could be enhanced by the fact that American legislation on starting up businesses is more flexible than European legislation. Dirk Pilat showed that the strong growth of total factor productivity seen in the United States is also due to an acceleration in some ICT-using service industries, such as wholesale and retail trade, finance and insurance. The discussant was Sally Srinivasan (Bank of England). She highlighted the fragility of the empirical findings by comparing United Kingdom data published by the Bank of England with Dirk Pilat's data. This comparison shows big differences in ICT capital services. She also highlighted the problems accounting for currency effects when compiling ICT price indices for European countries on the basis of indices compiled in the United States.

Information Technology and the G7 Countries

The growth of hourly labour productivity accelerated in the United States and Canada in 1989–1995 and 1995–2001, but it slowed down in the other G7 countries (Germany, France, Italy, Japan and the United Kingdom) over the same period. Dale Jorgenson's paper on the G7 countries illustrated the divergences in growth and the contributions of labour and capital by using harmonised prices compiled according to Paul Schreyer's method. The author does this to show that the differences in productivity growth between the United States, on one side, and the European countries, Canada and Japan, on the other side, mainly concern the contribution of non-ICT investment. Very rapid growth of the ICT contribution was observed in all countries from 1980 to 2001, especially during the last six years.

However, there were substantial differences between countries. On the other hand, only the United States showed more rapid growth of the contribution of accumulated non-ICT capital. Furthermore, the contribution that labour quality makes to hourly productivity growth followed a fairly similar pattern in all countries, with slower growth in 1989–1995 and 1995–2001. Dale Jorgenson concluded by showing that total factor productivity growth accelerated greatly in ICT-producing industries in all G7 countries. It outpaced total factor productivity growth in all other sectors,with the exception of Canada.

The discussant was Jacques Mairesse (CREST). He questioned the nature of total factor productivity, which can be seen as a residual or the reflection of technological progress. Ideally, shouldn't TFP be nil, if the production function is perfectly specified and all of the factors measured properly? He also stressed the partially conventional and somewhat approximate nature of the findings, stemming from the strong economic assumptions underlying growth accounting and how it contrasted with the inevitable weaknesses of the data used. For example, is the weighting of employment by sex, age groups and education in the labour quality index really reliable? Finally, he regretted the fact that research and development investment and its externalities are not taken explicitly into account in the standard growth accounting approaches.

Productivity, Innovation and ICT in Old and New Europe

Bart van Ark presented a revised version of the paper written for this seminar. Productivity in Central and Eastern European Countries (CEEC) seems to be converging with that of European Union countries, but improved labour productivity accounts for much of the convergence, as the old production structures in CEEC countries disappear. The authors compare labour productivity patterns in ICT producing and using industries and in other industries. Compared to EU countries, ICT-using industries make a larger contribution to productivity gains in the CEEC countries. According to the authors, this observation is characteristic of a first step in the convergence process; the CEEC countries make rapid productivity gains in specific and limited industries as a result of technology transfers. The effects wear off as these countries finish restructuring their economies. To build on these gains in the second phase of convergence with the EU countries, productivity gains will have to be more rapid in other industries, particularly in the service industries. This will require other improvements in job training and reorganisation of businesses.

Jean-Luc Schneider (French Ministry of Finance) was the discussant. He stressed the fact that the CEEC countries are indeed catching up, in strictly accounting terms. Their growth is faster than that of the 15 EU countries and ICT makes a positive contribution to this growth. There is less certainty about the assumption that ICT makes a greater contribution to growth in the CEEC countries than it does in the 15 EU countries. Bart van Ark's findings seem to point to the opposite conclusion. ICT does not seem to make a positive contribution to closing the productivity gaps between CEEC and EU countries, since productivity gains in CEEC countries still stem primarily from restructuring and job cuts. This means that the issue of technological specialisation is still an open question in these countries. For the time being, the CEEC countries are more similar to Greece than they are to Ireland. This suggests that it could take as long as thirty or so years for these countries to end the catching up process.

COUNTRY FOCUS

Outsourcing and Productivity Growth: Sectoral Evidence from Germany

Thomas Fuchs presented the next paper, which relies on a large industry-level productivity database for Germany compiled by IFO. The database is used for output accounting in order to determine the sources of productivity growth between 1993 and 2001. The authors contend that sectoral value added cannot be used as a proxy for gross output, because it would lead to overstated total factor productivity among other problems. The value added and output TFP measurements diverge, as the proportion of imported inputs used in production increases. International outsourcing explains the divergence between output growth and value added growth, as well as the divergence between output and value added TFP measurements, since the proportion of imported inputs in German output has risen substantially.

Soledad Nuñez (Bank of Spain) was the discussant. She pointed out that the divergence between value added and output productivity measurements could also stem from other sources, such as economies of scale. The authors' hypothesis would only hold if there were constant returns to scale. In the case of Spain, which Soledad Nuñez has analysed, only three sectors show economies of scale, which tempers the severity of this criticism.

Economic Growth of Japan and the United States in the Information Age

Kazuyuki Motohashi compared Japanese and US performances. This is done by means of a GDP adjustment of some JPY 20,000 billion (EUR 150 billion), which is about 3.7 per cent of the adjusted GDP. The standard growth accounting approach and a production possibility frontier approach are then used to analyse growth components. Japan stopped catching up with the United States at the end of the nineteen-nineties. According to the authors, this was not due to smaller TFP gains, since they were more rapid in Japan than in the United States. Nor was it due to differences in the contribution that ICT capital makes to growth, which is nearly the same in both countries. Instead, it was due to slower growth of labour quality and slower non-ICT capital deepening. These findings seem to be in line with the findings in the available literature on the subject, even though this literature often relies on old accounting methods from SNA 68, except in the case of the contribution that TFP makes to Japanese growth. This contribution is usually estimated to be much smaller.

Dirk Pilat (OECD) was the discussant. He stressed that it was necessary to provide a very careful description of the data sources and how they were put together (the devil is in the detail). The general discussion that followed evoked the links with the paper that Dale Jorgenson presented earlier. This paper supported his idea that the discontinuation of the catching-up process with the United States does not come from differences in TFP gains, but from differences in the quantities of capital and labour inputs.

DETERMINANTS

Labour Quality and Skill-Biased Technological Change in France

Both authors presented a paper which aims to describe changes in labour in France from 1982 to 2001. The authors explain the change in the share of hours worked (shift share) with a greater share for younger, more educated workers and a larger proportion of women. The hiring of college-educated workers has also led to a big improvement in labour quality. An industry-level breakdown of hours worked by educational attainment shows that ICT producing and using industries, which are already major employers of college graduates, are the ones where the proportion of college-educated employees is increasing most rapidly. Technological change could therefore offer an industry-level bias in favour of college-educated workers. Using industry-level data, the authors show that R&D spending and ICT capital accumulation have a significant positive impact on the share of aggregate payroll for college-educated employees. When a distinction is made between the impact of technological change on the payroll share of college-educated workers in ICT-producing industries and other industries, we see that this effect is particularly pronounced in ICT-producing industries, especially between 1996 and 2001. A breakdown of different categories of workers by educational attainment also shows that ICT has had the biggest impact on workers holding a Baccalaureate diploma in ICT producing industries. In other industries, ICT has had the biggest impact on workers with undergraduate degrees.

Pierre Biscourp (INSEE) was the discussant. He pointed out that the hourly wage of college-educated workers, compared to that of other workers could be included in the econometric regression in place of the dummy time variable, even though this could give rise to endogeneity problems. He laid particular emphasis on the interpretation of the findings. He felt that it was difficult to accept the thesis of technological bias because the findings may be skewed as a result of endogeneity problems.

Determinants of Productivity Per Employee: An Empirical Estimation Using Panel Data

Nicolas Belorgey and Rémy Lecat presented a paper which deals with the determinants of productivity per employee in two ways. It first estimates determinants of productivity change in a panel of twenty-five industrial countries during the nineteen-nineties, using the generalised method of moments. It then estimates determinants of productivity level for a broad sample of 77 countries and a narrower sample of 49 countries in 2000, in order to get a clearer picture of the impact of ICT. Productivity changes and levels seem to be positive functions of ICT spending and negative functions of the employment rate, since employment is concentrated on the most productive workers. The change in productivity per employee seems to be significantly linked to hours worked, even though the returns to the latter are decreasing. Productivity levels seem to be positively correlated to public infrastructures, education and price stability. The importance of ICT can be gauged either by the share of ICT-producing industries, or by their diffusion in the economy, which also has a significant influence on productivity.

Christopher Gust (Federal Reserve Bank of Washington) was the discussant. He started by underlining the contribution made by using the generalised method of moments. He then pointed out that the negative relationship between the employment rate and productivity has become increasingly pronounced, which opens up new avenues of research. The general discussion evoked the potential impact that structural rigidities have on productivity, which some OECD indicators are attempting to formalise.

CONCLUSIONS OF THE SEMINAR

The seminar concluded with a summary presented by Jacques Mairesse, Nicholas Oulton and Hans-Werner Sinn. Jacques Mairesse said that the comparison of productivity differences between the United States and Europe is a delicate task because of the 'fragility' of macroeconomic databases (especially when comparing levels). He then reviewed the avenues of research currently open to us: work on enterprise data, consideration of research and development externalities, introducing economies of scale that are not constant and labour and product market inefficiencies, and dynamic analysis. According to Jacques Mairesse, an analysis of enterprise data could help answer several questions. Why do established American firms show much more rapid growth than European firms do? Are they better prepared? Is the economic, financial and regulatory environment more favourable for their growth? Jacques Mairesse also pointed out that many of the papers presented at the seminar highlighted the importance of human capital. Organisational change and the complementary nature of capital and labour are some of the factors that can explain divergences in productivity growth between the United States and Europe. These factors now need to be studied using firm-level data. Nicolas Oulton emphasised the importance of new technology prices and their impact on ICT demand. As prices continue to drop, will they sustain demand growth so that the nominal share of ICT in factors of production continues to grow? Since many of the papers presented rely on growth accounting to identify the roles of the factors of production, Hans-Werner Sinn stressed that this approach could, in addition to the problems already mentioned, lead to an error of judgment: the shift from one optimal capital-labour mix to another in response to a change in relative factor costs is more direct and provides the same level of output in the long term. This shift can be sub-optimal, which would create a complex productivity dynamic during the adjustment phase, with a decrease in total factor productivity, followed by an increase. This means that one could draw the wrong conclusion from growth accounting, which assumes that adjustments are always optimal. The increase in total factor productivity could be interpreted as a lasting structural change, when it merely indicates a temporary catching-up phase.

1. Comparing Growth in GDP and Labour Productivity: Measurement Issues

Nadim Ahmad, François Lequiller, Pascal Marianna, Dirk Pilat, Paul Schreyer and Anita Wölfl

Growth and productivity are on the policy agenda in most OECD countries. Recent OECD work has highlighted large diversities in growth and productivity as well as a range of policies that could enhance them (OECD, 2001, 2003a, 2003b). In the United States, Gross Domestic Product (GDP) growth has increased substantially faster than in large European countries or Japan, partly because the US population expanded rapidly during the 1990s. Moreover, estimates of labour productivity growth, measured as GDP per hour worked, suggest that US labour productivity has grown faster than that of some large European Union countries such as Italy and Germany (see Figure 1.1). Also, US GDP per capita has grown more in comparative terms, since strong labour productivity growth was combined with increased labour utilisation over the 1990s, in contrast with several European countries.

This article highlights measurement issues that can affect international comparisons of GDP and productivity growth and therefore the validity of cross-country analysis.[1] These measurement issues do not undermine the strong performance of the United States compared to the large EU countries and Japan for real GDP growth during the period 1995–2002. However, differences in annual average growth of GDP per capita and labour productivity between these countries for the same period are small enough to fall within the range of statistical uncertainty.

1.1 MEASURING NOMINAL GDP

Comparability of nominal GDP is significantly dependent on the use of a common conceptual framework. The current framework is the 1993 version of the international 'System of National Accounts' (SNA), which nearly all OECD member countries now use as the basis of their national accounts. De-

spite this convergence, however, some differences still exist between countries regarding the degree to which the manual has been implemented.[2]

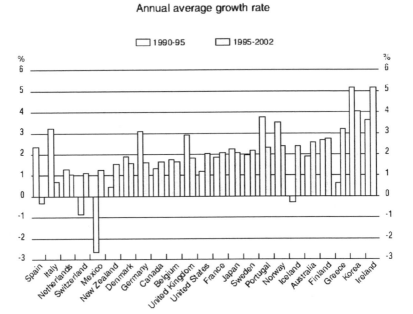

Annual average growth rate

Source: OECD estimates based on the OECD Productivity Database.

Figure 1.1   Growth of GDP per hours worked, 1990–95 and 1995–2002

Military Expenditures

The coverage of government investment in the US National Income and
Product Accounts (NIPA) is wider than that recommended by the SNA, since
it includes expenditures on military equipment that are not considered assets
by the SNA. The other OECD countries strictly follow the SNA in this matter.
As the amount of public investment affects the level of GDP, this results in a
statistical difference in the GDP measurement. Fortunately, the impact on
GDP growth tends to be relatively small. Over the past decade, this methodological difference has only reduced annual US GDP growth by 0.03 per cent
on average. Recent planned increases in US military expenditure may reverse
this effect, however. Convergence on this issue is expected in the next edition
of the SNA, in 2008. In the meantime, the OECD publishes data for the
United States in its Annual National Accounts Database, which adjusts for
this difference.

Financial Intermediation Services

Most banking services are not explicitly charged. Thus, in the SNA, the production of banks is estimated using the difference between interests received and paid, known as 'Financial Intermediation Service Indirectly Measured' (FISIM). All OECD member countries estimate total FISIM. While it is relatively straightforward to estimate FISIM, the key problem is breaking it down between final consumers (households) and intermediate consumers (businesses). Only the former has a direct impact on GDP. In the United States, Canada and Australia, such a breakdown has been estimated in the national accounts for some time, in accordance with the SNA. In Europe and Japan, however, the implementation of a breakdown between final and intermediate consumers has been delayed until 2005.

Before the NIPA was comprehensively revised in December 2003, imputed household consumption of financial services accounted for 2.3 per cent of US GDP compared to zero in Europe and Japan. Fortunately, the impact on GDP growth is limited to less than 0.1 per cent per year, the effect being positive in some years and negative in others. Furthermore, the recent revision of the US accounts has significantly reduced the difference in levels to probably just over 1 per cent of GDP, thus roughly halving the impact on growth. Preliminary estimates suggest that with the implementation of the allocation of FISIM between both sectors in 2005, GDP levels would increase by approximately 1.3 per cent in European countries and by nearly 3 per cent in Japan. With these changes, diversities arising from methodological differences should be mostly eliminated.

Investment in Software

Measurement of software investment is another significant issue in the comparability of GDP. The SNA recommends that software expenditures be treated as investment once the acquisition satisfies conventional asset requirements. When introduced, this change added nearly 2 per cent to GDP for the United States, around 0.7 per cent for Italy and France, 0.5 per cent for the United Kingdom. Doubts on the comparability of these data were raised when comparing 'investment ratios', which are defined as the share of total software expenditures that are recorded as investments. These ratios range from under 4 per cent in the United Kingdom to over 70 per cent in Spain (see Figure 1.2). One would have expected them to be roughly the same across OECD countries.

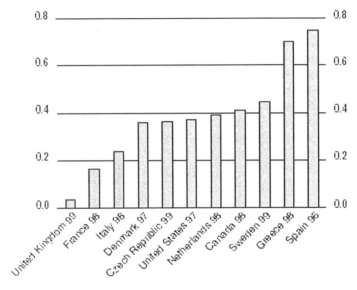

Source: OECD

Figure 1.2   Investment ratio of purchased software

An OECD/Eurostat Task Force established in October 2001 confirmed that different estimation procedures contributed significantly to the differences in software capitalisation rates, and a set of recommendations describing a harmonised method for estimating software was formulated (see Lequiller et al., 2003; Ahmad, 2003). Most of these recommendations eventually will be implemented by countries but until then differences in software and GDP measures will persist.

In practice, National Statistical Offices use one of two distinct methods to estimate software investment. The first derives data from business accounts. The second disregards business accounts, measures the total supply of computer services in an economy and estimates directly the amount of software with asset characteristics. The first approach tends to produce systematically lower estimates of investment than the second. This is mainly because businesses tend to use very prudent criteria when capitalising software, particularly if there are no tax incentives for doing so. Countries using the second approach, such as the United States, had a higher measured investment than countries such as France, the United Kingdom and Japan where statistical methods were more inspired by the first approach. As a result, while the amount of total software expenditures may be more or less similar, the amount of software expenditures recorded as investment, and thus included in GDP, is significantly higher in the United States than in France, the United Kingdom or Japan for purely methodological reasons.

The impact of these methodological differences on GDP growth can be substantial. Figure 1.3 shows the estimated impact on GDP growth in the United States, assuming an investment ratio of 0.04 (which is the one currently used in the United Kingdom), and for the United Kingdom, assuming an investment ratio of 0.4 (which is close to that used in the United States and some other countries). In both cases, the OECD Task Force procedure for own-account production is applied and a number of assumptions are made.

Annual growth rate

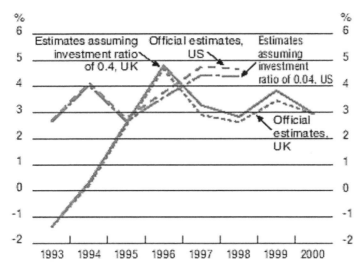

Source: OECD

Figure 1.3   Sensitivity of GDP growth rates to different investment ratios of purchased software

The results show that the impact on UK GDP growth can reach 0.2 per cent, and even 0.4 per cent, in some years. Similar results are likely to occur depending on the size of the investment ratio in each country and the approach used. Changes of between +/-0.25 per cent of GDP should thus be expected. However, the variations in growth arising from the different methodologies is unlikely to be as large from 2000 onwards, since expenditure on software before then was exceptionally high to address the Y2K problem.

1.2 MEASURING REAL GDP

Measurement becomes even more complicated when price and quality changes have to be accounted for. In this chapter only temporal price indices are discussed, not spatial price indices (see Box 1.1 'Purchasing power parities in comparisons of labour productivity growth').

Adjusting for Quality Change: The Role of Hedonic Price Indexes

A widely discussed issue at the height of the 'new economy' debate was the international comparability of rates of economic growth, given that the United States and some European countries apply very different statistical methodologies to the computation of price indices for information and communication technology (ICT) products. Because an alternative price index translates into a different measure of volume growth, the question has been posed whether some, or all, of the measured variation in growth between countries is a statistical illusion rather than reality.

The main challenge is to accurately account for quality changes in these high-technology goods, for example computers. The necessary quality adjustments are not standardised across countries. Consequently, between 1995 and 1999, the US price index of office accounting and photocopying equipment (which includes computers) dropped by more than 20 per cent annually, compared with 13 per cent in the United Kingdom and – at that time – a mere 7 per cent in Germany.[3] Because computers are internationally traded, their price changes should be similar across countries.

Another illustration of the difference in price indices is evident in Figure 1.4, which shows deflators for software investment. For example, the price index for Australia fell by about 30 per cent between 1995 and 2000, while the price index for Sweden rose by about the same amount. This does not reflect real price movements but rather the dearth of price information available in this area.

Thus, at least part of the differences in measured price changes appears to be due to methodological differences. The natural question is: how would GDP growth in Germany, the United Kingdom or any other country change if US methods were applied? Clearly, if the US price index for computers is applied to Italy's or the United Kingdom's investment expenditure, their investment volume will show more rapid growth, as will the volume measures of the computer industry's output. However, the direct effect on GDP growth of different price indices is limited owing to three factors.

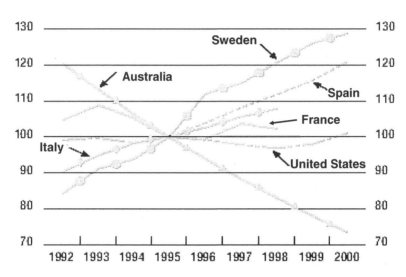

Source: OECD

Figure 1.4   Price indices for software investment

First, only final products have an impact on GDP. Thus, errors on the price index of an intermediate good such as semiconductors will only affect the contribution of the semiconductor industry to total GDP growth but not GDP growth itself. A second distinction is that, even for final demand products such as personal computers, the impact of an error on the price index will only affect GDP if the product is manufactured in the country. Third, if imported products are used as intermediate inputs then the absence of hedonic deflators in a country's national accounts will lead to an overstatement of real GDP growth (assuming that hedonic deflators represent the preferred measure) because imports will be lower and imports have a negative impact on GDP.

This is why simulations to obtain an order of magnitude for the impact of price adjustments of ICT products on the rate of change of real GDP lead, in general, to only modest effects, around +0.1 per cent (Lequiller, 2001; Deutsche Bundesbank, 2001; Schreyer, 2002). A review of the impact of hedonic price indices on aggregate volume growth in the United States found that the quality change in personal computers added 0.25 per cent to the estimate of annual real GDP growth over the period 1995–99 (Landefeld and Grimm, 2000). While quite high, this has to be put in proportion to a rate of real GDP growth of 4.15 per cent per year in the United States during this period.

Measuring Real Output in Services

The service sector now accounts for about 70 to 80 per cent of aggregate production and employment in OECD economies and continues to grow. But measuring output and productivity growth in many services is not straightforward. The measurement of non-market services is even more difficult, because, by definition, there is no output price and thus no deflator, other than costs. Health and education are the main non-market services and they have a significant impact on GDP because they contribute to final demand. This difficulty may raise doubts regarding the international comparability of the volume estimate of production of these sectors. In this paper we have focused on the health and social services sector quantity and quality of output, thereby mis-measuring productivity growth. Some countries have therefore tried to implement what are called output measures.

Indices, 1982 = 100

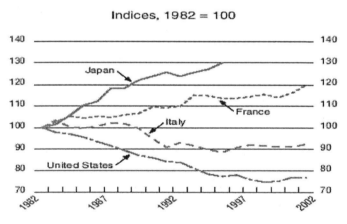

Source: OECD

*Figure 1.5   Real value-added per employed person in the health and social
              work industry*

Figure 1.5 shows that measured productivity in health and social services is in secular decline in the United States and Italy, while increasing slightly in France and steadily in Japan. Given the nature of the industry and given the difficulty in obtaining appropriate price and volume measures, it would seem that at least some of the cross-country differences in productivity growth are due to measurement differences. However, it is very difficult to quantify these effects.

Zero Productivity Simulations

Noting that certain service industries have been characterised by prolonged periods of negative measures of productivity growth, one could conclude that poor measurement may provide an explanation. Wölfl (2003) simulated what would happen if productivity growth in these services for France, the United States and Germany had not been negative but zero and further simulated the impacts on measured overall labour productivity growth. The empirical results suggest strong negative indirect effects on measured productivity growth for industries that use these services, partly outweighing the direct positive effect of the adjustment on productivity growth for the services themselves. The effect on aggregate productivity growth may be very small, depending on the type of measurement problem and the importance of the adjusted services for other industries and for the total economy. Setting negative productivity growth rates at zero, would lead, for instance, to a 0.19 percentage point change in measured aggregate productivity growth for France and a 0.08 percentage point change for the United States over the period 1990–2000. While these effects would directly translate into measured labour productivity growth, they are comparatively small.

The Choice of Index Numbers

GDP growth is a single number, drawn up as a combination of the change in volumes of the several hundred goods and services categories that constitute the classifications of national accounts. To compile this number, countries use different formulae in practice, even if the trend is toward using chained rather than fixed formulae. 'Fixed base' Laspeyres volume indices are currently still in use in some OECD countries (e.g. Japan, Germany, Finland, Spain, Sweden and Switzerland). Annually chained Laspeyres indices are the formula recommended by Eurostat for its Member countries. About half of the EU countries have changed their national accounts to a chained annually re-based Laspeyres method, and the remainder will change by 2005. The Australian and New Zealand accounts are also based on this index number formula. Annually weighted Fisher indices are currently used in the national accounts of the United States and Canada.

**Box 1.1: Purchasing Power Parities in comparisons of labour pro-
ductivity growth**

Purchasing Power Parities (PPPs) for GDP are spatial price indices that
compare levels of real GDP and its components internationally. As they
are associated with level comparisons, there is normally no need to in-
voke PPPs for comparisons of growth in GDP and productivity. Thus,
the method used by countries to compile the data discussed in the main
text does not involve PPP. However, in principle, it is possible to construct an index of relative output growth by using a time series of PPPs,
and applying them to one country's current-price GDP. The resulting
GDP level, expressed in current international prices, can then be related
to the GDP level of another country to form an index of relative GDP
growth between two countries. This method is based on different
weighting schemes and indeed, empirical differences can be sizable as
recently shown by Callow (2003). One might argue that the comparison
of the two methods should in itself be interesting because it reveals effects of different weighting schemes. This is true in a world of complete
and high-quality statistics. Practically, however, PPPs are based on a
smaller sample of prices and on less detailed weights than national price
indices. For purposes of comparing relative output and productivity
growth, the comparison based on constant national prices is preferred.
PPPs should be used when output and productivity levels are the object
of comparison across countries. For more detailed discussion of PPPs,
see OECD Statistics Brief No. 3.

With regard to international comparability, does it matter which index
number formula is chosen to compute volume GDP growth, given the same
set of prices and quantities for GDP components in two countries? Schreyer
(2001) used detailed final expenditure statistics to assess the effects of choos-
ing fixed Laspeyres index numbers over chained Fisher index numbers, in the
presence of significant relative price changes. The results confirmed that
chained Fisher indices tend to produce systematically lower figures for GDP
growth than fixed Laspeyres, ranging from -0.26 per cent per year in Japan to
-0.06 per cent per year in Canada, the US being at -0.15 per cent. In this case,
the statistical methods implemented in the United States have thus decreased
the estimate of GDP growth compared to other methods.

1.3 MEASURING LABOUR INPUT

Labour input can be measured using total employment, total hours worked, or a quality adjusted measure of labour input. Considering the importance of the change in the number of hours worked, adjusting for this is particularly important for cross country comparisons of labour productivity. Figure 1.6 illustrates that in most OECD countries, while productivity growth over the 1995–2002 period was much more rapid after adjustment for hours worked, this difference is not similar for all countries. It is negligible for the United States, but important for Japan, France and Germany. Unfortunately, adjustments for the composition of labour are not available.

Data on total hours worked (computed using surveys carried out on households or enterprises) are often not consistent with National Accounts. Some uncertainty remains regarding the comparability of measures of hours worked in OECD countries although this uncertainty is greater for the level of hours worked than for its growth rate. Nevertheless, comprehensive estimates of annual working time currently exist only for a limited number of OECD countries and the quality of data in this area therefore differs across Member countries, introducing some uncertainty in measures of labour productivity growth. Total hours worked can be derived by combining estimates of annual hours worked per person employed with average employment levels over the year that are in accordance with National Accounts production boundaries. Such employment series have not been collected systematically or examined very closely in the past. The quality of the labour productivity measures has relied on the vigilance of the analysts and their understanding of the annual hours and employment series. Work is currently underway at the OECD to develop a series of estimates of total hours worked that ensure the consistency over time of employment and annual hours worked in calculations of labour productivity.

1.4 CONCLUSION AND FUTURE WORK

This chapter cannot be considered to fully cover all statistical differences in GDP and productivity growth between countries. In particular, the comparability of imputed rents has not been explored and some methodological differences remain probably yet to be discovered. However, the impression is that the known differences remain small when compared to total growth differentials. Therefore, the assessment of a substantially more rapid growth in the US cannot be undermined by statistical defects. However, growth differentials for GDP per capita or labour productivity between the US and other countries have been smaller on average during 1995–2002. The diagnosis re-

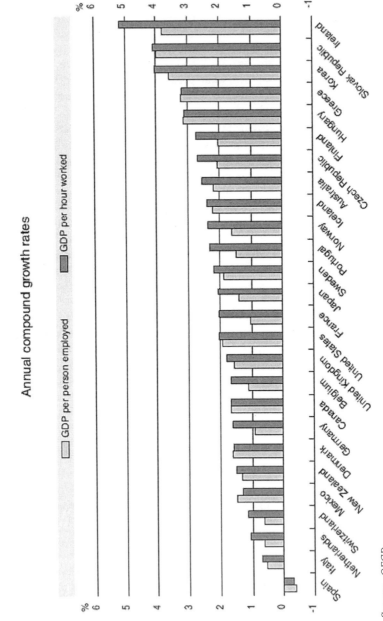

Source: OECD

Figure 1.6   Comparison of GDP per hours worked and GDP per person employed, 1995–2002

mains therefore more fragile for these variables, in particular considering the difficulties regarding the measurement of labour input. The OECD is highly committed to working with Member countries towards maximising convergence on statistical methodologies and to provide a better statistical base for such analyses. In this regard the organisation is currently developing a reference database on productivity at the aggregate level.

1.5 GLOSSARY

ICT: This stands for Information and Communication Technologies. It covers the range of new information goods and services, from software and computers to mobile phones, including semi-conductors.

Hedonic pricing: This refers to a technique which consists of using econometrics to price the different characteristics of a product, thus allowing price index compilers to take better account of the differences in the quality of the product. A good synonym would be 'fully quality adjusted price indices'. In general, hedonic pricing leads to price indices which grow slower (or decrease more) than non-hedonic pricing.

NOTES

1. For more detail on this subject, see Ahmad et al., 2003 at http://www.oecd.org/findDocument/0,2350,en_2649_33715_1_119684_1_1_1,00.html; *Statistics Brief*, Nr. 7, OECD.
2. An important issue not considered in this paper relates to valuing activities in the non-observed economy. This is the subject of *Statistics Brief*, No. 5, OECD.
3. Germany has recently introduced hedonic methods for IT products. The first publication of these data took place in 2002.

REFERENCES

Ahmad, N. (2003), 'Measuring Investment in Software', *STI Working Paper*, 2003–6, OECD, Paris.

Ahmad, N., F. Lequiller, P. Marianna, D. Pilat, P. Schreyer and A. Wölfl (2003), 'Comparing labour productivity growth in the OECD area: the role of measurement', *Statistics Directorate Working Paper*, 2003/5, OECD, Paris.

Callow, J. (2003), 'Getting Europe to work', *Credit Suisse First Boston Fixed Income Research*, 10 April.

Deutsche Bundesbank (2001), 'Problems of international comparisons of growth – a supplementary analysis', *Appendix to Monthly Report*, May.

Landefeld, S.J. and B.T. Grimm (2000), 'A Note on the Impact of Hedonics and Computers on Real GDP', *Survey of Current Business*, December.

Lequiller, F. (2001), 'La nouvelle économie et la mesure de la croissance du PIB', *Série des documents du travail de la Direction des Etudes et Synthèses Economiques* G2001/01, INSEE.

Lequiller, F., N. Ahmad, S. Varjonen, W. Cave and K.H. Ahn (2003), 'Report of the OECD Task Force on Software Measurement in the National Accounts', *Statistics Directorate Working Paper,* 2003/1, OECD, Paris.

OECD (2001), *The New Economy: Beyond the Hype*, Paris.

OECD (2003a), *The Sources of Economic Growth in OECD Countries*, Paris.

OECD (2003b), *ICT and Economic Growth – Evidence from OECD countries, Industries and Firms*, Paris, forthcoming.

Schreyer, P. (2001), 'Information and Communication Technology and the Measurement of Real Output, Final Demand and Productivity', *Economics of Innovation and New Technology*, Vol. 10.

Schreyer, P. (2002), 'Computer price indices and international growth and productivity comparisons', *Review of Income and Wealth*.

Wölfl, A. (2003), 'Productivity Growth in Service Industries: an Assessment of Recent Patterns and the Role of Measurement', *STI Working Paper,* 2003-6, OECD, Paris.

2. The Breaks in per Capita Productivity: Trends in a Number of Industrial Countries[1]

Tristan-Pierre Maury and Bertrand Pluyaud

2.1 ABSTRACT

The purpose of this chapter is to study the trends in per capita productivity in several major industrialised countries. The analysis is first based on annual data over a long period spanning the entire 20th century for the United States, France and the United Kingdom. Productivity trends are then studied over a shorter period, using quarterly data, for the United States, France, the United Kingdom, Germany, Spain, Japan and the Netherlands. There are already a large number of studies of this kind, but they are too often focused on presenting average productivity growth rates for given periods chosen on an ad hoc basis. In this chapter, we use a robust statistical method to endogenously identify possible breaks in per capita productivity trends. This method, developed by Bai and Perron (1998), brings out the following salient features:

- in the United States, per capita productivity growth accelerated following the trend break at the start of the 1920s, then slowed down at the end of the 1960s. This finding is in line with the 'Big Wave' concept developed by Gordon (1999, 2002) to describe the trends in US productivity growth throughout the 20th century.
- French and UK productivity started catching up with that in the United States around the end of the Second World War.
- Most of the countries under review recorded slower trend productivity growth in the first half of the 1970s. In the United States, this break occurred in 1966. This finding differs from that of other existing analyses, which point to 1974.
- Trend productivity growth in Europe and Japan slowed in the 1990s, whereas US productivity gained momentum over the same period.

2.2 INTRODUCTION

The various studies on long-term productivity trends have provided a couple of findings on American and European data. In particular, Gordon has analysed in his research papers the main phases of the American productivity growth since the beginning of the 20th century and the catching up of American productivity levels by European economies.

Gordon (1999) launched the expression 'Big Wave' to describe total factor productivity growth in the United States. He set the 'US take-off' at around 1913.[2] Productivity growth rose continuously until the mid-1960s, then declined from 1964[3] to the start of the 1990s, to reach a lower rate than that recorded during the inter-war period.

Gordon (2002) showed that the gap between European and US productivity growth widened until the mid-1950s,[4] when Europe started catching up with the United States. This catching-up process continued until the early 1990s and was not interrupted by the oil price shock in 1973.

Some studies (see Basu, Fernald and Shapiro, 2001, Hansen, 2001, Gust and Marquez, 2002, Lecat, 2004) went a step further by focusing on US and European productivity trends in the 1990s. These studies highlight the fact that the catching up process ended in the mid-1990s. Around 1995, productivity growth rates in the United States were close to those recorded in the 1950s, while European and Japanese growth rates were on a downturn.

However, the robustness of these stylised facts is questionable. Indeed, the statistical techniques used are generally not sufficiently rigorous, except in the case of Hansen's (2001). For example, Gordon merely calculates average productivity growth rates for given periods chosen on an ad hoc basis. The purpose of this study is therefore to determine whether the above-mentioned phases of US, European, and Japanese productivity growth can be validated using a trend break test. For each country, the study is conducted using two samples of per capita productivity:

- a long sample of annual data covering the 20th century;
- a short sample of quarterly data covering the post-war period.

The first sample enables us to detect possible trend breaks before the Second World War. We are therefore able to test whether the US take-off brought to light by Gordon (1999) corresponds to a productivity trend break.

More generally, we are able to check whether the trend break test enables us to identify Gordon's Big Wave. Furthermore, these tests make it possible to date the start of the catching up process.

The second sample enables us to test the existence of possible trend breaks at the time of the oil price shock and in the 1990s. Concerning this last point, Hansen (2001) highlighted a pronounced positive break in the US productivity trend between 1992 and 1996. Our objective is to determine whether this upswing corresponds to a fall in European and Japanese productivity growth.

By comparing the results obtained in both samples, we are able to compare the current US and European trend growth rates with those prior to the Second World War, and, like Gordon, establish whether the growth rates at the end of the Big Wave are comparable to those at the start of the period.

Given our many objectives, we require a method which will enable us to endogenously determine both the number and the date of the trend breaks. We have recourse to a technique recently put forward by Bai and Perron (1998), which is much more efficient than the methods previously used. The approach adopted in this paper is purely statistical. It does not put forward any economic interpretation of the identified trend breaks. Furthermore, it appears necessary to emphasise the weakness of some of the data, in particular long data which are derived from several accounting databases and sources. Caution should therefore be exercised when interpreting the results.

The chapter is structured as follows. In the next section, we present the econometric method and the data we use. The third section is divided in two parts: results on long samples are displayed in the first one, and results on short samples, as well as comments on the structural breaks detected in the 1970s and 1990s, are presented in the second one. Then, productivity trends computed on the period before World War II are compared to trends computed on short samples. Finally, the last section concludes briefly.

2.3   CHOSEN APPROACH

The Bai and Perron Method

Econometrics has increasingly focused on trend breaks over recent years. In the initial work on structural change (see Perron, 1989), modelling only allowed for a single trend break, for which the date of occurrence would be determined by econometrics. Andrews (1993) proposed a general method for endogenously determining the date of the break. However, this method had the same drawback: it only allowed for a single trend break. Since then, several methods for measuring the number of break points have been developed. The use of information criteria (AIC, BIC) has been largely criticized. The method for a sequential estimation of break dates elaborated by Bai and Perron (1998) has appeared to be much more efficient, given the fact that the AIC or BIC approaches tend to overestimate the number of breaks.

Four commonly used specifications are implemented in this study to detect trend breaks. Specifications 1 and 2 are written as follows:

Specification 1

$$Y_t = \mu + \beta_1 . t + \sum_{k=1}^{m} \beta_{k+1}(t - T_k)I(t > T_k) + u_t \qquad (2.1)$$

Specification 2

$$Y_t = \mu + \beta_1 . t + \sum_{k=1}^{m} \beta_{k+1}(t - T_k)I(t > T_k) + \sum_{i=1}^{p} c_i Y_{t-i} + u_t \qquad (2.2)$$

for $t=1,..., T$ where T is the sample size. $I(.)$ denotes the indicator function. For both specifications, productivity (Y_t) is expressed in log form. u_t is a residual term with a zero average. μ is a constant. β_i ($i=1, ...,m$) is the trend growth rate on the ith segment. And, c_i ($i=1,...,p$) are the autoregressive term coefficients. For the first specification, we use the method developed by Den Haan and Levin (2000) to estimate the variance-covariance matrix of the parameters (VARHAC method). For the second specification, the residual autocorrelation problem is solved by including autoregressive terms. The optimal number of lags p is calculated using the Perron method (1989).

Our objective is to assess the number (m) and the dates (T_k, $k=1,...,m$) of possible breaks in the trend. β (slope of the trend) is the only parameter to be subject to a break; the other parameters μ and c_i are assumed to be stable.

Specifications 3 and 4 are written as follows:

Specification 3

$$\Delta Y_t = \beta_1 + \sum_{k=1}^{m} \beta_{k+1}.I(t \succ T_k) + u_t \qquad (2.3)$$

Specification 4

$$\Delta Y_t = \beta_1 + \sum_{k=1}^{m} \beta_{k+1}.I(t \succ T_k) + \sum_{i=1}^{p} c_i \Delta Y_{t-i} + u_t \qquad (2.4)$$

This time, we are measuring the per capita productivity growth rate (ΔY is the variation in the logarithms of productivity levels). The definitions of β_i and c_i are the same as in the first two specifications.

In specification 3, we run a regression of productivity growth rates on a constant subject to a random number of breaks. Here again, β is the only parameter subject to a break. Once more, we use Den Haan and Levin's VARHAC method to estimate the long-term variance-covariance matrix of the parameters. In specification 4, the autocorrelation problem is solved by using autoregressive terms.

Once the number and the dates of the breaks are determined, each specification is estimated. For specifications 1 and 3, we use the VARHAC method again to evaluate the significance of the parameters. We use the analytic formulas given by Bai and Perron (2001a, 2001b) to estimate the confidence intervals associated with the break points.

2.4 PRESENTING AND PROCESSING THE DATA

Long Sample

The long sample includes data which go back to the start of the 20th century, or even the end of the 19th century. In this case, the only data available are for France, the United States and the United Kingdom; employment and gross domestic product (GDP) data for Germany and Japan are not available over a sufficiently long period to enable us to use the Bai and Perron method.[5]

The precise sources from which the data for France, the United States and the United Kingdom are derived are available from the authors upon request. In general, the data in long time series are less homogenous and robust than those in short time series. Pre-war data are highly volatile. Several factors account for this lack of homogeneity. First, data in long time series are drawn from a wide range of sources (censuses, industrial tribunals, trade unions, statistical surveys, etc). Second, the methods used for constructing series have changed considerably, in particular with regard to GDP deflators. Third, accounting conventions have also been considerably amended over time, for example with regard to the classification of farm workers[6] or the switch from national product to domestic product. Lastly, changing borders also account for the heterogeneity of the data. This problem occurs in the case of France (Alsace-Lorraine was not part of France prior to 1918) and the United Kingdom (Southern Ireland was included in the United Kingdom before 1920). For these three countries, the most recent data are drawn from the Groningen Growth and Development Centre (GGDC) database.[7] The older data are taken from Villa[8] for France, from Feinstein (1976) for the United Kingdom and from Mitchell (1998a/b) for the United States. Villa presents single long time series both for employment and GDP data. He makes the assumption of a variable territory but reprocesses the data in order to ensure that concepts and nomenclatures remain constant. Feinstein and Mitchell, on the other hand, present discontinuous time series, which vary according to territory, source and methodology. The various employment and GDP series put forward by both authors have the particularity of always having a date in common. For example, in the case of the United Kingdom, some employment and GDP series including Southern Ireland extend until 1920 and others excluding Southern Ireland start in 1920.

The two world wars, for which there are either no data or unreliable data, were processed successively by interpolation and through the use of buffer variables. Because both methods yielded the same results, we only present the interpolation method. The French sample deliberately runs up until 1990, as the short sample of French data is broken in the 1990s (see below). This break cannot be detected using annual data, because it is too close to the end of the sample. At the same time, it is likely to distort the results for the rest of the sample.[9]

Short Sample

The countries under review in the short time series covering the post war period are the United States, France, the United Kingdom, Germany, Japan, Spain and the Netherlands. We use quarterly series for all countries except for the Netherlands, where half-yearly series are used. These series have two advantages compared with the long time series: the data are more homogeneous and, unlike in the case of the annual series, we are able to test the presence of possible trend breaks in the 1990s.

The series used are mainly derived from the macroeconomic database of the Bank for International Settlements (BIS). This database is fed by various national bodies, such as national statistical institutes and central banks. We also used data from Villa for France, Eurostat data for Spain and data from the Organisation for Economic Cooperation and Development (OECD) for the Netherlands. We derived the productivity series from real GDP and employment series, except in the case of Germany, where we directly used per capita productivity series. All of the series were already seasonally-adjusted, with the exception of an employment series for the United Kingdom, which was adjusted for seasonality by the authors.

The problem posed by German reunification was handled in two stages. The same tests as those performed on the other countries under review were carried out on West Germany. However, we were unable to apply the Bai and Perron sequential procedure in the case of reunified Germany, as the available data sample was too short. We assumed that there could not be more than one break in this sample. In this case, there would be no sequential procedure and the test to be performed would be that of Andrews (1993).

2.5 RESULTS

Long Sample

Table 2.1 brings together all of the results obtained from the long sample. With annual time series, the autoregressive terms in specifications 2 and 4 are generally not significant. For this reason, only specifications 1 and 3 are included in Table 2.1. As regards the United States, we were able to identify the Big Wave brought to light by Gordon (1999). Productivity growth showed a positive trend break in 1922 or 1933 (depending on the chosen specification) and starts slowing in 1967. The date of the US 'take-off' is slightly later than that identified by Gordon, while the date of the slowdown is roughly the same.[10] However, a number of economists set the US slowdown at 1974 (see Zivot and Andrews, 1992). As we will see in the following section, the starting date of the US slowdown is not very different if one uses hourly productivity instead of per capita productivity.

Table 2.1   Trend productivity growth (GDP/employment) using long time series (annual) – results from the Bai and Perron method

For specifications 1 and 3, the table shows the dates of the breaks and the average annual productivity growth rate for each period, in %.

United States

Spec.1	1890	1922		1967	2002
	1.3%		2.5%	1.3%	
Spec.3	1890	1933		1967	2002
	1.1%		3.0%	1.3%	

France

Spec.1	1890	1945	1970	1990
	0.6%		5.4%	2.4%
Spec.3	1890	1945	1970	1990
	0.6%		5.4%	2.4%

United Kingdom

Spec.1	1875	1943	2002
	0.7%		1.9%
Spec.3	1875	1943	2002
	0.7%		1.9%

Sources: Authors' calculations.

Positive trend breaks occurred in the United Kingdom and France in 1943 and 1945 respectively. The date of the trend break in France corresponds to the start of the catching up process with the United States (according to Gordon, 2002, the catching-up process began in 1950). The average growth rate in France stood at 5.4 per cent, compared with 2.5 per cent or 3 per cent in the United States (depending on the chosen specification). France posted a negative productivity trend break in 1970, but this break did not interrupt the catching up process: the trend productivity growth rate in France was almost twice as high as that in the United States after 1970. It appears that this break corresponds to a GDP break (Le Bihan, 2002, finds a negative GDP break for France around 1973 by applying the Bai and Perron method).

It is also worth pointing out that the United Kingdom did not experience a trend break at the time of the oil price shock of 1973 (this result will be partly confirmed in the following section).

Short Sample

The results, presented in Table 2.2, confirm that there are never more than two breaks, irrespective of the country. These breaks can be divided into two clusters, around 1970 and in the 1990s (except in the case of the United States).

All of the countries under review, with the exception of the United States and the United Kingdom, posted a significant negative productivity trend break between 1972 and 1976, irrespective of the specification.[11] These results therefore confirm those obtained from the long sample. In the case of France, this productivity trend break coincides once again with a GDP break (Le Bihan, 2002). In the absence of any significant break in the employment trend over this period, the downturn in productivity can therefore be attributed to the break in GDP trend growth.

The United Kingdom only posted a negative productivity trend break, albeit very small, for specifications 1 and 2. These results are in line with those of Broadberry and Crafts (2003), who identified a pronounced slowdown in British productivity around 1973 for the manufacturing sector, but a much smaller slowdown for the economy as a whole. The United States experienced a sharp fall in labour productivity growth in the first quarter of 1966. This date is robust to the chosen specification. This may be surprising given that the economic literature generally sets the negative break at around 1974 (see the work of Zivot and Andrews on US GDP, for example).

To corroborate our results, we carried out the same tests on hourly productivity in the United States. Our objective was to estimate whether using the number of hours worked per employed person would alter our conclusions (the data series was supplied by the Bureau of Labour Statistics (BLS). The date of the break (last quarter of 1967 or first quarter of 1968 depending on the specification) is very close to that obtained using the productivity per employed person. The US slowdown can therefore not be attributed to the number of hours worked per employed person. The discrepancy between the results put forward in this article and those in the literature probably stems from our choice of method (multiple break test). The Zivot and Andrews test (1992), on the contrary, only allows for a single break.

Table 2.2   *Trend productivity growth (GDP/employment) using short time series (quarterly except for the Netherlands) – results from the Bai and Perron method*

NB: For each specification, the table shows the break dates and the average annual productivity growth rate for each period

United States – per capita GDP

	1948Q1	1966Q1		1983Q1	2002Q4
Spec.1	2.8%		0.7%		2.0%
Spec.2	1948Q1	1966Q1		1983Q1	2002Q4
	2.8%		0.7%		2.0%
Spec.3	1948Q1		1966Q1		2002Q4
	2.8%			1.3%	
Spec.4	1948Q1		1966Q1		2002Q4
	2.8%			1.3%	

United States – hourly productivity

	1964Q1	1967Q4		1995Q3	2002t4
Spec.1	3.2%		1.4%		2.2%
Spec.2	1964Q1	1967Q4		1995Q3	2002t4
	3.2%		1.4%		2.2%
Spec.3	1964Q1	1968Q1		1995Q3	2002Q4
	2.6%		1.5%		2.2%
Spec.4	1964Q1	1968Q1		1995Q3	2002Q4
	2.6%		1.5%		2.2%

France

	1959Q1	1973Q3		1991Q2	2002Q4
Spec.1	5.0%		2.1%		1.1%
Spec.2	1959Q1	1973Q1		1991Q1	2002Q4
	4.9%		2.2%		1.1%
Spec.3	1959Q1	1973Q2		1990Q1	2002Q4
	5.0%		2.2%		1.1%
Spec.4	1959Q1	1973Q2		1990Q1	2002Q4
	5.0%		2.2%		1.1%

Table 2.2 continued

United Kingdom

Spec.1	1955Q1		1972Q2		2002Q4
		2.7%		1.9%	

Spec.2	1955Q1		1972Q2		2002Q4
		2.7%		1.9%	

Spec.3	1955Q1				2002Q4
			2.2%		

Spec.4	1955Q1				2002Q4
			2.2%		

Japan

Spec.1	1961Q1		1973Q2		1990Q3		2002Q4
		8.0%		2.9%		1.2%	

Spec.2	1961Q1		1973Q2		1990Q3		2002Q4
		8.0%		2.8%		1.2%	

Spec.3	1961Q1		1973Q2		1990Q3		2002Q4
		8.0%		2.9%		1.2%	

Spec.4	1961Q1		1973Q2		1990Q3		2002Q4
		8.0%		2.8%		1.1%	

West Germany

Spec.1	1960Q1		1973Q4		1998Q4
		4.1%		1.9%	

Spec.2	1960Q1		1973Q4		1998Q4
		4.1%		1.9%	

Spec.3	1960Q1		1969Q4		1998Q4
		4.3%		2.2%	

Spec.4	1960Q1		1973Q1		1998Q4
		4.2%		2.0%	

Reunified Germany

Spec.1	1991Q1		1997Q3		2002Q4
		1.9%		0.8%	

Spec.2	1991Q1		1997Q3		2002Q4
		1.9%		0.8%	

Spec.3	1991Q1		1997Q3		2002Q4
		2.2%		0.8%	

Spec.4	1991Q1		1997Q3		2002Q4
		2.1%		0.8%	

Table 2.2 continued

Spain

Spec.1	1970Q1	1985Q4	1996Q1	2003Q2
	3.3%	1.5%		-0.4%

Spec.2	1970Q1	1985Q4	1996Q1	2003Q2
	3.3%	1.5%		-0.4%

Spec.3	1970Q1	1994Q1	2003Q2
	2.9%	-0.1%	

Spec.4	1970Q1	1994Q1	2003Q2
	2.9%	-0.1%	

Netherlands (half-yearly)

Spec.1	1960S1	1976S1	2003S1
	4.1%	1.4%	

Spec.2	1960S1	1976S1	2003S1
	4.1%	1.4%	

Spec.3	1960S1	1976S2	2003S1
	3.7%	1.3%	

Spec.4	1960S1	1976S2	2003S1
	3.7%	1.3%	

Sources: Authors' calculations.

The end of the catching up process can also be attributed to the fact that three countries, France, reunified Germany and Japan (see Gust and Marquez, 2002), experienced a negative labour productivity trend break in the 1990s. In France, it occurred in 1990 or 1991 depending on the chosen specification. The French trend growth rate dropped by approximately half. Unlike the 1973 break, this productivity trend break was not due to a GDP break (Le Bihan, 2002, rejects the hypothesis of a second GDP break in France). Instead, it can probably be attributed to the sharp rise in the employment growth rate in France at the start of the 1990s (in particular after the slump in 1993). We obtain similar results for Germany and Japan. Spain is a special case, since it experienced a negative trend productivity growth rate following the trend break in the mid-1990s.

Once again, the United Kingdom and the United States are in sharp contrast with the other industrialised countries under review. The United Kingdom and the Netherlands did not experience a productivity trend break in the 1990s. The fall in productivity growth around 1996–1997 is probably too close to the end of the sample and not sufficiently pronounced to be interpreted as a trend break. This slight fall may also correspond to a cyclical movement. It is also worth pointing out that, although the United Kingdom did not experience a negative trend break in the 1990s, it lagged further behind the United States than the other European countries (see Lecat, 2004).

In contrast to the other countries, the United States experienced an upward break in 1983. However, it is not very robust to the chosen specification, as it only appears when using productivity levels. This result is in line with the findings of Bassanini and Scarpetta (2002), according to whom US productivity growth started accelerating in the mid-1980s. Conversely, Hansen (2001) sets this acceleration in the mid-1990s. The reason for this is that Hansen uses hourly productivity in the manufacturing sector. By extending Hansen's analysis based on hourly productivity to the whole of the economy, we are able to confirm the presence of a positive trend break in 1995. Results obtained using hourly productivity are statistically more reliable than those obtained using per capita productivity, since they are robust to the chosen specification, which is not the case of the results based on per capita productivity.[12] This leads us to set the acceleration in the US growth rate at around 1995, rather than 1983.

This finding points to the end of the catching up process. For specifications 1 and 2, following the positive trend break in 1983, the United States posted a higher trend labour productivity growth rate than the other countries. This is also the case for specifications 3 and 4 if the United Kingdom is excluded from the sample. The widening gap between US and European and Japanese productivity therefore cannot be attributed to a cyclical movement, but, on the contrary, to shifts in productivity trends.

By bringing together the results derived from the long and short samples, we are now able to compare the growth rates before and after the Second World War. In the case of France, average per capita productivity growth before the war is significantly lower than that after the war, including the period following the slowdown of the early 1990s. Since 1991, the French trend growth rate has been twice as high as that recorded in the first half of the century. This also holds true for the United Kingdom, whose average per capita productivity growth after the Second World War is roughly three times as high as that recorded before.

The situation in the United States is markedly different. Average productivity growth before the 1930s was higher than that between the oil price shock and the economic recovery in the 1980s. On the other hand, it stands below the current trend productivity growth rate.

2.6 CONCLUSIONS

Using the Bai and Perron method to highlight the trend component of apparent labour productivity enabled us to bring out the following salient points:

* some of Gordon's conclusions (1999, 2002) were confirmed. We were able to identify the centennial wave brought to light by Gordon and to establish that France and the United Kingdom started catching up with the United States shortly after the Second World War.
* The test showed that most of the countries under review experienced slower trend productivity growth at the time of the oil price shock in the 1970s. In the United States, this break occurred around 1966 (both in terms of per capita productivity and hourly productivity). This finding contrasts with that of other existing analyses, which point to 1974.
* Lastly, we were able to establish that the end of the catching up process in the mid-1990s was part of the trend in productivity growth in these countries. European countries and Japan posted slower trend productivity growth in the 1990s, whereas US productivity gained momentum in the 1980s or 1990s (depending on whether one considers per capita productivity or hourly productivity).

This last result, which concerns the recent period, is certainly likely to be of interest to decision makers in charge of conducting monetary policy. It highlights the capacity of the US economy in recent years to raise its labour productivity, in particular via the development of new information and communication technologies (ICT). However, it also shows the need for European countries, in particular France, to foster structural policies designed to improve labour productivity.

NOTES

1. This study was prepared as part of the productivity-profitability network led by Gilbert Cette at the Banque de France. Comments on an earlier draft of the paper by Dirk Pilat (OECD), Jacques Mairesse (CREST) as well as participants to the seminar 'Productivity' (Paris, Nov. 2003) are gratefully acknowledged. All errors remain ours. The authors are solely responsible for the contents, which do not necessarily reflect the views of the Banque de France or the Eurosystem.
2. This date depends on the respective weightings of capital and labour in the calculation of total factor productivity.
3. This date is subject to debate: theoretical literature generally places the US slowdown at around the time of the oil crisis in 1973.
4. Europe had been lagging behind the United States since the middle of the 19th century.

5. Employment data for Germany are only available from 1921 onwards (Mitchell) and exclude the Second World War. In the case of Japan, the earliest available data go back to the 1930s.
6. In France, all persons living on farms who neither went to school nor had a job were automatically considered as farm workers until 1946. Today, only persons who declare themselves as farm workers are considered as such.
7. University of Groningen and The Conference Board, GGDC Total Economy Database, July 2003, http://www.eco.rug.nl/ggdc
8. http://www.cepii.fr//francgraph/bdd/villa.htm
9. This problem is well covered in econometric literature on trend breaks.
10. NB: Gordon uses total factor productivity series, whereas we use per capita productivity series.
11. Excluding the third specification applied to West Germany.
12. We were unable to repeat this exercise for Europe, as quarterly data on hours worked were not available.

REFERENCES

Andrews, D. (1993), 'Tests for Parameter Instability and Structural Change with Unknown Change Point', *Econometrica*, **61**, 821–56.
Bai, J. and P. Perron (1998), 'Estimating and Testing Linear Models with Multiple Structural Changes', *Econometrica*, **66**, 47–78.
Bai, J. and P. Perron (2001a), 'Multiple Structural Change Models: A Simulation Analysis', Unpublished Manuscript, Department of Economics, Boston University.
Bai, J. and P. Perron (2001b), 'Computation and Analysis of Multiple Structural Change Models', Unpublished Manuscript, Department of Economics, Boston University.
Bassanini, A. and S. Scarpetta (2002), 'Growth, technological change, and ICT diffusion: recent evidence from OECD countries', *Oxford Review of economic policy*, **18**, Oxford University Press.
Basu, S., J. Fernald and M. Shapiro (2001), 'Productivity Growth in the 1990s: Technology, Utilization, or Adjustment?', *Carnegie Rochester Conference Series on Public Policy*, **55**, 117–65.
Broadberry, S. and N. Crafts (2003), 'UK Productivity Performance from 1950 to 1979: A Restatement of the Broadberry-Crafts View', WP, University of Warwick.
Den Haan, W. and A. Levin (2000), 'Robust Covariance Matrix Estimation with Data-Dependent VAR Prewhitening Order', *NBER Technical Working Paper*, 255.
Feinstein, C. (1976), *Statistical Tables of National Income, Expenditure and Output of the UK, 1855–1965*.
Gordon, R. (1999), 'US Economic Growth since 1870: One Big Wave?', *American Economic Review, Papers and Proceedings*, **89**, 123–38.
Gordon, R. (2002), 'Two Centuries of Economic Growth: Europe Chasing the American Frontier', Paper Prepared for Economic History Workshop, WP Northwestern University.
Gust, C. and J. Marquez (2002), 'International comparison of productivity growth: the role of information technology and regulatory practise', *International Finance Discussion Papers*, 727, Board of Governors of the Federal Reserve System.
Hansen, B. (2001), 'The New Econometrics of Structural Changes: Understanding and Dating Changes in US Productivity', mimeo, University of Wisconsin.

Le Bihan, H. (2002), 'Le PIB Tendanciel Français: une Approche par les Ruptures de Tendance', *Note d'Etudes et de Recherche*, 89, Banque de France.

Lecat, R. (2004), 'Productivité du Travail des Grands Pays Industrialisés: la fin du Rattrapage des Etats-Unis?', *Monthly Bulletin of the Banque de France*, **121**, 47–67.

Mitchell, B. (1998a), *International Historical Statistics: the Americas, 1750–1993*, 4th Edition, Stockton Press.

Mitchell, B. (1998b), *International Historical Statistics: Europe, 1750–1993*, 4th Edition, Stockton Press.

Perron, P. (1989), 'The Great Crash, the Oil Price Shock, and the Unit Root Hypothesis', *Econometrica*, **57** (6), 1361–1401.

Zivot, E. and D. Andrews (1992), 'Further Evidence on the Great Crash, the Oil Price Shock, and the Unit-Root Hypothesis', *Journal of Business & Economic Statistics*, **10** (3), 251–70.

3. ICT Diffusion and Potential Output Growth

Gilbert Cette, Jacques Mairesse and Yusuf Kocogluc

3.1 ABSTRACT

The diffusion of ICTs may increase potential output growth in the medium to long term via capital deepening effects and total factor productivity gains and in the short to medium term via the lagged adjustment of wages to productivity gains.

3.2 INTRODUCTION

Due to rapid progress in performances price indices for computer hardware have declined on average by around 20 per cent every year for more than three decades. Quality changes on this scale, which may extend to other types of ICTs such as software and communications equipment, could significantly raise the potential output growth rate. ICT diffusion appears to have a lasting impact on medium to long-term potential output growth and a more temporary effect on short to medium-term potential output.

3.3 MEDIUM TO LONG-TERM EFFECTS

Let's assume a Cobb-Douglas function with constant returns to scale and Hicks-neutral technological change, that is, in growth rate terms:

$$\dot{Q} = T\dot{F}P + \alpha\dot{K} + (1-\alpha)\dot{N} \qquad (3.1)$$

where Q is the volume of output, K the volume of fixed productive capital, N the volume of employment, α the elasticity of output to capital, *TFP* the total factor productivity and a 'dot' (˙) above a variable denotes its growth rate.

In the long term, the capital coefficient remains constant in nominal terms at the potential output level (see Jorgenson and Stiroh's analysis (1999)):

$$\dot{P}_Q + \dot{Q}* = \dot{P}_K + \dot{K}*, \text{ or } \dot{K}* = \dot{Q}* + (\dot{P}_Q - \dot{P}_K) \qquad (3.2)$$

where P_Q is the price of output, P_K the price of investment in fixed productive capital and a 'star'(*) as an upper script of a variable denotes its potential level.

In theory, in the long-term equilibrium, there is no permanent divergence in the relative prices of different products, here investment and output. Empirically, however, such divergences have frequently been observed on the potential growth horizon being explored (which may extend over several decades). Additionally, it is assumed that ICT diffusion does not affect the medium to long-term level of potential employment, i.e. that it does not affect the medium to long-term NAIRU level or the potential labour supply N*. From the two previous relations, the following expression for potential output growth is thus obtained:[1]

$$\dot{Q}* = \frac{T\dot{F}P}{1-\alpha} + \frac{\alpha}{1-\alpha}(\dot{P}_Q - \dot{P}_K) + \dot{N}* \qquad (3.3)$$

The gain in the potential output growth rate from ICT diffusion is the sum of two components: the first one corresponds to the effect of changes in TFP gains and the second one to the impact of capital deepening caused by the decline in the relative price of investment. The accounting and statistical treatment used to break down the nominal investment and output series in their volume and price components have a crucial influence on the magnitude of the contributions to potential output growth imputed to TFP and capital deepening in any growth accounting analysis (see for example Gordon (2000), Stiroh (2001) or Cette et al. (2000, 2002)).

To offer an empirical evaluation for both USA and France, we suppose that (i) the levels reached in 2002 for the ICT investment share correspond to full ICT diffusion in the production system for the two countries; (ii) the annual divergence in price growth of about 2.5 points between non-residential investment and value added over the 1995–2002 period in the two countries is entirely explained by the divergence in ICT price trends; (iii) the corporate profit margin is of 1/3 in the two countries; (iv) the overall TFP gains for the USA are those evaluated by Oliner and Sichel (2002) and Jorgenson et al. (2002), and for France by Cette et al. (2004). We then consider two extreme cases. The first assumes that the ICT-induced TFP gains are the difference in the contribution to TFP gains between the producing and non-producing sectors, while the second assumes that all TFP gains are associated to ICTs. In the two cases, we find that ICT diffusion has a large overall effect on potential output growth in both the USA and France, but is significantly higher in the USA: in the first extreme case of about 1.4 per cent per year in the USA as against 0.8 per cent in France, and in the second one of about 2.2 per cent as against 1.3 per cent.

3.4 SHORT TO MEDIUM-TERM EFFECTS

During the ICT diffusion phase, the lagged adjustment of wages to productivity may reduce inflationary pressures. To propose a simplified formalisation of this mechanism, it is assumed that labour productivity grows at a constant rate before and after ICT diffusion and that productivity accelerates at a constant rate during the diffusion phase from date t1 to date t2.

Regarding wages, and more precisely the labour costs per capita, we follow Meyer (2000a) in assuming the following growth adjustment of wages to productivity:

$$\dot{W} = \beta_1 + \dot{P}_{C-1} + \phi(L)(Q/\dot{N}) - \beta_2 U_{-1} \text{ with } \phi(1) = 1 . \qquad (3.4)$$

where W is the per capita labour cost, P_C the price of household consumption, U the unemployment rate, $\phi(L)$ a polynomial of the time lag operator, and subscript '-1' denotes a variable that has been lagged by one period.

The 'long-term' NAIRU is then $U^* = \beta_1/\beta_2$. In the short run, during the ICT diffusion phase, we have $\phi(L)(Q/\dot{N}) \prec Q/\dot{N}$, owing to the lagged adjustment of wage growth to productivity growth. As a result, during the ICT's diffusion, the NAIRU falls temporarily below its long-term level, as demonstrated also by Meyer (2000a):

$$U^*_{ST} = U^* - \tfrac{1}{\beta_2}((1 - \phi(L))Q/\dot{N}) \qquad (3.5)$$

where $_{ST}$ as a subscript of a variable denotes its short-term value.

The fact that the NAIRU is temporarily lower than its long-term level paves the way for a temporary gain in potential output. We define employment by the relation: $N=(1-U)$. POP, where POP is the labour supply. On the basis of the previous relations and assumptions, the temporary gain in potential output is equal to: $(1-\alpha)(U^*_{ST} - U^*) = \tfrac{1-\alpha}{\beta_2}((1-\phi(L))Q/\dot{N})$. This gain in potential output is temporary because, if we start out from a situation of equilibrium, it appears when productivity accelerates and then declines and disappears as labour costs progressively adjust to their long-term equilibrium path.

This mechanism has been described in many studies (see Meyer (2000a,b), Blinder (2000), Ball and Moffit (2001) and Ball and Mankiw (2002)). The size of this temporary effect, for a given rise in growth rate of labour productivity, depends on the speed with which average wages adjust to productivity. In the case of the USA, Ball and Moffit (2001, 24 and 25) estimate that the NAIRU dropped temporarily by about one percentage point at the end of the 1990s, following the acceleration in productivity.

However, in contrast with these analyses, Cette and Sylvain (2003) show that for the private sector as a whole in the USA, real labour productivity grew by 2.1 per cent per year on average over the period 1995–2000 compared with 1.3 per cent over the period 1990–1995. At the same time, real per capita labour costs increased by 2.9 per cent per year over the period 1995–2000 (and even by 3.8 per cent over the sub-period 1997–2000) compared with 1.1 per cent per year over the period 1990–1995. Consequently, while the average profit margin for the private sector rose by 0.5 percentage points between 1990 and 1995, it declined by 2.7 percentage points between 1995 and 2000. It seems therefore not the case that the faster rate of USA labour productivity observed in the latter half of the 1990s led to lower inflation via a temporary decline in the NAIRU resulting from a lagged adjustment of wages to productivity.[2]

3.5 CONCLUSIONS

The diffusion of ICTs increases potential output growth in the medium to long term via capital deepening effects and total factor productivity gains, and in the short to medium term via the lagged adjustment of wages to productivity. The orders of magnitude of the medium to long-term effect could be significant. However, we do not find strong empirical support for the existence of the temporary short to medium-term effect that is often referred to in the economic literature in the case of the USA experience in the late 1990s.

NOTES

1. In case there is no divergence between output and investment price trends $\dot{P}_Q = \dot{P}_K$ we obtain the usual expression for potential output growth $\dot{Q}^* = \frac{TFP^*}{1-\alpha} + \dot{N}^*$

2. See Cette and Sylvain (2003) for the case of France where there was a productivity slowdown in the late 1990s, mainly related to a slowdown in the non ICT capital deepening contribution.

REFERENCES

Ball, L. and G. Mankiw (2002), The NAIRU in Theory and Practice, *NBER Working Paper,* 8940.

Ball, L. and R. Moffit (2001), Productivity Growth and the Phillips Curve, *NBER Working Paper,* 8421.

Blinder, A. (2000), 'The Internet and the new economy', *Brookings Institution Policy Brief* 60.

Cette, G. and A. Sylvain (2003), 'L'accélération de la productivité aux Etats-Unis y a-t-elle réellement permis une détente inflationniste?' *Bulletin de la Banque de France* 109 (Janvier).

Cette, G., J. Mairesse and Y. Kocoglu (2000), 'La mesure de l'investissement en technologies de l'information et de la communication: quelques considérations méthodologiques', *Economie et Statistique* 339–340 (2000-9/10).

Cette, G., J. Mairesse and Y. Kocoglu (2002), 'Croissance économique et diffusion des TIC: le cas de la France sur longue période [1980–2000]', *Revue Francaise d'Economie* XVI (3).

Cette, G., J. Mairesse and Y. Kocoglu (2004), 'ICT diffusion and potentiel output growth', Banque de France, *Notes d'Etudes et de Recherches*, no 112.

Gordon, R. (2000), 'Does the New Economy measure up to the great inventions of the past?' *Journal of Economic Perspectives*, **14** (4).

Jorgenson, D. and K. Stiroh (1999), 'Productivity growth: current recovery and longer-term trend', *The American Economic Review,* **89** (2).

Jorgenson, D., M.S. Ho and K. Stiroh (2002), 'Projecting productivity growth: lessons from the US growth resurgence', *Federal Reserve Bank of Atlanta Economic Review*, Third Quarter, 1–14.

Meyer, L.H. (2000a), 'The economic outlook and the challenges facing monetary policy – remarks at the century club breakfast series', Research Memorandum, 19 October.

Meyer, L.H. (2000b), 'The economic outlook and the challenges facing monetary policy – remarks before the Toronto association for business and economics', Research Memorandum, 12 April.

Oliner, S. and D. Sichel (2002), 'Information technology and productivity: where are we now and where are we going?' *Federal Reserve Bank of Atlanta Economic Review*, Third Quarter, 15–44.

Stiroh, K. (2001), 'What drives productivity growth?' *FRBNY Economic Policy Review*, March, 37–59.

4. Yeasty Investment and Mushroom Productivity Growth: an Industry Perspective on European and American Performance, 1987–2003

Robert Inklaar and Marcel P. Timmer

4.1 INTRODUCTION

Since the mid-1990s, European labour productivity growth has been lower than in earlier decades, as well as lower than in the United States. This has attracted a large amount of research (e.g. O'Mahony and van Ark, 2003) and attention by policy makers (European Commission, 2004). Figure 4.1 sketches the outline of the situation.[1] Already over the course of a full business cycle, US labour productivity growth has outpaced European growth, suggesting a structural growth deficit.[2] The reasons for the US growth advantage are higher investment in information and communication technologies (ICT) assets as well as faster total factor productivity (TFP) growth. In addition, the pace of investment in non-ICT assets has slowed down noticeably in Europe, depressing growth.[3]

In this chapter we analyze these developments from an industry perspective. Specifically, we aim to determine whether the differences between Europe and the US are due to only a few industries or whether the broader patterns of growth are very different. To answer this question we use data on 25 industries covering the entire market economy in France, Germany, Netherlands, UK and the US for the period 1987–2003. Our main tool to analyze the broad patterns of growth is the Harberger (1998) diagram. Following Harberger's terminology, balanced growth is referred to as 'yeasty', while unbalanced growth is said to follow a 'mushroom' pattern. We find that investment in ICT and non-ICT capital is quite yeasty. Especially the growth of ICT capital services progresses at a very similar rate across industries but non-ICT capital deepening is also quite broad-based. This suggests that changes in (relative) factor prices and other macroeconomic developments may play an important role. TFP growth however, shows a more mushroom-like process, with a limited number of industries making large contributions and many industries making smaller or even negative contributions. An important difference between Europe and the US is that in the US, large TFP contributions do not just originate in the ICT producing sector but also in key market services like wholesale trade, retail trade and finance. Although this explains much of the difference in aggregate growth between Europe and the US, the industry growth pattern is nearly identical.

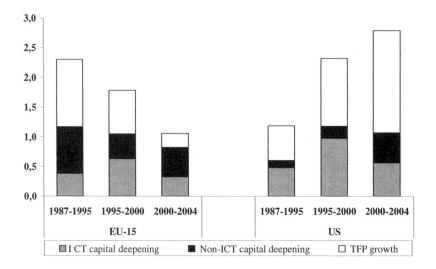

Figure 4.1   Sources of total economy labour productivity growth, EU-15 and US, 1987–2004

The main contribution of this chapter is to provide up-to-date evidence on European and US growth from an industry perspective. However, to our knowledge we are also the first use the Harberger diagram to analyze investment patterns across industries.

While the mushroom pattern of TFP growth is similar to the evidence shown in Harberger (1998), the yeasty nature of investment has received much less attention in the literature.

The rest of this chapter is organised as follows. The next section describes the database and the methods used to analyze the data. In the next four sections, we cover the aggregate growth pattern in more detail and subsequently the patterns of ICT capital deepening, TFP growth and non-ICT capital deepening. The final section summarises and makes some concluding remarks.

4.2   DATA AND METHODOLOGY

In this chapter we follow a basic growth accounting framework to identify the sources of labour productivity growth at the industry level. This requires an extensive dataset covering output, labour and capital input for each industry.[4] For the most part, we build on a previous database, described in detail in Inklaar, O'Mahony and Timmer (2005) but extended to cover the period 1979–2003 using mostly similar methods as for earlier years.

There is data for 25 industries, covering the entire market economy[5] for France, Germany, the Netherlands, United Kingdom and United States. In this paper, we focus on the period 1987–2003, centred around 1995 as the start of the US productivity revival.[6]

For data on output and total hours worked, we rely on the GGDC (2005) 60-industry database. In addition, data has been collected on employment and wages for different worker types, distinguished by the level of educational attainment, from national labour force surveys.[7] To cover capital input, investment data for six assets for each industry have been constructed. Investment data covers three ICT categories (computers, communication equipment and software) and three non-ICT assets (buildings, transport equipment and other, non-ICT equipment). The data are mostly available directly in detailed tables from statistical offices, but in some cases additional survey material was used.[8]

Calculating Capital Stocks and Rental Prices

Capital input is measured by capital service flows, following the methodology pioneered by Jorgenson and Griliches (1967) and more recently implemented in Jorgenson, Ho and Stiroh (2005). With investment for a sufficiently long period of time, capital stocks can be calculated using the perpetual inventory method (PIM) as:

$$K_t^i = (1 - \delta^i)K_{t-1}^i + I_t \qquad (4.1)$$

where K_t^i is the capital stock at constant prices of asset i at time t, δ^i is the geometric depreciation rate of capital good i and I_t is investment at constant prices. The capital stocks for each asset are combined into aggregate service flows using the share of each asset in capital compensation. Capital compensation is calculated as the capital stock at current prices times the gross rate of return of a capital asset:

$$r_t^i = R_t + \delta_t^i - \dot{p}_t^i \qquad (4.2)$$

where the gross return r_t^i of asset i at time t is determined by the rate of return R, the depreciation rate of the asset and its rate of price change $\dot{p}_t^i$. Growth in capital input is measured by capital service flows as follows:

$$\Delta \ln K_t = \sum_j \overset{-K}{v}_{j,t} \Delta \ln K_t \qquad (4.3)$$

where $\overset{-K}{v}_{j,t}$, is the two-period average share of asset type j in total nominal capital compensation. In the results below, ICT capital services and non-ICT capital services are distinguished. ICT capital services are calculated by weighting each of the ICT capital stocks by the share of the asset in total ICT capital compensation. Non-ICT capital services are calculated analogously. The labour input services from different types of workers are similarly calculated by weighting the growth in hours worked by the average share of each worker type in labour compensation.

Growth Accounting

To assess the contribution of the various inputs to aggregate growth, a growth accounting framework is followed as developed by Jorgenson and associates and used in for example Jorgenson et al. (2005). For each industry gross value added (Y) is produced from an aggregate input X, consisting of ICT capital services (K^{ICT}), non-ICT capital services (K^N) and labour services (L). Productivity is represented as a Hicks-neutral augmentation of the aggregate input (A). The industry production function (industry and time subscripts are omitted) takes the following form:

$$Y = AX(L, K^N, K^{ICT}) \qquad (4.4)$$

with superscript ^{N} indicating services from non-ICT capital and superscript ^{ICT} indicating services from ICT capital. Under the assumption of price-taking on factor markets, cost minimisation by firms and full input utilisation, the growth of output can be expressed as the (compensation share) weighted growth of inputs and total factor productivity, denoted by A, which is derived as a residual:

$$\Delta \ln Y = \overset{-L}{v} \Delta \ln L + \overset{-K}{v} \Delta \ln K + \overset{-ICT}{v} \Delta \ln ICT + \Delta \ln A \qquad (4.5)$$

where $\overset{-L}{v}$ denotes the two-period average share of input i in total factor income. Imposing constant returns to scale implies $1 = \overset{-L}{v} + \overset{-K}{v} + \overset{-ICT}{v}$.

As in Jorgenson et al. (2005), labour composition change ($\Delta \ln q^L$) is defined as the difference between the growth of labour input and the growth of total hours worked:

$$\Delta \ln q^L = \sum_h \overset{-L}{v}_h \Delta \ln L_h - \Delta \ln \sum_h L_h = \Delta \ln L - \Delta \ln H \qquad (4.6)$$

here L is the labour input index, aggregated over the h labour types using labour compensation shares and H_t is total hours worked, summed over the different labour types.

By rearranging equation (4.5), the results can be presented in terms of average labour productivity growth defined as the growth of value added minus growth of hours worked, $\Delta \ln y = \Delta \ln Y - \Delta \ln H$, the growth in capital services per hour worked, $\Delta \ln k = \Delta \ln K - \Delta \ln H$, labour composition change and TFP growth as follows:

$$\Delta \ln y = v^{-L} \ln q^{L} + v^{-K} \ln k^{N} + v^{-ICT} \ln k^{ICT} + \ln A \qquad (4.7)$$

Aggregation and Industry Contributions

The focus in this chapter is on the contribution of industry input growth and TFP growth to aggregate labour productivity growth. Jorgenson et al. (2005) distinguish three methods to aggregate output and inputs across industries, namely the aggregate production function, the aggregate production possibility frontier and aggregation over industries.

Here the third method is employed, which does not assume that the prices of value added and inputs are equal across industries.[9] This means that industry growth rates of output and inputs are weighted by their share in aggregate value added to calculate contributions to aggregate labour productivity growth.

As Stiroh (2002) shows, aggregate labour productivity growth can be decomposed into contributions from industries as:

$$\Delta \ln y = \sum_i \overline{w}_i \Delta \ln y_i + \left(\sum_i \overline{w}_i \ln H_i - \ln \sum_i H_i \right) = \sum_i \overline{w}_i \ln y_i + R \qquad (4.8)$$

In equation (4.8), w_i is the share of industry i in total value added and a bar over a variable denotes the two-period average. Aggregate labour productivity growth is the weighted sum of industry productivity growth plus a reallocation term R. This reallocation term gives the differences between the output-weighted growth of hours and (roughly) the employment-weighted growth of hours. If this term is positive, industries where the output share is larger than the employment share are showing faster employment growth than industries where the reverse is true. In other words, the reallocation term is positive if employment shifts towards high productivity industries.

Combining the decomposition of aggregate labour productivity in (4.8) with equation (4.7), the full decomposition of aggregate labour productivity growth can be written as:

$$\Delta \ln y = \sum_i \overline{w}_i \left(v_i^{-L} \ln q^{L} + v_i^{-N} \ln k^{N} + v_i^{-ICT} \ln k^{ICT} + \ln A_i \right) + R \qquad (4.9)$$

In this way, the contribution of each industry from ICT and non-ICT investment and TFP growth to aggregate labour productivity growth can be calculated. For example, the contribution of ICT-capital deepening in industry i to aggregate labour productivity growth is given by:

$$LPCON_i^{ICT} = \overline{w}_i (\overline{v}_i^{ICT} \Delta \ln k_i^{ICT}) \qquad (4.10)$$

which is the growth of ICT capital per hour worked in industry i weighted by the share of ICT capital compensation of industry i in aggregate nominal value added. The weight is the product of the share of industry i in aggregate value added ($\overline{w}_i$) and the share of ICT capital compensation in industry value added ($\overline{v}_i^{ICT}$).

Similar calculations can be carried out for the contributions of non-ICT capital, labour composition and TFP.[10]

Harberger Diagrams

As can be imagined, the wealth of data makes it challenging to present the results in a comprehensive, yet insightful fashion. One instrument to do this is the Harberger diagram (see Harberger, 1998). The Harberger diagram provides a convenient graphical summary of the industry pattern of growth. The diagram shows the cumulative contribution of the industries to aggregate growth on the y-axis and the cumulative share of these industries on the x-axis. The industries are first ranked by growth rate to ensure a concave diagram.

The resulting pattern can have a more yeasty or mushroom character, depending on the number of industries contributing positively to aggregate growth and the distribution of growth rates. Growth is yeasty when it is broad-based and taking place in many industries or firms. Mushroom growth indicates a pattern in which only a limited number of industries contribute positively to aggregate growth.

For illustration purposes, Figure 4.2 shows two examples of Harberger diagrams. For easy comparison, the sum of the industry contributions is the same for both diagrams, implying equal aggregate growth. The top line is an example of 'mushroom'-type growth. Not all industries have positive growth, as the downward sloping part of the diagram implies some industries have negative growth. The second diagram is an example of more yeasty, balanced growth. It is closer to the straight diagonal line, so the growth rates of the industries are relatively close to each other and in addition, all industries have positive growth.

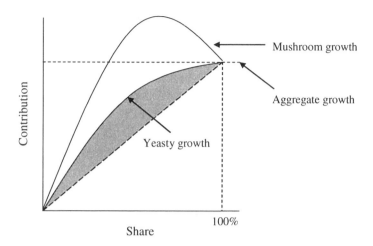

Figure 4.2   Illustration of Harberger diagrams

Diagrams such as these can be useful to quickly identify how important certain industries are in achieving growth. To compare diagrams of different shapes and with different levels of aggregate growth, it is useful to devise some summary statistics of the Harberger diagram. Figure 4.2 suggests that the general shape of the diagram can be summarised by three statistics, namely:

1. aggregate growth, which is the sum of industry contributions,
2. the cumulative share of industries with positive contributions, as an indicator of the pervasiveness of growth[11] and
3. the curvature as measured by the area between the diagram and the diagonal line (the shaded area in the case of the yeasty diagram) divided by the total area beneath the diagram. This relative area measure lies between zero and one. It is zero when all industries have equal growth and when industry growth rates start to diverge, the relative area increases.[12]

Aggregate Results

To focus the subsequent analysis, it is useful to identify the main contributors to the divergence between Europe and the US. Figure 4.1 already showed that labour productivity growth in Europe slowed down after 1995 from a combination of lower TFP growth and lower non-ICT capital deepening, while the US accelerated due to faster investment, both in ICT and non-ICT assets, and higher TFP growth. However, Figure 4.1 covered the total economy, which includes the hard-to-measure non-market services and it is based on a top-down view of each of the economies.

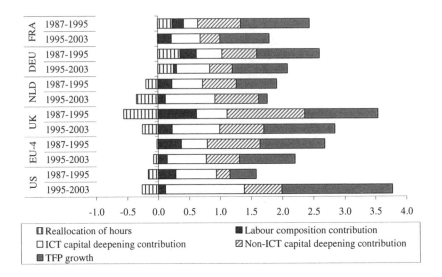

Figure 4.3   Sources of market economy labour productivity growth, EU-4 and US, 1987–2003

Table 4.1 and Figure 4.3 present a decomposition of labour productivity growth for the market economies, which excludes non-market services, in the four European countries we cover and the United States. An aggregate of the European countries, dubbed EU-4, is also added to facilitate the comparison. Figure 4.3 shows broadly the same sources of divergence as Figure 4.1, but especially the performance of the US economy is more striking due to the larger share of market services in the market economy than in the total economy. Furthermore, the EU-4 slowdown in TFP growth is less pronounced than for the EU-15, mostly because the EU-4 does not include Italy and Spain. The two categories that were not distinguished in Figure 4.1, namely the reallocation of hours and labour composition change are relatively less important as a source of divergence than the other contributors to growth. Table 4.1 shows the data underlying Figure 4.3.

The growth performance of individual European countries is of course not perfectly captured by the EU-4 aggregate. For example, UK labour productivity growth after 1995 is relatively close to the rates achieved in the US, while especially France and the Netherlands show considerably slower growth than the EU-4 average. The Netherlands also shows a more pronounced deceleration in TFP growth than the EU-4, but little change in the pace of non-ICT deepening. Despite some of the differences between the countries, in general the main observations about EU-US differences also hold for the individual countries. In the remainder of the chapter, the main focus is on the differences between Europe and the US, but individual country results will be covered in the summary statistics. From the point of view of the EU–US differences, the most interesting questions are on the industry patterns of ICT capital deepening, TFP growth and non-ICT capital deepening. The following three sections deal with each of these in turn.

Table 4.1   Sources of market economy labour productivity growth in Europe and the US, 1987–2003

	Labour productivity growth	Reallocation of hours	Labour composition contribution	ICT capital deepening contribution	Non-ICT capital deepening contribution	TFP growth
			Panel A: 1987–1995			
EU-4	2.7	0.0	0.4	0.4	0.9	1.0
US	1.4	-0.2	0.3	0.7	0.2	0.4
France	2.4	0.2	0.2	0.2	0.7	1.1
Germany	2.6	0.4	0.3	0.4	0.6	1.0
Netherlands	1.7	-0.2	0.2	0.5	0.5	0.6
UK	3.0	-0.6	0.6	0.5	1.2	1.2
			Panel B: 1995–2003			
EU-4	2.1	-0.1	0.1	0.6	0.5	0.9
US	3.5	-0.3	0.1	1.3	0.6	1.8
France	1.8	0.0	0.2	0.5	0.3	0.8
Germany	2.1	0.3	0.0	0.5	0.4	0.9
Netherlands	1.4	-0.4	0.1	0.8	0.7	0.1
UK	2.6	-0.3	0.2	0.8	0.7	1.1

ICT Capital Deepening

Figure 4.4 shows Harberger diagrams for the EU-4 and the US on the ICT capital deepening contribution of each industry to market economy labour productivity growth over the period 1995–2003. These charts are not typical Harberger diagrams because they show the capital deepening contribution to labour productivity growth instead of TFP or labour productivity growth. As a result, the shares on the x-axis do not add up to 100 per cent, but instead to the share of ICT capital in value added. The aggregate growth line in these diagrams corresponds to the ICT capital deepening contribution from Table 4.1.

Judging by the nearly diagonal diagrams, ICT diffusion is a balanced process, with the growth in ICT capital per hour worked comparable across industries. The level of investment is very different across industries, though. In both regions, business services, finance and communications make the largest contributions. The most important difference between the two diagrams is the total ICT contribution. In the EU-4, the ICT share in value added is about half as large as in the US, and as a result, the ICT contribution to labour productivity growth is also half as large.

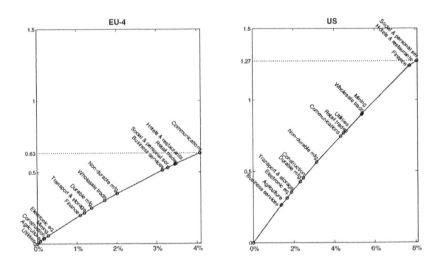

Figure 4.4   Harberger diagram of EU-4 and US ICT capital deepening contribution to labour productivity growth, 1995–2003

Table 4.2 shows the summary statistics for ICT capital deepening in the US and the individual European countries. This table reveals that ICT diffusion is also a 'yeasty' process in each of the EU-countries.[13] In the 1995–2003 period all industries make positive contributions to aggregate growth and the relative areas are close to zero, which means that all Harberger diagrams are close to the diagonal. Furthermore, the differences between the 1987–1995 and the 1995–2003 period are relatively small, which is why Figure 4.4 only shows the 1995–2003 results. After 1995, ICT investment has become a bit more balanced, but there has been a largely uniform shift upwards in the level of the ICT contribution. An important part of the reason for this homogeneity is that prices of ICT assets have been decreasing by around 10–15 per cent per year over the entire period. This means that even with unchanging investment at current prices, investment in constant prices increases by this amount each year.[14]

Table 4.2   Harberger diagrams of ICT capital deepening, 1987–2003, summary statistics

	Sum of contributions	Share of positive contributions	Relative area under Harberger
Panel A: 1987–1995			
EU-4	0.4	100	0.12
US	0.7	94	0.17
France	0.2	100	0.15
Germany	0.4	100	0.22
Netherlands	0.5	100	0.13
UK	0.5	100	0.10
Panel B: 1995–2003			
EU-4	0.6	100	0.07
US	1.3	100	0.07
France	0.5	100	0.14
Germany	0.5	100	0.13
Netherlands	0.8	100	0.10
UK	0.8	100	0.05

TFP growth Figures 4.5a and 4.5b show Harberger diagrams of TFP growth for the 1987–1995 and the 1995–2003 periods respectively. In the 1987–1995 period, European TFP growth outpaced US growth, for a considerable part due to faster growth in durable and nondurable manufacturing. Similar industries show positive growth in both regions, like transport and storage and retail trade. Likewise, industries such as business services and finance can be found on the downward sloping part of the diagram in both the EU-4 and the US. The main difference is that many of the industries with positive growth have higher growth rates in Europe than the US and this leads to a more balanced growth pattern in Europe.

This pattern changed considerably after 1995. European growth became more reliant on a number of industries, notably the ICT producing sector, although the overall TFP growth rate stayed roughly constant. Growth in the US accelerated sharply, leading to a relatively more balanced growth pattern. Again, most industries are in a similar location on the diagrams in both regions, but a number of key market services show much faster growth in the US than in Europe. Retail trade and wholesale trade also had positive growth before 1995, but finance had declining TFP before 1995 and throughout the period in Europe. The large contribution of finance in the US therefore represents perhaps the clearest break with previous trends.

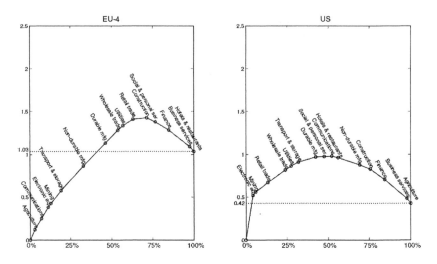

Figure 4.5a   Harberger diagram of EU-4 and US TFP growth, 1987–1995

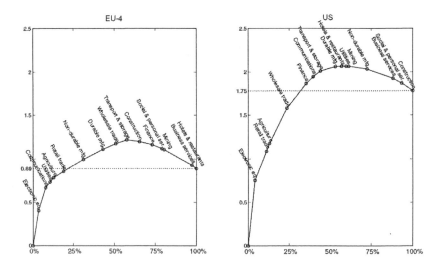

Figure 4.5b   Harberger diagram of EU-4 and US TFP growth, 1995–2003

There are some concerns that statistical practices in the US, chiefly the use of constant-quality price indices, has led to an overstatement of growth in the trade sector (e.g. European Commission 2004). Timmer and Inklaar (2005) show that when harmonising trade output measurement between US and EU, differences are smaller but the US lead in productivity growth remains. Similar scepticism has been voiced about productivity measurement in financial services and specifically securities trade (Stiroh, 2002). Despite limited (internationally comparable) research into these problems, improved statistical practices in the US (BEA, 2004) have probably increased the robustness of these findings. Still, output measurement in services in both Europe and the US is far from straightforward and many potentially important issues remain to be resolved in future research.[15]

Table 4.3   Harberger diagrams of TFP growth, 1987–2003, summary statistics

	Sum of contributions	Share of positive contributions	Relative area under Harberger
Panel A: 1987–1995			
EU-4	1.0	71	0.48
US	0.4	52	0.73
France	1.1	69	0.54
Germany	1.0	65	0.53
Netherlands	0.6	53	0.60
UK	1.2	65	0.54
Panel B: 1995–2003			
EU-4	0.9	58	0.55
US	1.8	60	0.49
France	0.8	54	0.60
Germany	0.9	73	0.61
Netherlands	0.1	51	0.86
UK	1.1	65	0.51

Table 4.3 shows the summary statistics of the Harberger diagrams for all countries. Again, the first column, showing the sum of contributions, corresponds to the aggregate growth rates in Table 4.1. The statistics confirm some of the observations for the EU-4 and US: after 1995 US growth became more balanced, judging by the greater share of positive contributions and the smaller relative area. The EU-4 shows the reverse pattern: while aggregate growth is similar throughout the period, a smaller share of industries makes positive contributions and the relative area has increased. It is interesting to see that these trends have led to a similar TFP growth pattern.

Of the European countries, France fits the change in growth pattern most closely with both a strongly decreasing share of positive contributions and a larger relative area. Germany and the Netherlands also show clear increases in the relative area under the diagram though. The UK is the one country with a mostly unchanged pattern of TFP growth over time. Overall though, Table 4.3 makes clear that TFP growth follows a mushroom pattern everywhere.

Non-ICT Capital Deepening

The previous two sections covered the reasons why US labour productivity growth outpaced European growth after 1995, namely higher levels of ICT investment and faster TFP growth. This still leaves the third source of divergence: non-ICT capital deepening.

In Table 4.1, it could be seen that non-ICT capital deepening contributed about as much to EU-4 growth as to US growth after 1995, but this is the result of increased investment in the US and a deceleration in the EU-4. Figures 4.6a and 4.6b show Harberger diagrams of, respectively, EU-4 and US non-ICT capital deepening for the two periods.

The first observation is that non-ICT investment is relatively yeasty, although to a lesser extent for non-ICT deepening in the US for the 1987–1995 period. When comparing the pre-1995 and post-1995 period for the EU-4, the same industries make large positive contributions, most notably business services and non-durable manufacturing. This suggests that not only investment patterns are yeasty in both periods, but also that the slowdown has been relatively evenly distributed across industries.

Table 4.4   Harberger diagrams of Non-ICT capital deepening, 1987–2003, summary statistics

	Sum of contributions	Share of positive contributions	Relative area under Harberger
Panel A: 1987–1995			
EU-4	0.9	100	0.25
US	0.2	75	0.48
France	0.7	87	0.33
Germany	0.6	78	0.43
Netherlands	0.5	78	0.42
UK	1.2	100	0.27
Panel B: 1995–2003			
EU-4	0.5	100	0.24
US	0.6	96	0.27
France	0.3	80	0.44
Germany	0.4	98	0.32
Netherlands	0.7	96	0.31
UK	0.7	90	0.27

Similar observations can be made for the US, although some industries showed declining capital intensity over the 1987–1995 period. Here too, many industries make relatively similar contributions in both periods, suggesting a more or less uniform acceleration. Table 4.4 shows that for each country the relative area is larger than in Table 4.2 for ICT capital deepening but smaller than in Table 4.3 for TFP growth. In our view though, the very high share of positive contributions makes yeast the best description of the non-ICT growth pattern.

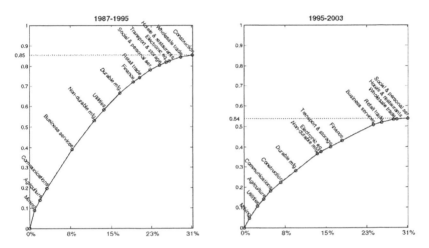

*Figure 4.6a   Harberger diagram of EU-4 Non-ICT capital deepening,
              1987–1995 and 1995–2003*

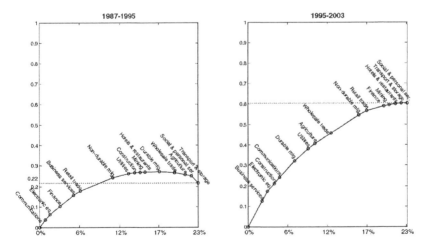

*Figure 4.6b   Harberger diagram of US Non-ICT capital deepening,
              1987–1995 and 1995–2003*

4.3 CONCLUSIONS

In this chapter we have looked at the industry pattern of growth in four major European countries (France, Germany, Netherlands and UK) and the US. We have focused on the main drivers of the divergence in labour productivity growth after 1995 between Europe and the US. Compared to the 1987–1995 period, the US had faster labour productivity growth than Europe in the 1995–2003 period because of higher levels of ICT investment and faster total factor productivity (TFP) growth. In addition, investment in non-ICT assets accelerated in the US and slowed down in Europe, further contributing to the divergence.

Our main tool for analyzing industry growth patterns is the Harberger (1998) diagram that shows the cumulative contribution of the industries to aggregate growth. This way, the contributions from many industries can conveniently be summarised and compared. While originally the Harberger diagram has mostly been used to look at the industry pattern of TFP growth, we show that it can also shed light on industry investment patterns.

Our analysis shows that investment in both ICT assets and non-ICT assets is quite balanced, or yeasty in nature. In other words, capital services per hour worked grow at comparable rates across industries, especially in the case of ICT investment. Furthermore, there are considerable similarities in the importance of different industries across countries. For example, finance and business services are two of the most important ICT investors in Europe and the US. Likewise, non-durable manufacturing and business services are among the more important investors in non-ICT assets in both regions throughout the period. As a result, the European slowdown and American acceleration in non-ICT deepening is a broad-based phenomenon just like the diffusion of ICT.

The yeastiness of investment suggests that macroeconomic developments, such as changes in relative factor prices are important drivers of investment patterns. One narrative that could explain the observed investment patterns is that ICT assets have become much cheaper over time, leading to substitution away from non-ICT assets and (unskilled) labour. Wage moderation in Europe may have made non-ICT assets even less attractive. Technological opportunities differ across industries leading to differences in the level of investment. However, investment prices are the same across industries so if elasticities are similar, changes in investment over time should be comparable too. Evidence on these hypotheses has been less easy to come by, although Estevao (2004) does find some support for the wage moderation story.[16]

In contrast to the yeasty nature of investment, TFP growth is much more localised or 'mushroom'-like. The ICT producing industries are important in this respect, but especially in the US, key market services like wholesale trade, retail trade and finance also contribute much. Indeed, due to faster growth in these market services, US TFP growth has become more balanced after 1995, and now closely resembles European growth patterns. But while the growth pattern is comparable, the level of TFP growth has been much higher in the US since 1995.

It is much harder to tell a plausible story of why TFP growth shows a mushroom pattern. As the original Harberger (1998) article pointed out, our understanding of the driving forces of TFP growth is still limited. Especially in services, our lack of understanding is pressing, since the US experience shows it can be an important source of growth. An agenda towards better understanding productivity growth in services should include efforts to improve output measurement in services, as well as better measurement of innovative activities. For example, firm-level work by Brynjolfsson and Hitt (2000, 2003) shows that TFP growth can be partly explained by a combination of ICT investment and investments in non-technical innovation like organisational change.

However, recent evidence suggests that the productive returns to ICT investment are in line with their marginal cost, so there is no evidence on TFP spillovers at the industry level.[17] An additional ingredient of the productivity research agenda should therefore include reconciling new firm-level research with industry and macroeconomic evidence.

NOTES

1. These data are from the GGDC Total Economy Growth Accounting Database. See www.ggdc.net and Timmer and van Ark (2005) for further details.
2. The figure shows the EU-15 or the 15 European member countries before the Accession round in May 2004.
3. See Timmer and van Ark (2005).
4. In this paper, we use value added as our measure of industry output instead of gross output. The input-output tables that are necessary for growth accounting analysis on a gross output basis are not available yet.
5. Non-market services (government, education and health) are not included in the analysis here, mostly due to measurement problems related to the output of these industries. The real estate industry is also left out because most of the output of this industry consists of imputed housing rents.
6. See Inklaar et al. (2005) for results extending back to 1979. See also www.ggdc.net.
7. No data have been collected for years after 2000, so the composition of the workforce of each industry is assumed to have stayed constant since then.
8. See Inklaar et al. (2005) for further details. The main difference with the database described in that paper is that for the US, new data based on the 1997 Capital Flow Table, with mostly more detailed data on software have been incorporated (see Meade et al., 2003 for more details).
9. An aggregate production function exists only if gross output prices, and hence value added prices, as well as input prices are equal across industries. For an aggregate production possibilities frontier, input prices need to be equal.

10. For a more extensive description of methodology, see Inklaar et al. (2005).
11. Harberger (1998) stresses the importance of the share of industries that together make up aggregate growth. In other words, he focuses on the crossing of the aggregate growth line in Figure 4.2. We feel that a split between industries with positive growth and with negative growth is a more natural distinction.
12. In practice, the diagrams are not smooth as in Figure 4.2 as we have a discrete number of industries. Instead they consist of piecewise linear plots. This means the area underneath the diagram can be calculated as the sum of triangles and squares.
13. Instead of all individual manufacturing industries, a group of non-durable and durable manufacturers is formed. Electronic equipment manufacturing is shown separately. Calculations based on all industries are nearly identical and available upon request.
14. A reason for the similar growth rates across countries is that we use harmonised US deflators for ICT assets (as well as for ICT producing industries). For more details, see Inklaar et al. (2005).
15. Triplett and Bosworth (2004) discuss many of the most important issues.
16. In the survey of Caballero (1999), a number of explanations are advanced for why it is hard to find a relationship between investment and the cost of capital.
17. See Inklaar and van Ark (2005). Stiroh (2003) surveys the literature on estimated output elasticities of ICT capital and comes to similar conclusions. O'Mahony and Vecchi (2003) show recent estimates that do suggest positive TFP spillovers.

REFERENCES

BEA (2004), 'Updated Summary NIPA Methodologies', *Survey of Current Business*, November 2004, 15–32.

Brynjolfsson, E. and L. Hitt (2000), 'Beyond computation: information technology, organizational transformation and business performance', *Journal of Economic Perspectives*, **14** (4), 23–48.

Brynjolfsson, E. and L. Hitt (2003), 'Computing productivity: firm-level evidence', *Review of Economics and Statistics*, **85** (4), 793–808.

Caballero, R.J. (1999), 'Aggregate Investment', in J.B. Taylor and M. Woodford (eds), *Handbook of Macroeconomics*, North Holland, Amsterdam, 813–862.

Estevao, M.M. (2004), 'Why is productivity growth in the euro area so sluggish?' *IMF Working Paper* WP/04/200.

European Commission (2004), 'The EU Economy 2004', *Review, European Economy* No 6, 2004, Office for Official Publications of the EC, Luxembourg.

Groningen Growth and Development Centre (2005), *60-industry database*, October, downloadable at www.ggdc.net.

Harberger, A.C. (1998), 'A Vision of the Growth Process', *American Economic Review*, **88** (1), 1–32

Inklaar, R. and B. van Ark (2005), 'Catching Up or Getting Stuck? Europe's Troubles to Exploit ICT's Productivity Potential', *GGDC Research Memorandum*, GD-79

Inklaar, R., M. O'Mahony and M.P. Timmer (2005), 'ICT and Europe's Productivity Performance, Industry-level Growth Account Comparisons with the United States', *Review of Income and Wealth*, **51** (3).

Jorgenson, D.W. and Zvi Griliches (1967), 'The Explanation of Productivity Change', *Review of Economic Studies*, **34**, 249–83.

Jorgenson, D.W., Mun Ho and K.J. Stiroh (2005), 'Growth of US Industries and Investments in Information Technology and Higher Education', forthcoming in Corrado, Haltiwanger and Sichel (eds), *Measuring Capital in the New Economy*, University of Chicago Press, Chicago.

Meade, D.S., S.J. Rzeznik and D.C. Robinson-Smith (2003), 'Business Investment by Industry in the US Economy for 1997', *Survey of Current Business*, November 2003, 18–70.

O'Mahony, M. and B. van Ark, eds. (2003), *EU Productivity and Competitiveness: An Industry Perspective. Can Europe Resume the Catching-up Process?* Office for Official Publications of the European Communities, Luxembourg.

O'Mahony, M. and M. Vecchi (2003), 'Is there an ICT impact on TFP? A heterogeneous dynamic panel approach', *NIESR Discussion Paper*, 219, downloadable at http://www.niesr.ac.uk/pubs/dps/dp219.pdf

Stiroh, K.J. (2002), 'Information Technology and the US Productivity Revival: What Do the Industry Data Say?', *American Economic Review* **92** (5), 1559–1576.

Stiroh, K.J. (2003), 'Reassessing the Role of IT in the Production Function: A Meta-Analysis', downloadable at http://www.newyorkfed.org/research/economists/stiroh/ks_meta.pdf

Timmer, M.P., and B. van Ark (2005) 'Does Information And Communication Technology Drive Productivity Growth Differentials? A Comparison Of The European Union Countries And The United States', forthcoming in *Oxford Economic Papers.*

Timmer, M.P., and R. Inklaar (2005), 'Productivity Differentials in the US and EU Distributive Trade Sector: Statistical Myth or Reality?' *GGDC Research Memorandum*, GD-76, downloadable at www.ggdc.net.

Triplett, J.E. and B.P. Bosworth (2004), *Productivity in the US Services Sector, New Sources of Economic Growth*, Brookings Institution, Washington DC.

5. Growth Patterns in the OECD Area: Evidence from the Aggregate, Industry and Firm Level

Dirk Pilat

5.1 INTRODUCTION

The promotion of growth and productivity are on the policy agenda in most OECD countries, as governments seek to address problems related to sluggish growth, such as low employment growth, high unemployment or fiscal deficits. This agenda has also affected the work of the OECD. A comprehensive study of growth performance in the OECD area, including a set of policy recommendations, was presented to the OECD Ministerial meeting in May 2001 (OECD, 2001). Further findings and policy recommendations, focusing on the role of firm dynamics, regulatory factors and information and communications technology (ICT), were released in 2003 (OECD, 2003a; 2003b).

This chapter returns to the findings of these OECD studies and presents new empirical evidence on economic growth and its key drivers at the aggregate, industry and firm level. It particularly focuses on the different growth experience of the main OECD regions, notably Europe and the United States. The next section discusses aggregate growth patterns in the OECD area and the main drivers of growth at the aggregate, industry and firm level. It also examines some of the factors that influence the impact of these drivers on growth performance and the policies that may help strengthen growth. The third section focuses on multi-factor productivity (MFP) growth, or the overall efficiency of labour and capital, and some of the factors that may have influenced the pick-up in MFP growth in certain OECD countries. The final section draws some conclusions.

5.2 GROWTH PATTERNS IN THE OECD AREA

Growth Diverged in the OECD Area

The interest of many OECD countries in economic growth over the past years was linked to the strong performance of the United States over the second half of the 1990s and the reversal of the catch-up pattern that had characterised the OECD area over the 1950s and the 1960s. During much of the early post-war period, most OECD countries grew rapidly as they recovered from the war and applied US technology and knowledge to upgrade their economies. For most OECD countries, this catch-up period came to a halt in the 1970s; average growth rates of GDP per capita over the 1973–1992 period for much of the OECD area were only half that of the preceding period, and many OECD countries no longer grew faster than the United States (Maddison, 2001).

During the 1990s, a different pattern emerged. Even though the United States already had the highest level of GDP per capita in the OECD area at the beginning of the decade, it expanded its lead on many of the other major OECD countries during the second half of the 1990s. A few other OECD countries, including Australia, Canada, Finland, Greece, Ireland, Portugal and Sweden, also registered markedly stronger growth of GDP per capita over the 1995–2002 period compared with the 1980–1995 period (OECD, 2003a; De Serres, 2003). The increase in GDP per capita in several other OECD countries, including Japan, Germany and Italy, slowed sharply over the second half of the 1990s, leading to a divergence with the United States (Figure 5.1).

Even though US growth performance is no longer considered to be as exceptional as was claimed during the 'new economy' hype, its strong performance over the second half of the 1990s has increased interest in the analysis of economic growth and the sources of growth differentials across countries. The OECD work suggests that the divergence in growth performance in the OECD area is not due to only one cause, but that it reflects a wide range of factors. These are discussed below in more detail. Differences in the measurement of growth and productivity might also be contributing to the observed variation in performance. A recent OECD study (Ahmad et al., 2003) suggests that such differences probably only account for a small part of the variation in growth performance. Moreover, to reduce the uncertainty of empirical analysis related to the choice of data, OECD has developed a new Productivity Database, which is used in this chapter (Box 5.1).

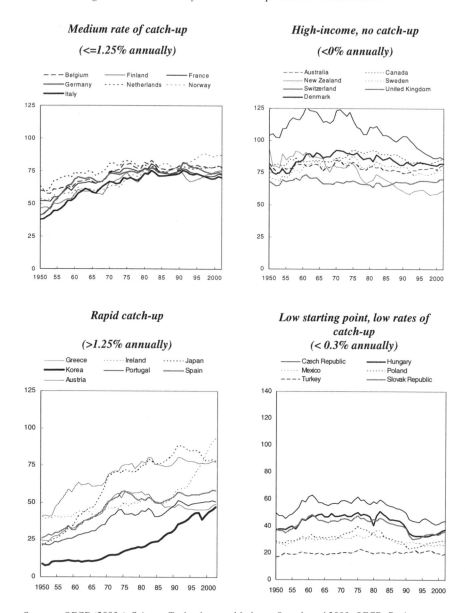

Source: OECD (2003c), Science, Technology and Industry Scoreboard 2003, OECD, Paris.

Figure 5.1   Catch up and convergence in OECD income levels, 1950–2002, United States = 100

Box 5.1: The OECD Productivity Database

Productivity comparisons constitute an important focus of OECD work. It includes both efforts to improve the measurement of productivity growth, and efforts to improve the understanding of the drivers of productivity performance and the policies that governments could undertake to strengthen productivity performance. Such analysis reflects a strong interest in many OECD Member countries. The OECD Productivity Database aims at meeting the demand of inside and outside users of OECD statistics by bringing together those series that are judged best suited for productivity analysis. Where possible, data has been complemented with methodological information to facilitate an assessment of its quality and its international comparability.

The productivity database has been developed in co-operation between several parts of the organisation to streamline efforts and to bring together relevant expertise. At this point, and concerning measures of productivity growth, the database comprises the following series: (i) Measures of output growth (GDP); (ii) labour input growth (index of total hours worked); (iii) labour productivity growth (index of GDP per hour worked); (iv) capital services growth; (v) growth of combined labour and capital inputs; (vi) cost shares of inputs; (vi) multi-factor productivity growth.

Presently, these data are available at the level of the total economy, covering about 26 countries for measures of labour productivity and about 14 OECD countries, including the G7 countries, for capital services and multi-factor productivity. The data for labour productivity typically cover the period 1970–2002, whereas those for capital services and MFP are available for the period 1985–2002 (or the latest year available).

The Productivity database can be accessed from the Statistics Portal of the OECD web pages (http://www.oecd.org/home/) under the entry 'Productivity measures' as of March 15, 2004.

Labour Utilisation Plays a Key Role

The first factor affecting growth differences concerns labour utilisation (Figure 5.2).

In the first half of the 1990s, most European countries, with the exception of Ireland and the Netherlands, were characterised by a combination of high labour productivity growth and declining labour utilisation. The high productivity growth of these EU countries may thus have been achieved by a greater use of capital or by dismissing (or not employing) low-productivity workers. In contrast, the United States, Australia, Ireland and the Netherlands experienced a combination of strong productivity growth and stable or growing labour utilisation. In the second half of the 1990s, most European countries improved their performance in terms of labour utilisation, as unemployment rates fell and labour participation increased. However, this was accompanied by a sharp decline in labour productivity growth. In contrast, some other OECD countries, such as Canada, Ireland and the United States experienced

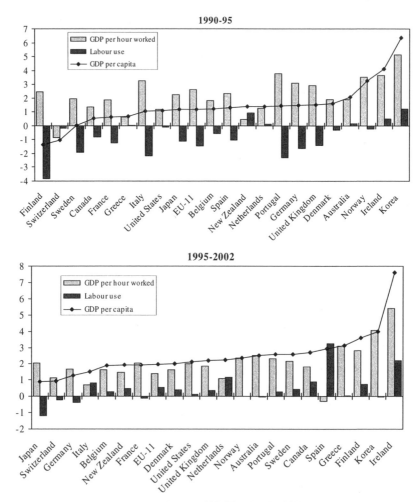

Note: Percentage change at annual rates, 1990–95 and 1995–2002.

Source: OECD, Productivity Database, see De Serres (2003) for estimates adjusted for the business cycle.

Figure 5.2   Changes in labour utilisation contribute to growth in GDP per capita

a pick-up in both labour utilisation and labour productivity growth from 1990–95 to 1995–2002, showing that there need not be a trade-off between labour productivity growth and increased use of labour.[1]

Achieving a combination of labour productivity growth and growing labour utilisation requires well-functioning labour markets that permit and enable reallocation of workers. This is particularly important during times of rapid technological change. Labour market institutions have to ensure that affected workers are given the support and the incentives they need to find new jobs and possibly to retrain. In many countries, institutions and regulations hinder the mobility of workers and prevent the rapid and efficient reallocation of labour resources (OECD, 1999). In most of the countries characterised by a combination of increased labour utilisation and labour productivity, reforms over the 1980s and 1990s improved the functioning of labour markets, effectively enabling more rapid growth.

Despite the progress in enhancing labour utilisation that has been made in many OECD countries over the 1990s, further improvements will be needed, in particular as the population in many OECD countries is ageing rapidly. Moreover, for several European countries, there is still a large scope for improvement in labour utilisation, as it accounts for the bulk of the gap in GDP per capita with the United States (Figure 5.3).

A range of policies may be beneficial to increase labour utilisation, and should not just focus on reducing unemployment, but also on increasing participation in the labour force, notably from women and older workers (De Serres, 2003; OECD, 2003d). The key influences on labour utilisation include tax and benefit systems as well as regulations in labour and product markets (OECD, 2003e). Reform in these areas may help enhance both the incentives for firms to hire workers and for would-be workers to take up work. Efforts to enhance labour utilisation should also include policies to make work pay. For example, schemes under which in-work benefits such as tax reductions are conditional on employment, or where employers are exempt from social security charges if they hire low-skilled workers have been effective when properly targeted (OECD, 2003d). It is also important to increase the opportunities for women to participate in the labour market, for example by enhancing access to child-care facilities and enabling greater flexibility in working time for family workers. Improving prospects for older workers will also require a range of measures, including the removal of incentives for early retirement.

The Impact of Human Capital on Labour Productivity Growth

Labour productivity is the other main driver of GDP per capita shown in Figure 5.2. It can be increased in several ways: by improving the quality of labour used in the production process, increasing the use of capital and im-

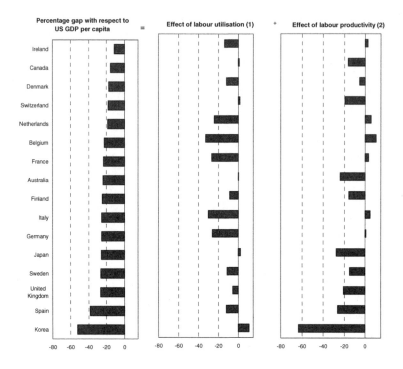

Notes:
Percentage point differences with respect to the United States
1. Based on hours worked per capita.
2. GDP per hour worked.

Source: OECD, National Accounts and Labour Force Statistics, 2003. Hours worked from
OECD Employment Outlook.

Figure 5.3   Income and productivity levels, 2002

proving its quality, and attaining greater overall efficiency in how these factors of production are used together, or multi factor productivity (MFP). The
quality of labour is the first of these, and plays a key role in labour productivity growth. The available empirical evidence suggests that improvements in
the quality of labour have directly contributed to labour productivity growth
in virtually all OECD countries (Bassanini and Scarpetta, 2001; Jorgenson,
2003). This is partly because in all OECD countries, educational policies
have ensured that young entrants to the job market are better educated and
trained on average than those who are retiring from it. For example, in most
OECD countries, more 25–34 year olds have attained tertiary education than
45–54 year olds (Figure 5.4). The OECD Productivity Database does not yet

include estimates of labour quality, although their inclusion is planned for the future. Estimates of labour quality for the G7 countries are included in a recent study by Prof. Dale Jorgenson, however (Jorgenson, 2003). These suggest that the contribution of labour quality to labour productivity growth has declined in most G7 countries over the second half of the 1990s, Italy being the only exception.

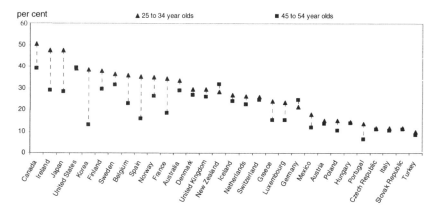

Source: OECD, Education at a Glance, 2002.

Figure 5.4   Percentage of the population that has attained tertiary level education, 2001

This finding can partly be attributed to the large number of low-skilled workers that were integrated into the labour force in several OECD countries over the second half of the 1990s. Moreover, the decline in the contribution of labour quality has also declined over time since the gap in education levels between cohorts of new and retiring workers has declined over time. Growth accounting estimates, such as those presented by Dale Jorgenson, point to an important contribution of human capital to economic growth. They can only take account of changes in educational attainment, however; increases in the level of post-educational skills may also help enhance labour quality, but few hard measures are available.

The Role of Investment

Investment in physical capital is the second factor that plays an important role in labour productivity growth. It expands and renews the existing capital stock and enables new technologies to enter the production process. While some countries have experienced an overall increase in the contribution of capital to growth over the past decade, ICT has typically been the most dynamic area of investment. This reflects rapid technological progress and strong competitive pressure in the production of ICT goods and services and a consequent steep decline in prices. This fall, together with the growing scope for application of ICT (including the impact of Y2K), has encouraged investment in ICT, at times shifting investment away from other assets. The available data show that ICT investment rose from less than 15 per cent of total non-residential investment in the business sector in the early 1980s, to between 15 and 30 per cent in 2001 (OECD, 2003b).

While ICT investment accelerated in most OECD countries, the pace of that investment and its impact on growth differed widely. For the countries for which data are available, ICT investment accounted for between 0.2 and 0.8 percentage points of growth in GDP per capita over the 1995–2001 period (Figure 5.5).[2] The United States and Canada received the largest boost; Australia, the Netherlands and the United Kingdom a sizeable one; and Germany, France and Italy a much smaller one (OECD, 2003b). In some OECD countries, e.g. Australia and Japan, the growing contribution of ICT capital was accompanied by a decline in the contribution of non ICT capital (Figure 5.5).

Investment primarily relies on good fundamentals. Stable macroeconomic policies play a critical role. Evidence for a wide range of OECD countries shows that fiscal discipline, low inflation rates and the reduction in the variability of inflation over the 1990s have helped to boost national savings, reducing uncertainty and enhancing the efficiency of the price mechanisms in allocating resources (OECD, 2001). This has resulted in an improved environment for decision making and has unleashed resources for private investment.

At the same time, the way public finances are improved influences growth. In particular, government is a direct investor in the economy. Although the volume of this investment may be small compared with that of the private sector, it can be of crucial importance. For example, public investment in R&D, transport, communication and infrastructure, to the extent it is of high quality and generates high economic and social returns, can help to create an environment conducive to entrepreneurship, innovation and private sector activity. Similarly, efficient government spending on education should improve the stock of human capital. The pursuit of fiscal consolidation should of course remain a priority in many OECD countries, particularly in view of population ageing, but neglecting public spending in high-return physical and human capital investments can lead to negative economic effects in the medium term. Investment in these areas should thus be given due consideration in public budgets.

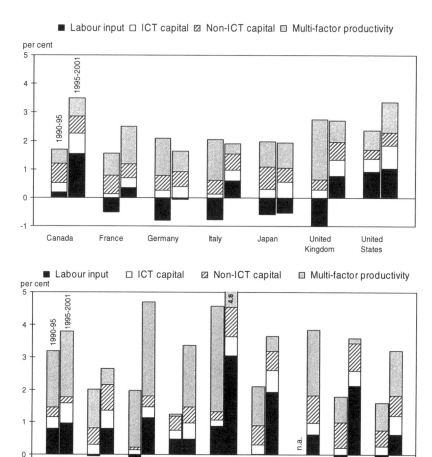

Note: Annual average multi factor productivity growth in Ireland for 1995–2001 was 4.8%, annual average growth of labour input in Finland over 1990-95 was -2.65%.

Source: OECD, Productivity Database and Database on Capital Services, June 2003; Wölfl and Hajkova, 2004.

Figure 5.5   *Contributions of growth to GDP, 1990–95 and 1995–2001, in percentage points*

An important difference between OECD countries is the extent to which countries have invested in ICT (Figure 5.6). A range of indicators on ICT use show that the highest rate of uptake of ICT can typically be observed in the

United States, Canada, New Zealand, Australia, the Nordic countries and the Netherlands (OECD, 2003c). The question that follows concerns the reason why the diffusion of ICT is so different across OECD countries. All countries have been faced with a rapid decline in ICT prices and with growing opportunities for efficiency-enhancing investment in ICT. A number of reasons can be noted. In the first place, firms in countries with higher levels of income and productivity typically have greater incentives to invest in efficiency-enhancing technologies than countries at lower levels of income, since they are faced with higher labour costs. High-income economies have therefore invested significantly more in ICT than OECD economies at lower levels of income. But more specifically, the decision of a firm to adopt ICT depends on the balance of costs and benefits that may be associated with the technology. There is a large range of factors that affect this decision.

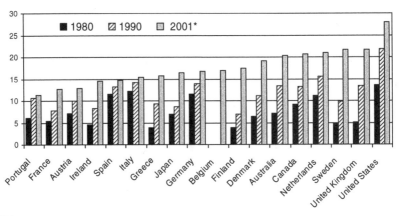

Notes:
*Or latest available year.
Percentage of non residential gross fixed capital formation, total economy.
Estimates of ICT investment are not yet fully standardised across countries, mainly due to differences in the capitalisation of software in different countries. See Ahmad (2003).

Source: OECD, Database on capital services.

Figure 5.6   ICT investment in selected OECD countries

The empirical evidence points to several of these factors (OECD, 2003b; OECD, 2004). This includes the direct costs of ICT, e.g. the costs of ICT equipment, telecommunications or the installation of an e-commerce system. Considerable differences in the costs of ICT persist across OECD countries, despite strong international trade and the liberalisation of the telecommunications industry in OECD countries. Moreover, costs and implementation barriers related to the ability of the firm to absorb new technologies are also important. This includes the availability of know-how and qualified personnel, the scope for organisational change and the capability of a firm to innovate. In addition, competition and regulatory factors are of key importance. A competitive environment is more likely to lead a firm to invest in ICT, as a way to strengthen performance and survive, than a more sheltered environment. Moreover, excessive regulation in product and labour markets may make it difficult for firms to draw benefits from investment in ICT and may thus hold back such spending. These issues will be further discussed below.

5.3 STRENGTHENING MFP GROWTH

The final component that accounts for some of the pick-up in labour productivity growth in the 1990s in certain OECD countries is the acceleration in multi factor productivity (MFP) growth (Figure 5.5). MFP growth rose particularly in Australia, Canada, Finland, France, Greece, Ireland, Sweden and the United States. In other countries, including Germany, Italy, the United Kingdom, Denmark, the Netherlands and Spain, MFP growth slowed down over the 1990s.[3]

The improvement in MFP in some countries reflects a break with slow MFP growth in the 1970s and 1980s and may be due to several sources. Better skills and better technology may have caused the blend of labour and capital to produce more efficiently, organisational and managerial changes may have helped to improve operations, and innovation may have led to more valuable output being produced with a given combination of capital and labour. MFP growth is measured as a residual, however, and it is difficult to provide evidence on such factors. Some is available, though.

Production of ICT – A Boon to MFP Growth in Some Countries

First, in some OECD countries, MFP reflects rapid technological progress in the production of ICT. Technological progress at Intel, for instance, has enabled the amount of transistors packed on a microprocessor to double every 18 months since 1965, and even more rapidly between 1995 and 1999. While the ICT manufacturing sector is relatively small in most OECD countries, it can make a large contribution to growth if it expands much more rapidly than other sectors. Some OECD countries, such as Finland, Ireland, Korea and the United States, benefited from rapid productivity growth in the ICT producing sector in the 1990s (Pilat, Lee and Van Ark, 2002; Figure 5.7).[4]

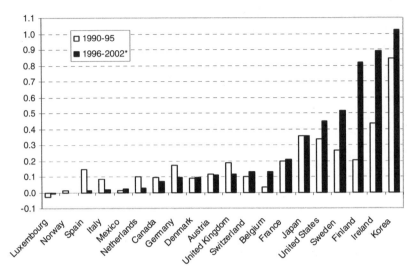

Notes:
1991–95 for Germany; 1992–95 for France and Italy and 1993–95 for Korea; 1996–98 for Sweden, 1996–99 for Korea and Spain, 1996–2000 for Ireland, Norway and Switzerland, 1996–2001 for France, Germany, Japan, Mexico, the Netherlands, the United Kingdom and the United States.
Total economy, value added per person employed, contribution in percentage points.

Source: Estimates on the basis of the OECD STAN database, February 2004.

Figure 5.7   Contribution of ICT manufacturing to aggregate labour productivity growth

The ICT-producing services sector, notably the telecommunications sector, also made an important contribution to aggregate productivity growth in certain OECD countries over the second half of the 1990s (OECD, 2003b). Partly, this is linked to the liberalisation of telecommunications markets and the high speed of technological change in this market. Some of the growth in ICT-producing services is also due to the emergence of the computer services industry, which has accompanied the diffusion of ICT in OECD countries. The ICT-producing sector should continue to contribute to aggregate productivity growth in many OECD countries, given ongoing technological progress in this area. Further efforts to strengthen competition in this sector will be needed, however, as liberalisation has been an important driver of technological progress in this sector and has allowed its benefits to be diffused across the economy.

Competition and Firm Turnover Boost Productivity Growth

MFP also reflects the effects of competition. Analysis of productivity growth at the firm level shows that the impacts of competition, such as the entry and exit of firms and changes in market shares are important drivers of productivity growth (OECD, 2003a). New firms may use a more efficient mix of labour, capital and technology than existing firms, which in the long term has a positive effect on MFP growth. This is particularly true of industries that have grown rapidly in response to the new technological opportunities, such as the ICT sector, where new firms play a key role (Brandt, 2004). In contrast, growth in mature industries is typically driven by productivity growth within existing firms or by the exit of obsolete firms. This factor might potentially also help explain low MFP growth in certain OECD countries. Some evidence is available on this issue, both from previous OECD work (OECD, 2003a) and from more recent work, based on a new dataset from Eurostat (Brandt, 2004). Both studies suggest that rates of firm creation and destruction in OECD countries are fairly similar (Figure 5.8), in particular after they have been adjusted for differences in the composition of the economy. Moreover, the available estimates show that the entry and exit of firms made a sizeable contribution to MFP growth in the early 1990s (OECD, 2003a).

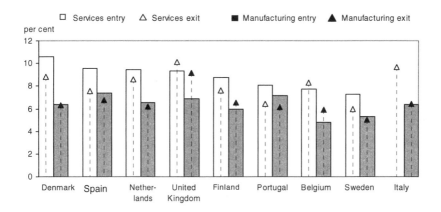

Notes:
Average over 1998–2000.
Entry and exit rates are calculated as the number of entering and exiting firms respectively as a proportion of the total number of firms in the same sector.

Source: Brandt (2004), based on Eurostat.

Figure 5.8   Firm entry and exit rates in EU countries

While firm creation as such does not appear to be a problem for MFP growth in many OECD countries, the growth of firms once they have been created appears problematic in many European countries. Compared with the European Union, the United States appears to be characterised by: (i) a smaller (relative to the industry average) size of entering firms; (ii) a lower labour productivity level of entrants relative to the average incumbent; and (iii) a much stronger (employment) expansion of successful entrants in the initial years which enable them to reach a higher average size (OECD, 2003a). These differences in firms' performance can only partly be explained by statistical factors or differences in the business cycle (OECD, 2003a; Brandt, 2004), and seem to indicate a greater degree of experimentation amongst entering firms in the United States. US firms take higher risks in adopting new technology and opt for potentially higher results, whereas European firms take fewer risks and opt for more predictable outcomes. This is likely related to differences in the business environment between the two regions; the US business environment permits greater experimentation as barriers to entry and exit are relatively low, in contrast to many European countries.

A dynamic business environment is important for good growth performance. A striking feature of the US economy in the 1990s was the large number of new firms that was created. In conditions of rapid technological change, such firms have an advantage in that they can come on to the market with the latest technology and hope to benefit from both the cost advantage that this gives them, and strongly rising demand in the early phases of the product cycle. There are risks as well as benefits, of course, as high entry rates go hand-in-hand with high exit rates. But provided that the barriers to both entry and exit are low, that innovation is rewarded and that displaced human and capital resources can be quickly re-allocated, this continuing process of creative destruction brings strong productivity gains. In turn, this requires both a social culture in which entrepreneurship is respected and encouraged. The ease and speed with which new firms can be created varies strikingly between OECD countries, while bankruptcy legislation can have an important impact on the speed with which resources can be re-allocated as well as on the willingness of managers to invest in risky but possibly very rewarding projects (OECD, 2001; Brandt, 2004).

Making Innovation More Effective

Innovation is the third important driver of MFP growth (Guellec and Van Pottelsberghe, 2001). Foreign research and development (R&D) is particularly important for most OECD countries (the United States being an exception), since the bulk of innovation and technological change in small countries is based on R&D that is performed abroad.[5] But domestic R&D, i.e. business, government and university research, is also an important driver of MFP growth. It is also the key in tapping into foreign knowledge; countries that invest in their own R&D appear to benefit most from foreign R&D.

R&D thus plays an important role as an input for technological progress and MFP growth. The major OECD regions have experienced considerable differences in the role of R&D over the past decade, however (Figure 5.9). In the United States, R&D spending increased considerably over the 1990s, both in absolute terms and as a share in GDP. In Japan, R&D intensity also increased, but this was partly due to a sluggish economy as absolute spending changed only little. In the European Union, the R&D intensity increased in the second half of the 1990s, but remains at a much lower level than in the United States.

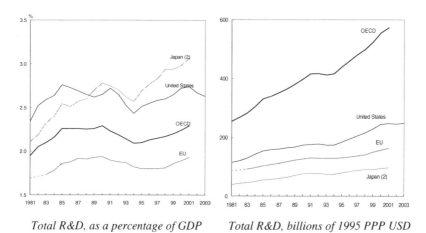

Total R&D, as a percentage of GDP   Total R&D, billions of 1995 PPP USD

Source: OECD (2003), Main Science and Technology Indicators 2003–2, December.

Figure 5.9   Trends in R&D intensity by area, 1981–2002

The R&D patterns shown above mainly reflect the development of business R&D; in the EU and the United States, government R&D declined over the past decade, while it increased only slightly in Japan. Changes in business R&D are affected by a broad range of factors (Guellec and Ioannides, 1997), including growth in business GDP, changes in interest rates as well as changes in government funding of business R&D. Structural factors also play a role, notably the contribution of high-technology sectors, such as the ICT-producing sector, to overall R&D. Several of these factors have had a positive influence on US R&D spending over the second half of the 1990s; high R&D spending thus reflects the strong performance of the US economy and has helped to reinforce technological progress over the past years. In contrast, the low growth of R&D spending in the European Union largely reflects more modest growth performance over the second half of the 1990s.

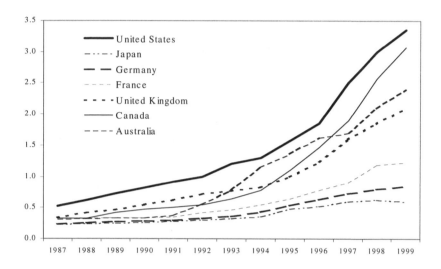

Note:
Science-innovation links have developed rapidly in some OECD countries.
The graph shows that patents increasingly cite the findings of scientific research as an impor-tant ingredient for new innovations. Language is not the explanation for these differences; in-novation in non-English speaking countries such as Finland, the Netherlands and Sweden also draws increasingly on scientific research carried out inside the country. The graph is based on US patents, since the estimates are not available for European and Japanese patents.

Source: CHI Research, http://www.chiresearch.com; see also OECD (2002).

Figure 5.10   Average number of scientific papers cited in patents taken in
the US, by country of origin

Lack of innovation in the services sector can also contribute to low MFP growth. For example, compared to OECD countries such as Australia and the United States, many OECD countries carry out relatively little R&D in the services sector (OECD, 2003d). Insufficiently developed links between sci-ence and industry is another factor limiting innovation in several OECD coun-tries. Innovation in key sectors such as biotechnology, in particular, is closely linked to advances in basic science. Interaction within the innovation system, notably between science and industry, has grown in recent years. Neverthe-less, there are considerable differences among OECD countries in the extent to which innovation draws on science. The growth in science-industry links over the 1990s, as measured by patent citations has been much more rapid in the United States, Canada, the United Kingdom and Australia than in France, Germany or Japan (OECD, 2002; Figure 5.10). Policy plays a role in explaining these cross-country differences. In the United States, for example, the linkages have been strengthened by initiatives in the 1980s and 1990s, like the extension of patent protection to publicly funded research, and the introduction of co-operative research and development agreements to facilitate technology transfer from the public sector to private industry.

Providing a good climate for innovation also requires sufficient public funding for basic research. This is also the case in smaller countries, as the benefits from foreign sources of knowledge are higher in countries that also invest in their own scientific efforts. Clearly, governments cannot fund all efforts equally, they should therefore complement funding of scientific research with more focused efforts to build capacity, e.g. by creating 'centres of excellence'. Aside from the direct creation of scientific knowledge and innovation, the creation of world class research centres plays an important role in the formation of research networks and clusters. They help establish a collaborative environment between industry and university researchers and provide a critical mass of people who can extend research further and diffuse the resulting technology.

Seizing Greater Benefits From the Use of ICT

The fourth driver of MFP that can be identified is the use of ICT in the production process. This effect can be interpreted in several ways. For example, ICT may help firms gain market share at the cost of less productive firms, which could raise overall productivity. In addition, the use of ICT may help firms to expand their product range, to customise the services offered, to respond better to client demand, or in short, to innovate. Moreover, ICT may help reduce inefficiency in the use of capital and labour, e.g. by reducing inventories. The diffusion of ICT may also help establish ICT networks, which can give rise to spill-over effects. These effects have proven difficult to identify over the past decade, even though ICT has diffused rapidly.

In recent years more evidence has emerged that ICT use can indeed help raise MFP growth. First, certain ICT intensive services, such as wholesale and retail trade and finance, have experienced an above-average pick-up in labour productivity growth in recent years, e.g. in the United States, Canada and Australia (Pilat, Lee and Van Ark, 2002; Figure 5.11). Second, there is growing evidence at the firm level from a wide range of studies in many OECD countries that ICT can help to improve the overall efficiency of capital and labour (OECD, 2003b; OECD, 2004). Third, there is evidence for a few countries, notably Australia and the United States, that certain ICT-using in-

dustries have indeed benefited from the efficiency-enhancing impacts of ICT
(Gretton et al., 2004; Bosworth and Triplett, 2003).

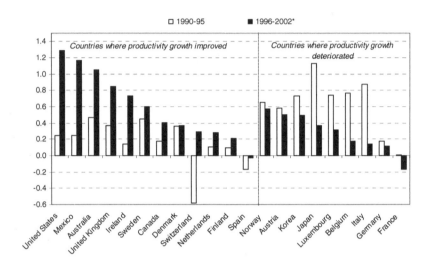

Notes:
Total economy, value added per person employed, contributions in percentage points.
See Figure 5.7 for period coverage. Data for Australia are for 1996–2001.

Source: Estimates on the basis of the OECD STAN database, February 2004.

*Figure 5.11 Contribution of ICT-using services to aggregate labour produc-
tivity growth, 1990–95 and 1996–2002*

Stronger growth in labour productivity in ICT-producing and ICT-using
industries could simply be due to capital deepening, i.e. greater use of capital
by workers. Estimates of MFP growth, as opposed to labour productivity
growth, adjust for this factor. Breaking aggregate MFP growth down in its
sectoral contributions can also help show whether changes in MFP growth
should be attributed to ICT producing sectors, to ICT-using sectors, or to
other sectors. Figure 5.12 shows the contribution of all activities to aggregate
MFP growth for the 8 countries for which estimates of capital stock at the industry level are available in the OECD STAN database. It shows that the
ICT-producing sector provided an important contribution to the acceleration
in MFP growth in Finland, with both ICT-producing manufacturing and ICT
producing services providing a strong contribution. In France and Germany,
the contribution of ICT production to MFP growth also increased over the

1990s, in both ICT-producing manufacturing and ICT-producing services, confirming rapid technological progress in this sector.

If ICT were to have effects on productivity growth over and above its contribution to capital deepening, MFP in sectors that are intensive users of ICT would need to increase. The estimates of Figure 5.12 show that the contribution of ICT-using services to aggregate MFP growth has slightly increased in Denmark and Germany, and substantially in Finland. In the other countries shown in the figure, MFP growth in the ICT-using services was zero or negative over the 1990s, suggesting that there appear to be no additional effects of ICT use in these sectors above those due to capital deepening. This may also be because some of the productivity changes in these sectors are not sufficiently picked up in the statistics, or because the adjustments that may be required to make ICT work have actually led to a (often temporary) drop in productivity growth (see also OECD, 2003b; OECD, 2004).

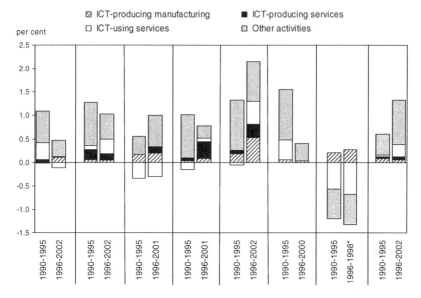

Notes:
Total economy, contributions to annual average growth rates, in percentage points.
*Or latest available year, i.e. 2001 for Germany and France, 2000 for Italy, and 1998 for Japan.
Estimates are based on official estimates of capital stock and sector-specific labour shares (adjusted for labour income from self-employment). No adjustment is made for capital services.

Source: OECD STAN database, February 2004.

Figure 5.12 Contribution of key sectors to MFP growth, 1990–95 and 1996–2002*

The OECD STAN database does not yet include capital stock for the United States, which implies that MFP estimates for the United States can not be derived from this source. Several studies provide estimates of the sectoral contributions to US MFP growth, however, that show considerable variation. For example, Oliner and Sichel (2002) found no contribution of non-ICT producing industries to MFP growth; Gordon (2002) and Jorgenson, Ho and Stiroh (2002) found a relatively small contribution, while Baily (2002) and the US Council of Economic Advisors (2001) found a much more substantive contribution.[6] The problem with some of these studies (e.g. Oliner and Sichel, 2002 and Gordon, 2002) is that all non-ICT producing sectors are combined, and the contribution of the non ICT-producing sector to aggregate MFP growth is calculated as a residual.

More detailed examination for the United States provides a different perspective (Bosworth and Triplett, 2003). This study finds, for example, that MFP growth in wholesale trade accelerated from 1.5 per cent annually to 3.1 per cent annually from 1987–95 to 1995–2001. In retail trade, the jump was from 0.2 per cent annually to 2.9 per cent, and in securities the acceleration was from 3.1 per cent to 6.6 per cent. Several other service sectors also experienced an increase in productivity growth over this period. On average, Bosworth and Triplett estimate that the contribution of service producing industries to aggregate MFP growth increased from 0.27 per cent over the 1987–95 period to 1.2 per cent over the 1995–2001 period, with the largest contributions coming from the sectors mentioned above (Figure 5.13).

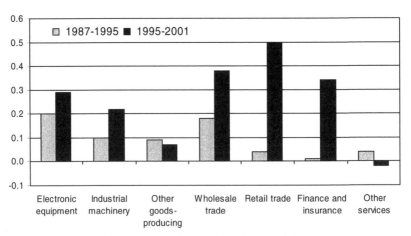

Note: Trend-adjusted, in percentage points, based on Domar weights.

Source: Bosworth and Triplett (2003).

Figure 5.13   Contribution of key industries to US MFP growth

There is therefore good evidence for strong MFP growth in the United States in ICT-using services. More detailed studies suggest how these productivity changes due to ICT use in the United States could be interpreted. First, a considerable part of the pick-up in productivity growth can be attributed to retail trade, where firms such as Walmart used innovative practices, such as the appropriate use of ICT, to gain market share from its competitors (McKinsey, 2001). The larger market share for Walmart and other productive firms raised average productivity and also forced Walmart's competitors to improve their own performance. Among the other ICT-using services, securities account also for a large part of the pick-up in productivity growth in the 1990s. Its strong performance has been attributed to a combination of buoyant financial markets (i.e. large trading volumes), effective use of ICT (mainly in automating trading processes) and stronger competition (McKinsey, 2001; Baily, 2002). These impacts of ICT on MFP are therefore primarily due to efficient use of labour and capital linked to the use of ICT in the production process. They are not necessarily due to network effects, where one firms' use of ICT has positive spill-overs on the economy as a whole.

For many other OECD countries, firm-level studies have also shown that ICT use can have positive effects on productivity (OECD, 2003b). However, in most of these countries, these benefits are not yet very visible at the sectoral level, which suggests that some of the conditions for this investment to become effective in improving aggregate productivity growth may not yet have been fully established. In fact, productivity growth in the United States in financial services and wholesale and retail trade has outperformed almost all other OECD countries (Figure 5.14). There are several reasons why productivity in ICT-using services has not increased in other OECD countries. First, ICT networks in many OECD countries may not yet have been sufficiently diffused, or for a sufficiently long period, and companies may therefore not yet have been able to achieve productivity returns from their investments. Given the relatively high rate of diffusion of ICT networks at this time (see OECD, 2003c), this explanation would imply that the returns of ICT investment on productivity might still emerge in the near future.

However, this is not the only possible explanation. There is some evidence from cross-country comparisons of the productivity impacts of ICT that the firm-level impacts of ICT may be smaller in European countries such as Germany, than in the United States (Haltiwanger et al., 2003). Productivity gains in ICT-using services might be smaller since the necessary complementary investments, e.g. in organisational change, skills and innovation, have not occurred to a sufficient degree. The lack of such changes in many OECD countries could be due to difficulties in changing organisational set-ups linked to relatively strict employment protection legislation, in particular for regular employment (De Serres, 2003). Another factor limiting the gains from ICT, already discussed above, may be lack of complementary process innovation in the service sector (OECD, 2003b). Innovation is important since users of ICT often help make their investments more valuable through their own experimentation and innovation, e.g. the introduction of new processes, products and applications. Without this process of 'co-invention', which often has a slower pace than technological innovation, the economic impact of ICT could be more limited.

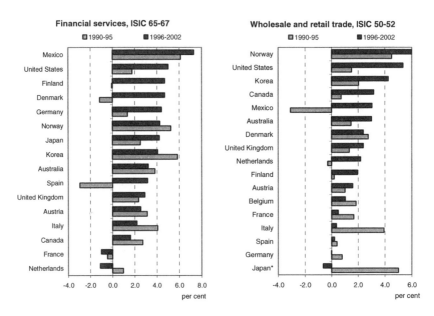

Notes:
Total economy, value added per person employed, annual average growth rates in per cent.
See Figure 5.7 for period coverage. Wholesale and retail trade includes hotels and restaurants for Japan.

Source: Estimates on the basis of the OECD STAN database, February 2004.

*Figure 5.14 Labour productivity growth in selected ICT-using services,
1990–95 and 1996–2002*

The aggregate impacts of ICT might also be smaller in Europe if firms that succeed in increasing productivity thanks to their investment in ICT do not grow sufficiently to gain market share. The US-Germany comparison highlighted above suggested that US firms had much greater variation in their productivity outcomes than German firms with some US firms experiencing very strong productivity gains from ICT (Haltiwanger et al., 2003). This may be because US firms engage in much more experimentation than their German counterparts; they take greater risks and opt for potentially higher outcomes. Lack of competition and lack of new firm creation in ICT-using services may also play a role. Competition is important in spurring ICT investment as it forces firms to seek ways to strengthen performance relative to competitors. In addition, newly created firms are often the first to take up new technologies; a lack of new firm creation and a lack of subsequent growth of these firms may therefore also be linked to poor performance in turning ICT investment into productivity gains.

Product market regulations may also play a role as they can limit firms in the ways that they can extract benefits from their use of ICT and reduce the incentives for firms to innovate and develop new ICT applications. For example, product market regulations may limit firms' ability to extend beyond traditional industry boundaries. The impact of product market regulations on ICT investment is confirmed by several studies. For example, OECD countries that had a high level of regulation in 1998 have had lower shares of investment in ICT than countries with low degrees of product market regulation (Gust and Marquez, 2002; OECD, 2003b). Moreover, countries with a high degree of product market regulation have not seen the same pick-up in productivity growth in ICT-using services as countries with low levels of regulation (Figure 5.15).

Spillover effects may also play a role, as ICT investment started earlier, and was stronger, in the United States than in most OECD countries (Colecchia and Schreyer, 2001; OECD, 2003b). Moreover, previous OECD work has pointed out that the US economy might be able to achieve greater benefits from ICT since it got its fundamentals right before many other OECD countries (OECD, 2001). Indeed, the United States may have benefited first from ICT investment ahead of other OECD countries, as it already had a high level of competition in the 1980s, which it strengthened through regulatory reforms in the 1980s and 1990s. For example, early and far-reaching liberalisation of the telecommunications sector boosted competition in dynamic segments of the ICT market. The combination of sound macroeconomic policies, well-functioning institutions and markets, and a competitive economic environment may thus be at the core of the US success.

The United States is not the only country where ICT use may already have had impacts on MFP growth. Studies for Australia (Gretton et al., 2004), suggest that a range of structural reforms have been important in driving the strong uptake of ICT by firms and have enabled these investments to be used in ways that generate productivity gains. This is particularly evident in wholesale and retail trade and in financial intermediation, where most of the Australian productivity gains in the second half of the 1990s have occurred. In some other countries, including Canada and the United Kingdom, there is evidence that certain ICT-using industries have experienced a pick-up in labour productivity growth, though not in MFP growth. But for most other OECD countries, there is little evidence that ICT-using industries are experiencing an improvement in labour productivity growth, let alone any change in MFP growth.

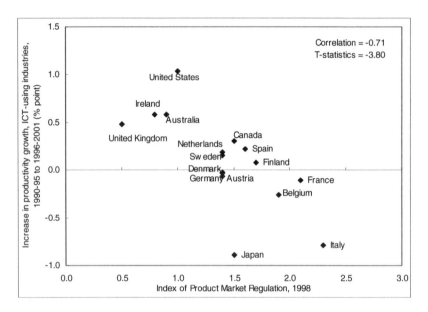

Source: OECD (2003), ICT and Economic Growth: Evidence from OECD Countries, Industries and Firms.

Figure 5.15 Relationship between growth in the contribution of ICT-using services to aggregate productivity growth and the state of product market regulation

Seizing the benefits from ICT therefore crucially depends on complementary investments in organisational change, skills and innovation (OECD, 2003b). These investments and changes, in turn, require a business environment that is sufficiently flexible for firms to make the necessary changes. Many OECD countries still require further reform of product and labour markets to foster such an environment.

5.4 CONCLUDING REMARKS

This chapter updates some of the previous OECD work on economic growth and brings together some of the recent evidence at the aggregate, industry and firm level. It also points to some of the factors that have influenced the diversity in growth performance of OECD countries over the past years. There are obviously other factors that may have contributed to higher growth in the 1990s, and it will take further research to understand better why the United States and some other countries did so well over this period. One important driving factor may have been the increased level of competition in many OECD countries, due to regulatory reform and greater openness to international trade and investment. This has likely increased the incentives for firms to increase overall efficiency, and may also have facilitated the diffusion of new technologies and knowledge. The available evidence suggests that regulatory reform has indeed improved productivity, in particular in services sectors such as distribution, financial services, transport and telecommunications.

The chapter demonstrated that in several countries with strong growth in the 1990s, ICT investment has been important. This has led to a rapid diffusion of ICT, which has also affected overall efficiency, at least in a few OECD countries. Innovation and technology diffusion are also important, as a possible way to higher MFP and to future technological breakthroughs. Education and skills have also gained new significance, partly due to the diffusion of new technologies. In addition, MFP growth in new industries has been accompanied by the creation of start-up firms. While these factors play an important role, they also rely on sound fundamentals – macroeconomic stability, openness and competition, as well as economic and social institutions – if they are to work properly. Many of the countries that improved growth performance in the 1990s did so because they had been able to create an environment that could take advantage of the new technologies and business opportunities when they emerged. Moreover, strong fundamentals allowed these countries to improve productivity while simultaneously drawing more people into productive employment.

At the macroeconomic level, countries that enjoyed faster growth also had policies aimed at keeping inflation low and reducing the burden of public debt. Stable macroeconomic conditions make it easier for established businesses to plan ahead and for new businesses to survive their early years. Public spending geared to improving infrastructure and human capital also helps entrepreneurship flourish. But the successful countries also had other policies in place – or policy reforms – that reinforced the impact of prudent demand-management policies. Competition and openness to trade, investment and ideas encourage firms to search for new and better ways of satisfying consumer demands, while a liquid and competitive financial sector helps ensure that scarce financial resources are channelled to their most productive uses. Moreover, a combination of social and labour market policies and institutions that enables and encourages people of all ages and skill levels to find jobs easily and quickly is an all-important element in making it easier for societies to embrace change. Giving the right incentives to people to remain employable through life ensures that they can share the fruits of growth.

Further policy actions to improve these fundamentals will still be needed in many OECD countries, in particular to further increase labour participation, as well as to reduce regulatory burdens and further strengthen competition in the economy. More can be done also to strengthen innovation, investment in human capital and firm creation. These areas still offer a potential to move closer to best policy practices and could help improve growth performance.

Finally, further empirical research will be needed to clear up several gaps in our current understanding of growth patterns in the OECD area. At the aggregate level, better measures of software investment and hedonic deflators adapted to each country could provide more comparable estimates of MFP growth. At the industry level, a better understanding of the performance of the services sector, notably as regards productivity growth, is sorely needed to inform the policy discussion. Moreover, a complete growth accounting at the industry level, as was carried out by Bosworth and Triplett (2003) for the United States, would be very helpful if carried out for other OECD countries. Finally, much more information can be derived from firm-level data in OECD countries, as these can point to the underlying competitive dynamics of OECD economies, the interrelation of various factors at the firm level, and the differences between OECD countries at this fundamental level of economies. The recent development of longitudinal databases in several OECD countries offers a wide range of opportunities for research with firm level data. Productivity researchers have a lot of exciting work ahead of them in the years to come.

NOTES

1. The estimates shown in Figure 5.2 are not adjusted for the business cycle. Trend-adjusted estimates prepared by the OECD Economics Department broadly confirm the findings of Figure 5.2. They suggest that the United States had slightly more rapid growth of GDP per capita than the European Union over the 1990s and that the difference in labour productivity growth between the two regions is relatively small. The bulk of the difference in growth performance between the two regions is therefore explained by labour utilisation, where the United States experienced stronger performance than the European Union.
2. These estimates are based on official data on ICT investment from individual countries' national accounts. They are based on a harmonised deflator for ICT investment, which adjusts for cross country differences in the measurement of ICT prices (see Colecchia and Schreyer, 2001 and OECD, 2003b). Methodological differences in the measurement of software investment may affect the results, however (Ahmad, 2003).

3. The MFP estimates in Figure 5.5 are not adjusted for labour quality. Moreover, for some countries, capital input may be underestimated due to underestimation of software investment (Ahmad, 2003). Adjusting for both factors would lead to a substantially smaller contribution of MFP to total output growth in OECD countries.
4. Figure 5.7 shows the contribution of these sectors to labour productivity growth, since data for capital input by industry are only available for some OECD countries. However, the contribution of the ICT-producing sector to MFP growth is also very large in some countries where data are available, e.g. Finland, Japan and the United States (Figure 5.12; Pilat and Wölfl, 2004).
5. OECD estimates suggest that a 1 per cent increase in the global stock of R&D increases MFP growth by 0.4-0.5 per cent; a 1 per cent increase in business R&D increases MFP by 0.13 per cent; and 1 per cent increase in government and university performed R&D increased MFP by 0.2 %. Embodied technology has only a small impact on MFP: a 1 per cent increase leads to a 0.02 per cent increase in MFP. See Guellec and Van Pottelsberghe (2001) for more detail.
6. The differences between the various US studies are partly due to the data sources and methodology used, as well as the timing of various studies.

REFERENCES

Ahmad, N. (2003), 'Measuring Investment in Software', *STI Working Paper,* 2003/6, OECD, Paris.

Ahmad, N., F. Lequiller, P. Marianna, D. Pilat, P. Schreyer and A. Wölfl (2003), 'Comparing Labour Productivity Growth in the OECD Area: The Role of Measurement', *STI Working Paper,* 2003/14, OECD, Paris.

Baily, M.N. (2002), 'The New Economy: Post Mortem or Second Wind', *Journal of Economic Perspectives,* **16** (2), 3–22.

Bassanini, A. and S. Scarpetta (2001), 'Does human capital matter for growth in OECD Countries? Evidence from pooled mean-group estimates', *OECD Economics Department Working Paper,* 289, OECD, Paris.

Bosworth, B.P. and J.E. Triplett (2003), 'Services Productivity in the United States: Griliches' Services Volume Revisited', Paper prepared for CRIW Conference in Memory of Zvi Griliches, Brookings Institution, Washington, DC, September.

Brandt, N. (2004), 'Business Dynamics in Europe', *STI Working Paper,* OECD, Paris, forthcoming.

Colecchia, A. and P. Schreyer (2001), 'The Impact of Information Communications Technology on Output Growth', *STI Working Paper,* 2001/7, OECD, Paris.

De Serres, A. (2003), 'Structural Policies and Growth: A Non-Technical Overview', *Economics Department Working Paper,* 355, OECD, Paris.

Gordon, R.J. (2002), 'Technology and Economic Performance in the American Economy', *NBER Working Paper,* 8771, National Bureau of Economic Research.

Gretton, P., Jyothi Gali and D. Parham (2004), 'The Effects of ICTs and Complementary Innovations on Australian Productivity Growth', in: OECD (2004), *The Economic Impact of ICT – Measurement, Evidence and Implications,* OECD, Paris.

Guellec, D. and B. van Pottelsberghe De la Potterie (2001), 'R&D and productivity growth: A panel analysis of 16 OECD countries', *STI Working Paper,* 2001/3, OECD, Paris.

Guellec, D. and E. Ioannidis (1997), 'Causes of Fluctuations in R&D Expenditures: A Quantitative Analysis', *OECD Economic Studies,* **29** (1997/II), 123–138.

Gust, C. and J. Marquez (2002), 'International Comparisons of Productivity Growth: The Role of Information Technology and Regulatory Practices', *International Finance Discussion Papers*, No. 727, Board of Governors of the Federal Reserve System, Washington, DC.

Haltiwanger, J., R. Jarmin and T. Schank (2003), 'Productivity, Investment in ICT and Market Experimentation: Micro Evidence from Germany and the United States', *Center for Economic Studies Working Paper*, CES-03-06, US Bureau of the Census, Washington, D.C.

Jorgenson, D.W. (2003), 'Information Technology and the G7 Economies', Harvard University, December, mimeo, http://post.economics.harvard.edu/faculty/jorgenson/

Jorgenson, D.W., M.S. Ho and K.J. Stiroh (2002), 'Information Technology, Education, and the Sources of Economic Growth across US Industries', mimeo.

Maddison, A. (2001), *The World Economy: A Millennial Perspective*, OECD, Paris.

McKinsey (2001), *US Productivity Growth 1995–2000: Understanding the Contribution of Information Technology relative to Other Factors*, McKinsey Global Institute, Washington, DC.

OECD (1999), *Implementing the OECD Jobs Strategy – Assessing Performance and Policy*, OECD, Paris.

OECD (2001), *The New Economy: Beyond the Hype*, OECD, Paris.

OECD (2002), *Benchmarking Industry-Science Relationships*, OECD, Paris.

OECD (2003a), *The Sources of Economic Growth in OECD Countries*, OECD, Paris.

OECD (2003b), *ICT and Economic Growth – Evidence from OECD Countries, Industries and Firms*, OECD, Paris.

OECD (2003c), *OECD Science, Technology and Industry Scoreboard*, OECD, Paris.

OECD (2003d), *OECD Employment Outlook*, OECD, Paris.

OECD (2003e), *Structural Policies and Growth*, OECD Economic Outlook No. 73, OECD, Paris.

OECD (2004), *The Economic Impact of ICT – Measurement, Evidence and Implications*, OECD, Paris.

Oliner, S.D. and D.E. Sichel (2002), 'Information Technology and Productivity: Where are We Now and Where Are We Going?', *Finance and Economics Discussion Series*, No. 2002–29, Federal Reserve Board.

Pilat, D., F. Lee and Bart van Ark (2002), 'Production and use of ICT: A sectoral perspective on productivity growth in the OECD area', *OECD Economic Studies* **35**, 47–78.

Pilat, D. and A. Wölfl (2004), 'ICT production and ICT use – what role in aggregate productivity growth?', in: OECD (2004), *The Economic Impact of ICT – Measurement, Evidence and Implications*, OECD, Paris.

United States Council of Economic Advisors (2001), *Economic Report of the President 2001*, United States Government Printing Office, Washington, DC.

Wölfl, A. and D. Hajkova (2004), 'Growth Accounts for OECD Countries', *STI Working Paper*, OECD, Paris, forthcoming.

6. Information Technology and the G7 Economies

Dale W. Jorgenson

6.1 INTRODUCTION

In this chapter I present international comparisons of economic growth among the G7 nations – Canada, France, Germany, Italy, Japan, the UK, and the US. These comparisons focus on the impact of investment in information technology (IT) equipment and software over the period 1980–2001. In 1998 the G7 nations accounted for nearly sixty per cent of world output[1] and a much larger proportion of world investment in IT. Economic growth in the G7 has experienced a strong revival since 1995, driven by a powerful surge in IT investment.

The resurgence of economic growth in the United States during the 1990s and the crucial role of IT investment has been thoroughly documented and widely discussed.[2] Similar trends in the other G7 economies have been more difficult to detect, partly because of discrepancies among official price indexes for IT equipment and software identified by Andrew Wyckoff.[3] Paul Schreyer has constructed 'internationally harmonized' IT prices that eliminate many of these discrepancies.[4]

Using internationally harmonized prices for France, Germany, Italy, and the UK, I have analyzed the role of investment and productivity as sources of growth in the G7 countries over the period 1980–2001. I have subdivided the period in 1989 and 1995 in order to focus on the most recent experience. I have decomposed growth of output for each country between growth of input and productivity. Finally, I have allocated the growth of input between investments in tangible assets, especially information technology and software, and human capital.

Growth in IT capital input per capita jumped to double-digit levels in the G7 nations after 1995. This can be traced to acceleration in the rate of decline of IT prices, analyzed in my Presidential Address to the American Economic Association.[5] The powerful surge in investment was most pronounced in Canada, but capital input growth in Japan, the US, and the UK was only slightly lower. France, Germany, and Italy also experienced double-digit growth, but lagged considerably behind the leaders.

During the 1980s productivity played a minor role as a source of growth for the G7 countries except Japan, where productivity accounted for thirty per cent of economic growth. Productivity accounted for only fifteen per cent of growth in the US, thirteen per cent in France and the UK, and twelve per cent in Germany; only two per cent of growth in Canada was due to productivity, while the decline of productivity retarded growth by fourteen per cent in Italy. Between 1989 and 1995 productivity growth declined further in the G7 nations, except for Italy and Germany. Productivity declined for France and the UK but remained positive for the US, Canada, and Japan.

Productivity growth revived in all the G7 countries after 1995, again with the exception of Germany and Italy. The resurgence was most dramatic in Canada, the UK, and France, partly offsetting years of dismal productivity growth. Japan exhibited the highest growth in output per capita among the G7 nations from 1980 to 1995. Japan's level of output per capita rose from the lowest in the G7 to the middle of the group in 2001. Although this advance owed more to input per capita than productivity, Japan's productivity growth far outstripped the other members of the G7. Nonetheless, Japan's productivity remained the lowest among the G7 nations. The US led the G7 in output per capita for the period 1989–2001. Canada's edge in output per capita in 1980 had disappeared by 1989.

The US led the G7 countries in input per capita during 1980–2001, but US productivity languished below the levels of Canada, France, and Italy.

In Section 6.2 I outline the methodology for this study, based on my Presidential Address. I have revised and updated the US data presented there through 2001. Comparable data on investment in information technology have been have been constructed for Canada by Statistics Canada.[6] Data on IT for France, Germany, Italy, and the UK have been developed for the European Commission by Bart Van Ark et al.[7] Finally, data for Japan have been assembled by myself and Kazuyuki Motohashi for the Research Institute on Economy, Trade, and Industry.[8] I have linked these data by means of the OECD's purchasing power parities for 1999.[9]

In Section 6.3 I consider the impact of IT investment and the relative importance of investment and productivity in accounting for economic growth among the G7 nations. Investments in human capital and tangible assets, especially IT equipment and software, account for the overwhelming proportion of growth. Differences in the composition of capital and labour inputs are essential for identifying persistent international differences in output and accounting for the impact of IT investment.

In Section 6.4 I consider alternative approaches to international comparisons. The great revival of interest in economic growth among economists dates from Maddison's (1982) updating and extension of Simon Kuznets' (1971) long-term estimates of the growth of national product and population for fourteen industrialized countries, including the G7 nations. Maddison (1982, 1991) added Austria and Finland to Kuznets' list and presented growth rates covering periods beginning as early as 1820 and extending through 1989.

Maddison (1987, 1991) also generated growth accounts for major industrialized countries, but did not make level comparisons like those presented in Section 6.2 below. As a consequence, productivity differences were omitted from the canonical formulation of 'growth regressions' by William Baumol (1986). This proved to be a fatal flaw in Baumol's regression model, remedied by Nazrul Islam's (1995) panel data model. Section 6.5 concludes the chapter.

6.2   INVESTMENT AND PRODUCTIVITY

My papers with Laurits Christensen and Dianne Cummings (1980, 1981) developed growth accounts for the United States and its major trading partners – Canada, France, Germany, Italy, Japan, Korea, The Netherlands, and the United Kingdom for 1947–1973. We employed GNP as a measure of output and incorporated constant quality indices of capital and labour input for each country. Our 1981 paper compared levels of output, inputs, and productivity for all nine nations.

I have updated the estimates for the G7 – Canada, France, Germany, Italy, Japan, the United Kingdom, and the United States – through 1995 in earlier work. The updated estimates are presented in my papers with Chrys Dougherty (1996, 1997) and Eric Yip (2000). We have shown that productivity accounted for only eleven per cent of economic growth in Canada and the United States over the period 1960–1995.

My paper with Yip (2000) attributed forty-seven per cent of Japanese economic growth during the period 1960–1995 to productivity growth. The proportion attributable to productivity approximated forty per cent of growth for the four European countries – France (.38), Germany (.42), Italy (.43), and the United Kingdom (.36). Input growth predominated over productivity growth for all the G7 nations.

I have now incorporated new data on investment in information technology equipment and software for the G7. I have also employed internationally harmonized prices like those constructed by Schreyer (2000). As a consequence, I have been able to separate the contribution of capital input to economic growth into IT and Non-IT components. While IT investment follows similar patterns in all the G7 nations, Non-IT investment varies considerably and helps to explain important differences in growth rates among the G7.

Comparisons of Output, Input, and Productivity

My first objective is to extend my estimates for the G7 nations with Christensen, Cummings, Dougherty, and Yip to the year 2001. Following the methodology of my Presidential Address, I have chosen GDP as a measure of output. I have included imputations for the services of consumers' durables as well as land, buildings, and equipment owned by non-profit institutions. I have also distinguished between investments in information technology equipment and software and investments in other forms of tangible assets.

A constant quality index of capital input is based on weights that reflect differences in capital consumption, tax treatment, and the rate of decline of asset prices. I have derived estimates of capital input and property income from national accounting data. Similarly, a constant quality index of labour input is based on weights by age, sex, educational attainment, and employment status. I have constructed estimates of hours worked and labour compensation from labour force surveys for each country.

In Table 6.1 I present output per capita for the G7 nations from 1980 to 2001, taking the US as 100.0 in 2000. Output and population are given separately in Tables 6.2 and 6.3. I use 1999 purchasing power parities from the OECD to convert output from domestic prices for each country into US dollars. The US maintained its lead among the G7 countries in output per capita after 1989. Canada led the US in 1980, but fell behind during the 1980s. The US-Canada gap widened considerably during the 1990s.

The four major European nations – the UK, France, Germany, and Italy – had very similar levels of output per capita throughout the period 1980–2001. Japan rose from last place in 1980 to fourth among the G7 in 2001, lagging considerably behind the US and Canada, but only slightly behind the UK. Japan led the G7 in the growth of output per capita from 1980–1995, but fell behind the US, Canada, the UK, France, and Italy after 1995.

In Table 6.1 I present input per capita for the G7 over the period 1980–2001, taking the US as 100.0 in 2000. I express input per capita in US dollars, using purchasing power parities constructed for this study.[10] The US was the leader among the G7 in input per capita throughout the period. In 2001 Canada ranked next to the US with Japan third and Germany fourth. France and Italy started at the bottom of the ranking and remained there throughout the period.

Table 6.1   Levels of output and input per capita and total factor productivity

Year	US	Canada	UK	France	Germany	Italy	Japan
				Output Per Capita			
1980	63.9	67.6	45.0	45.9	49.3	45.9	43.6
1989	79.7	78.8	56.5	54.1	58.6	57.3	58.4
1995	85.6	79.6	61.4	57.0	65.0	62.1	65.4
2001	100.3	91.9	71.3	64.0	69.2	68.8	70.4
				Input Per Capita			
1980	70.5	64.2	50.2	46.5	61.0	43.1	61.9
1989	83.9	74.4	61.2	53.3	71.1	55.5	74.8
1995	88.8	75.2	67.0	57.0	73.7	58.8	78.8
2001	100.8	83.7	73.6	61.7	79.0	67.2	81.1
				Total Factor Productivity			
1980	90.6	105.4	89.5	98.6	80.8	106.6	70.4
1989	94.9	105.9	92.3	101.5	82.4	103.2	78.0
1995	96.4	105.9	91.7	99.9	88.1	105.6	83.0
2001	99.5	109.7	96.9	103.6	87.6	102.5	86.8

Note: US = 100.0 in 2000, Canada data begin in 1981.

Table 6.2   Growth rate and level of output

Year	US	Canada	UK	France	Germany	Italy	Japan
				Growth Rate (percentage)			
1980–1989	3.38	3.10	2.69	2.38	1.99	2.51	3.83
1989–1995	2.43	1.39	1.62	1.30	2.34	1.52	2.23
1995–2001	3.76	3.34	2.74	2.34	1.18	1.90	1.45
				Level (billions of 2000 US Dollars)			
1980	5 361.2	618.4	934.0	932.0	1 421.7	955.7	1 875.9
1989	7 264.2	792.6	1 190.3	1 154.3	1 700.2	1 197.4	2 648.7
1995	8 403.3	861.4	1 311.8	1 247.8	1 956.3	1 311.5	3 027.1
2001	10 530.4	1 052.3	1 545.9	1 436.0	2 099.8	1 470.1	3 301.3
				Level (US = 100.0 in 2000)			
1980	51.6	5.9	9.0	9.0	13.7	9.2	18.0
1989	69.9	7.6	11.4	11.1	16.3	11.5	25.5
1995	80.8	8.3	12.6	12.0	18.8	12.6	29.1
2001	101.3	10.1	14.9	13.8	20.2	14.1	31.7

Note: Canadian data begin in 1981.

Table 6.3   Growth rate and level in population

Year	US	Canada	UK	France	Germany	Italy	Japan
			Growth Rate (percentage)				
1980–1989	0.92	1.18	0.16	0.54	0.05	0.05	0.59
1989–1995	1.23	1.22	0.24	0.45	0.62	0.18	0.33
1995–2001	1.12	0.95	0.24	0.41	0.14	0.18	0.22
			Level (millions)				
1980	227.7	24.8	56.3	55.1	78.3	56.4	116.8
1989	247.4	27.3	57.1	57.9	78.7	56.7	123.1
1995	266.3	29.4	58.0	59.4	81.7	57.3	125.6
2001	284.8	31.1	58.8	60.9	82.3	57.9	127.2
			Level (US = 100.0 in 2000)				
1980	80.7	8.8	20.0	19.5	27.8	20.0	41.4
1989	87.7	9.7	20.3	20.5	27.9	20.1	43.6
1995	94.4	10.4	20.5	21.1	28.9	20.3	44.5
2001	101.0	11.0	20.8	21.6	29.2	20.5	45.1

Note: Percentage, Canadian data begin in 1981.

In Table 6.1 I also present productivity levels for the G7 over the period 1980–2001. Productivity is defined as the ratio of output to input, including both capital and labour inputs. Canada was the productivity leader during the period 1989–2001 with France and Italy close behind, despite the drop in productivity in Italy. Japan made the most substantial gains in productivity, while there were more modest increases in the US, Canada, the UK, France, and Germany.

I summarize growth in output and input per capita and productivity for the G7 nations in Table 6.4. I present growth rates of output and population for the period 1980–2001 in Tables 6.2 and 6.3. Output growth slowed in the G7 after 1989, but revived for all nations except Japan and Germany after 1995. Output per capita followed a similar pattern with Canada barely expanding during the period 1989–1995.

Japan led in growth of output per capita through 1995, but fell to the lower echelon of the G7 after 1995. Japan led in productivity growth during 1980–1989, Germany led from 1989–1995, and the UK led from 1995–2001. For all countries and all time periods, except for Germany during the period 1989–1995 and Japan after 1989, the growth of input per capita exceeded growth of productivity by a substantial margin. Productivity growth in the G7 slowed during the period 1989–1995, except for Germany and Italy, where productivity slumped after 1995.

Table 6.4   Growth in output and input per capita and total factor productivity

Year	US	Canada	UK	France	Germany	Italy	Japan
				Output per Capita			
1980–1989	2.46	1.92	2.54	1.84	1.93	2.46	3.25
1989–1995	1.20	0.17	1.38	0.85	1.72	1.33	1.90
1995–2001	2.64	2.38	2.50	1.93	1.04	1.72	1.23
				Input Per Capita			
1980–1989	1.94	1.86	2.20	1.52	1.71	2.82	2.10
1989–1995	0.94	0.17	1.49	1.11	0.60	0.96	0.86
1995–2001	2.10	1.80	1.59	1.33	1.14	2.21	0.48
				Total Factor Productivity			
1980–1989	0.52	0.06	0.34	0.32	0.23	-0.36	1.15
1989–1995	0.26	0.00	-0.11	-0.26	1.12	0.37	1.04
1995–2001	0.54	0.58	0.91	0.60	-0.10	-0.49	0.75

Note: Percentage, Canadian data begin in 1981.

Italy led the G7 in growth of input per capita for the periods 1980–1989 and 1995–2001, but relinquished leadership to the UK for the period 1989–1995. Differences among input growth rates are smaller than differences among output growth rates, but there was a slowdown in input growth during 1989–1995 throughout the G7. After 1995 growth of input per capita increased in every G7 nation except Japan.

Comparisons of Capital and Labour Quality

A constant quality index of capital input weights capital inputs by property compensation per unit of capital. By contrast an index of capital stock weights different types of capital by asset prices. The ratio of capital input to capital stock measures the average quality of a unit of capital. This represents the difference between the constant quality index of capital input and the index of capital stock employed, for example, by Kuznets (1971) and Robert Solow (1970).

In Table 6.5 I present capital input per capita for the G7 countries over the period 1980–2001 relative to the US in 2000. The US was the leader in capital input per capita throughout the period, while Japan was the laggard. Canada led the remaining six countries in 1980, but was overtaken by Germany and Italy in 1995. Italy led the rest of the G7 through 2001, but lagged considerably behind the United States.

The picture for capital stock per capita has some similarities to capital input, but there are important differences. Capital stock levels do not accurately reflect the substitutions among capital inputs that accompany investments in tangible assets, especially investments in IT equipment and software. Japan led the G7 in capital stock per capita throughout the period 1980–2001. The UK lagged the remaining countries of the G7 throughout the period.

Table 6.5   Levels of capital input and capital stock per capita and capital quality

Year	US	Canada	UK	France	Germany	Italy	Japan
			Capital Input Per Capita				
1980	57.7	56.0	25.8	36.3	44.6	35.6	32.8
1989	73.7	67.1	37.9	48.3	62.1	62.4	43.5
1995	81.6	68.3	50.0	52.7	72.3	73.1	50.7
2001	103.9	78.0	56.1	58.1	83.5	89.4	58.3
			Capital Stock Per Capita				
1980	76.8	40.7	24.1	36.2	60.2	36.0	93.1
1989	88.4	48.5	31.2	42.4	67.9	52.4	104.1
1995	92.2	50.8	35.9	47.0	77.0	62.3	114.8
2001	101.7	55.1	44.5	52.0	85.5	72.3	122.2
			Capital Quality				
1980	75.1	137.5	107.0	100.1	74.0	98.8	35.2
1989	83.4	138.2	121.7	114.0	91.5	119.1	41.8
1995	88.5	134.6	139.3	112.2	94.0	117.4	44.2
2001	102.2	141.5	126.1	111.9	97.7	123.6	47.7

Note: US = 100.0 in 2000, Canadian data begin in 1981.

The behaviour of capital quality highlights the differences between the constant quality index of capital input and capital stock. There are important changes in capital quality over time and persistent differences among countries, so that heterogeneity in capital input must be taken into account in international comparisons of economic performance. Canada was the international leader in capital quality in 1980 and 2001, relinquishing the lead to the UK in 1995, while Japan ranked at the bottom of the G7 throughout the period.

I summarize growth in capital input and capital stock per capita, as well as capital quality for the G7 nations in Table 6.6. Italy was the international leader in capital input growth from 1980–1989, while the Canada was the laggard. The UK led from 1989–1995, while Canada lagged considerably behind the rest of the G7. The US took the lead after 1995. There was a slowdown in capital input growth throughout the G7 after 1989, except for the UK, and a revival after 1995 in the US, Canada, France, and Italy.

A constant quality index of labour input weights hours worked for different categories by labour compensation per hour. An index of hours worked fails to take quality differences into account. The ratio of labour input to hours worked measures the average quality of an hour of labour, as reflected in its marginal product. This represents the difference between the constant quality index of labour input and the index of hours worked employed, for example, by Kuznets (1971) and Solow (1970).

Table 6.6   Growth in capital input and capital stock per capita and capital quality

Year	US	Canada	UK	France	Germany	Italy	Japan
			Capital Input Per Capita				
1980–1989	2.72	2.26	4.28	3.19	3.70	6.25	3.16
1989–1995	1.70	0.31	4.61	1.46	2.53	2.63	2.55
1995–2001	4.03	2.20	1.92	1.63	2.40	3.35	2.31
			Capital Stock Per Capita				
1980–1989	1.56	2.19	2.85	1.74	1.34	4.18	1.25
1989–1995	0.70	1.05	2.36	1.74	2.09	2.87	1.63
1995–2001	1.63	1.36	3.57	1.67	1.75	2.49	1.04
			Capital Quality				
1980–1989	1.17	0.07	1.43	1.45		2.36	2.07
1989–1995	0.99	-0.74	2.25	-0.27	0.44	-0.24	0.92
1995–2001	2.40	0.84	-1.65	-0.04	0.65	0.86	1.26

Note: Percentage, Canadian data begin in 1981.

In Table 6.7 I present labour input per capita for the G7 nations for the period 1980–2001 relative to the US in 2000. Japan was the international leader throughout the period 1980–2001. Labour input in Japan was nearly double that in Italy. The US led the remaining G7 nations. The UK ranked third among the G7 through 1995, but fell slightly behind Canada in 2001. Italy and France lagged behind the rest of the G7 for the entire period.

The picture for hours worked per capita has some similarities to labour input, but there are important differences. Japan was the international leader in hours worked per capita. The US, Canada, and the UK moved roughly in parallel. The UK ranked second in 1980 and 1989, while the US ranked second in 1995 and 2001. France and Italy lagged the rest of the G7 from 1980 to 2001.

The behaviour of labour quality highlights the differences between labour input and hours worked. Germany was the leader in labour quality throughout the period 1980–2001. The US ranked second in labour quality, but Canada, France, the UK, and Japan approached US levels in 2001. Labour quality levels in these four countries moved in parallel throughout the period. Italy was the laggard among the G7 in labour quality as well as hours worked.

Table 6.7   Levels of labour input and hours worked per capita and labour quality

Year	US	Canada	UK	France	Germany	Italy	Japan
			Labour Input Per Capita				
1980	81.1	73.0	78.9	63.0	75.4	48.8	94.8
1989	91.9	82.1	85.4	59.4	78.7	51.0	107.5
1995	94.2	82.3	82.4	61.7	75.2	50.6	105.5
2001	98.8	89.3	89.2	65.3	75.9	55.1	100.9
			Hours Worked Per Capita				
1980	89.7	91.4	92.0	79.3	82.3	71.4	111.9
1989	97.1	96.6	97.7	71.2	82.7	72.1	115.6
1995	95.9	90.9	89.8	67.6	76.4	68.9	109.9
2001	98.3	96.3	94.2	69.7	75.3	72.3	101.1
			Labour Quality				
1980	90.4	79.9	85.7	79.5	91.6	68.3	84.7
1989	94.7	85.0	87.4	83.5	95.2	70.7	93.0
1995	98.2	90.6	91.7	91.2	98.4	73.5	96.0
2001	100.5	92.7	94.7	93.7	100.9	76.1	99.9

Note: US = 100.0 in 2000, Canadian data begin in 1981.

Table 6.8   Growth in labour input and hours worked per capita and labour quality

Year	US	Canada	UK	France	Germany	Italy	Japan
			Labour Input Per Capita				
1980–1989	1.38	1.47	0.88	-0.65	0.48	0.49	1.40
1989–1995	0.41	0.04	-0.59	0.61	-0.78	-0.13	-0.32
1995–2001	0.79	1.35	1.32	0.95	0.17	1.40	-0.73
			Hours Worked Per Capita				
1980–1989	0.87	0.69	0.67	-1.20	0.06	0.10	0.36
1989–1995	-0.21	-1.02	-1.41	-0.86	-1.33	-0.75	-0.84
1995–2001	0.41	0.98	0.79	0.50	-0.25	0.81	-1.39
			Labour Quality				
1980–1989	0.51	0.78	0.21	0.55	0.42	0.39	1.04
1989–1995	0.61	1.06	0.81	1.47	0.55	0.63	0.52
1995–2001	0.38	0.38	0.53	0.45	0.41	0.60	0.66

Note: Percentage, Canadian data begin in 1981.

I summarize growth in labour input and hours worked per capita, as well as labour quality for the period 1980–2001 in Table 6.8. Canada and Japan led the G7 nations in labour input growth during the 1980s, France led from

1989–1995 but relinquished its leadership to Italy after 1995. Labour input growth was negative for France during the 1980s, for the UK, Germany, Italy, and Japan during the period 1989–1995, and for Japan after 1995.

Hours worked per capita fell continuously through the 1989–2001 period for Japan and declined for all the G7 nations during the period 1989–1995. Growth in labour quality was positive for the G7 nations in all time periods. Japan was the leader during the 1980s, relinquishing its lead to France during the early 1990s, but regaining its lead in the 1995–2001 period. Growth in labour quality and hours worked are equally important as sources of growth in labour input for the G7.

6.3   INVESTMENT IN INFORMATION TECHNOLOGY

Using data from Tables 6.1 and 6.2, I can assess the relative importance of investment and productivity as sources of economic growth for the G7 nations. Investments in tangible assets and human capital greatly predominated over productivity during the period 1980–2001. While productivity fell in Italy during this period, the remaining G7 countries had positive productivity growth.

Similarly, using data from Table 6.5 I can assess the relative importance of growth in capital stock and capital quality. Capital input growth was positive for all countries for the period 1980–2001 and all three sub-periods. Capital quality growth was positive for the period as a whole for all G7 countries. Although capital stock predominated in capital input growth, capital quality was also quantitatively significant, especially after 1995.

Finally, using data from Table 6.7 I can assess the relative importance of growth in hours worked and labour quality. Hours worked per capita declined for France, Germany, and Japan, while labour quality rose in these nations during the period 1980–2001. For the US, Canada, the UK, and Italy, both hours worked per capita and labour quality rose. I conclude that labour quality growth is essential to the analysis of growth in labour input.

Investment in IT Equipment and Software

The final step in the comparison of patterns of economic growth among the G7 nations is to analyze the impact of investment in information technology equipment and software. In Table 6.9 I present levels of IT capital input per capita for the G7 for the period 1980–2001, relative to the US in 2000. The US overtook Germany in 1989 and remained the leader through 2001. Canada lagged behind the rest of the G7 through 1995, but France fell into last place in 2001.

Table 6.9 reveals substantial differences between IT capital stock and IT capital input. The G7 nations began with very modest stocks of IT equipment and software per capita in 1980. These stocks expanded rapidly during the period 1980–2001. The US led in IT capital stock throughout the period, while Japan moved from the fourth highest level in 1980 to the third highest in 2001.

Table 6.9   Levels of IT capital input and IT capital stock per capita and IT capital quality

Year	US	Canada	UK	France	Germany	Italy	Japan
			IT Capital Input Per Capita				
1980	4.5	1.0	3.0	4.2	7.1	6.7	1.7
1989	19.3	3.9	10.9	11.9	18.7	18.8	10.3
1995	38.1	11.2	20.9	19.1	31.1	31.2	19.0
2001	115.3	45.6	53.6	38.1	59.7	60.3	46.0
			IT Capital Stock Per Capita				
1980	9.8	0.8	2.5	3.5	6.1	4.6	3.5
1989	27.4	3.7	9.6	9.9	15.5	13.1	12.7
1995	46.8	9.7	19.2	18.0	28.2	23.8	22.9
2001	110.7	31.8	44.9	33.4	49.7	44.1	47.8
			IT Capital Quality				
1980	46.4	118.4	118.5	117.5	117.4	146.8	47.8
1989	70.4	107.4	112.7	119.7	120.4	143.2	81.1
1995	81.3	115.0	108.9	106.2	110.1	131.0	83.0
2001	104.1	143.4	119.3	114.1	120.2	136.6	96.1

Note: US = 100.0 in 2000, Canadian data begin in 1981.

IT capital quality reflects differences in the composition of IT capital input, relative to IT capital stock. A rising level of capital quality indicates a shift toward short-lived assets, such as computers and software. This shift is particularly dramatic for the US, Canada, and Japan, while the composition of IT capital stock changed relatively less for the UK, France, Germany, and Italy. Patterns for Non-IT capital input, capital stock, and capital quality largely reflect those for capital as a whole, presented in Table 6.5.

I give growth rates for IT capital input per capita, capital stock per capita, and capital quality in Table 6.10. The G7 nations have exhibited double-digit growth in IT capital input per capita since 1995. Canada was the international leader during this period with the US close behind. Japan was the leader in growth of IT capital input during the 1980s, another period of double-digit growth in the G7. However, Japanese IT growth slowed markedly during 1989–1995 and Canada gained the lead.

Table 6.10   Growth in IT capital input and capital stock per capita and IT capital quality

Year	US	Canada	UK	France	Germany	Italy	Japan
			IT Capital Input Per Capita				
1980–1989	16.09	17.66	14.43	11.66	10.71	11.44	20.19
1989–1995	11.35	17.42	10.91	7.92	8.47	8.44	10.22
1995–2001	18.47	23.42	15.69	11.55	10.87	10.98	14.71
			IT Capital Stock Per Capita				
1980–1989	11.47	18.88	14.98	11.46	10.43	11.72	14.32
1989–1995	8.94	16.28	11.50	9.91	9.97	9.94	9.84
1995–2001	14.34	19.73	14.16	10.35	9.40	10.28	12.25
			IT Capital Quality				
1980–1989	4.63	-1.22	-0.56	0.20	0.28	-0.27	5.88
1989–1995	2.41	1.14	-0.58	-1.99	-1.50	-1.49	0.38
1995–2001	4.12	3.69	1.53	1.20	1.47	0.70	2.46

Note: Percentage, Canadian data begin in 1981.

Patterns of growth for IT capital stock per capita are similar to those for IT capital input for the four European countries. Changes in the composition of IT capital stock per capita were important sources of growth of IT capital input per capita for the US, Canada, and Japan. IT capital stock also followed the pattern of IT capital input with substantial growth during the 1980s, followed by a pronounced lull during the period 1989–1995. After 1995 the growth rates of IT capital stock surged in all the G7 countries, but exceeded the rates of the 1980s only for the US and Canada.

Finally, growth rates for IT capital quality reflect the rates at which shorter-lived IT assets are substituted for longer-lived assets. Japan led in the growth of capital quality during the 1980s, but relinquished its lead to the US in 1989. IT capital quality growth for the US, Canada, and Japan outstripped that for the four European countries for most of the period 1980–2001. Patterns of growth in Non-IT capital input per capita, Non-IT capital stock per capita, and Non-IT capital quality given in Table 6.11 largely reflect those for capital as a whole presented in Table 6.6.

Table 6.12 and Figure 6.1 present the contribution of capital input to economic growth for the G7 nations, divided between IT and Non-IT.

Table 6.11   Growth in Non-IT capital input and Non-IT capital stock per capita and Non-IT capital quality

Year	US	Canada	UK	France	Germany	Italy	Japan
			Non-IT Capital Input Per Capita				
1980–1989	1.83	1.60	3.85	2.97	3.36	5.97	2.21
1989–1995	0.68	-0.66	4.22	1.20	2.09	2.17	1.95
1995–2001	2.00	0.85	0.15	1.30	1.52	2.57	0.96
			Non-IT Capital Stock Per Capita				
1980–1989	1.27	1.94	2.62	1.61	1.20	4.03	1.16
1989–1995	0.41	0.47	2.07	1.58	1.92	2.68	1.53
1995–2001	1.11	1.32	3.12	1.87	1.59	2.56	0.88
			Non-IT Capital Quality				
1980–1989	0.56	-0.35	1.23	1.36		2.16	1.94
1989–1995	0.27	-1.13	2.15	-0.38	0.17	-0.51	0.42
1995–2001	0.88	-0.47	-2.97	-0.57	-0.06	0.01	0.08

Note: Percentage, Canadian data begin in 1981.

Table 6.12   Contribution of total capital, IT capital and Non-IT capital to output growth

Year	US	Canada	UK	France	Germany	Italy	Japan
			Total Capital				
1980–1989	1.53	1.71	1.80	2.12	1.44	2.55	1.49
1989–1995	1.19	0.76	1.96	1.12	1.31	1.12	1.19
1995–2001	2.10	1.67	0.94	1.15	1.11	1.47	1.01
			IT Capital				
1980–1989	0.45	0.39	0.24	0.18	0.19	0.24	0.44
1989–1995	0.49	0.49	0.27	0.19	0.26	0.26	0.32
1995–2001	0.99	0.86	0.76	0.42	0.46	0.49	0.58
			Non-IT Capital Quality				
1980–1989	1.08	1.32	1.56	1.94	1.25	2.31	1.05
1989–1995	0.70	0.27	1.69	0.93	1.05	0.86	0.87
1995–2001	1.11	0.81	0.18	0.73	0.65	0.98	0.43

Note: Percentage, Canadian data begin in 1981.

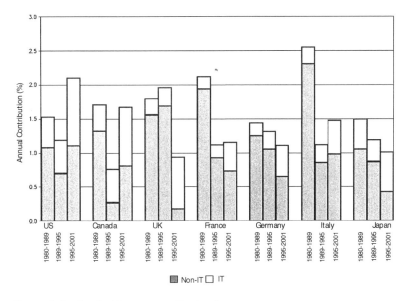

Figure 6.1   Capital input contribution by country

The powerful surge of IT investment in the US after 1995 is mirrored in similar jumps in growth rates of the contribution of IT capital through the G7. The contribution of IT capital input was similar during the 1980s and the period 1989–1995 for all the G7 nations, despite the dip in rates of economic growth after 1989. Japan is an exception to this general pattern with a contribution of IT capital comparable to that of the US during the 1980s, followed by a decline in this contribution from 1989–1995, reflecting the sharp downturn in Japanese economic growth.

The contribution of Non-IT capital input to economic growth after 1995 exceeded that for IT capital input for four of the G7 nations; the exceptions were Canada, the UK, and Japan. The US stands out in the magnitude of the contribution of capital input after 1995. Both IT and Non-IT capital input contributed to the US economic resurgence of the last half of the 1990s. Despite the strong performance of IT investment in Japan after 1995, the contribution of capital input declined substantially; the pattern for the UK is similar.

The Relative Importance of Investment and Productivity

Table 6.13 and Figure 6.2 present contributions to economic growth from productivity, divided between the IT-producing and Non-IT-producing industries.

Table 6.13   Contributions of productivity from IT and Non-IT production to output growth

Year	US	Canada	UK	France	Germany	Italy	Japan
				Productivity			
1980–1989	0.52	0.06	0.34	0.32	0.23	-0.36	1.15
1989–1995	0.26	0.00	-0.11	-0.26	1.12	0.37	1.04
1995–2001	0.54	0.58	0.91	0.60	-0.10	-0.49	0.75
			Productivity from IT Production				
1980–1989	0.23	0.14	0.23	0.29	0.28	0.32	0.15
1989–1995	0.23	0.14	0.32	0.29	0.43	0.38	0.20
1995–2001	0.48	0.17	0.82	0.56	0.65	0.68	0.46
			Productivity from Non-IT Production				
1980–1989	0.29	-0.08	0.11	0.03	-0.05	-0.68	1.00
1989–1995	0.03	-0.14	-0.43	-0.55	0.69	-0.01	0.84
1995–2001	0.06	0.41	0.09	0.04	-0.75	-1.17	0.29

Note: Percentage, Canadian data begin in 1981.

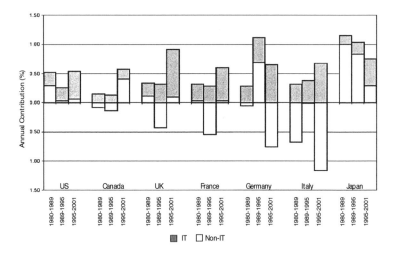

Figure 6.2   Sources of total factor productivity growth by country

The methodology for this division follows Triplett (1996). The contribution of IT-producing industries was positive throughout the period 1980–2001 and jumped substantially after 1995. Since the level of productivity in Italy was higher in 1980 than in 2001, it is not surprising that the contribution of productivity growth in the Non-IT industries was negative throughout the period. Productivity in these industries declined during the period 1989–1995 in Canada and Germany as well as Italy. The decline affected Canada, the UK, France, and Italy from 1989–1995 and became very steep in Germany and Italy from 1995–2001.

Table 6.14 and Figure 6.3 give a comprehensive view of the sources of economic growth for the G7. The contribution of capital input alone exceeds that of productivity for most nations and most time periods. The contribution of Non-IT capital input predominates over IT capital input for most countries and most time periods with Canada in 1989–1995, and the UK and Japan after 1995 as exceptions.

Table 6.14   Contributions of productivity from IT and Non-IT production to output growth

Year	US	Canada	UK	France	Germany	Italy	Japan
				Output			
1980–1989	3.38	3.10	2.69	2.38	1.99	2.51	3.83
1989–1995	2.43	1.39	1.62	1.30	2.34	1.52	2.23
1995–2001	3.76	3.34	2.74	2.34	1.18	1.90	1.45
				Labour			
1980–1989	1.33	1.33	0.56	-0.06	0.32	0.32	1.20
1989–1995	0.98	0.62	-0.24	0.44	-0.09	0.03	0.00
1995–2001	1.12	1.08	0.88	0.59	0.17	0.93	-0.31
				IT Capital			
1980–1989	0.45	0.39	0.24	0.18	0.19	0.24	0.44
1989–1995	0.49	0.49	0.27	0.19	0.26	0.26	0.32
1995–2001	0.99	0.86	0.76	0.42	0.46	0.49	0.58
				Non-IT Capital			
1980–1989	1.08	1.32	1.56	1.94	1.25	2.31	1.05
1989–1995	0.70	0.27	1.69	0.93	1.05	0.86	0.87
1995–2001	1.11	0.81	0.18	0.73	0.65	0.98	0.43
				Productivity from IT Production			
1980–1989	0.23	0.14	0.23	0.29	0.28	0.32	0.15
1989–1995	0.23	0.14	0.32	0.29	0.43	0.38	0.20
1995–2001	0.48	0.17	0.82	0.56	0.65	0.68	0.46
				Productivity from Non-IT Production			
1980–1989	0.29	-0.08	0.11	0.03	-0.05	-0.68	1.00
1989–1995	0.03	-0.14	-0.43	-0.55	0.69	-0.01	0.84
1995–2001	0.06	0.41	0.09	0.04	-0.75	-1.17	0.29

Note: Percentage, contributions, Canadian data begin in 1981.

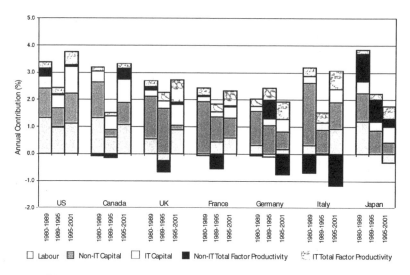

Figure 6.3   Sources of economic growth by country

This can be attributed to the unusual weakness in the growth of aggregate demand in these countries. The contribution of labour input varies considerably among the G7 nations with negative contributions after 1995 in Japan, during the 1980s in France, and during the period 1989–1995 in the UK and Germany.

Finally, Table 6.15 and Figure 6.4 translate sources of growth into sources of growth in average labour productivity (ALP).

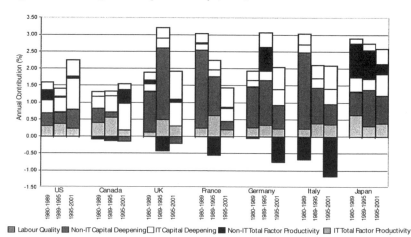

Figure 6.4   Sources of labour productivity growth by country

Table 6.15   Sources of labour productivity growth

Year	US	Canada	UK	France	Germany	Italy	Japan
				Output			
1980–1989	3.38	3.10	2.69	2.38	1.99	2.51	3.83
1989–1995	2.43	1.39	1.62	1.30	2.34	1.52	2.23
1995–2001	3.76	3.34	2.74	2.34	1.18	1.90	1.45
				Labour			
1980–1989	1.33	1.33	0.56	-0.06	0.32	0.32	1.20
1989–1995	0.98	0.62	-0.24	0.44	-0.09	0.03	0.00
1995–2001	1.12	1.08	0.88	0.59	0.17	0.93	-0.31
				IT Capital			
1980–1989	0.45	0.39	0.24	0.18	0.19	0.24	0.44
1989–1995	0.49	0.49	0.27	0.19	0.26	0.26	0.32
1995–2001	0.99	0.86	0.76	0.42	0.46	0.49	0.58
				Non-IT Capital			
1980–1989	1.08	1.32	1.56	1.94	1.25	2.31	1.05
1989–1995	0.70	0.27	1.69	0.93	1.05	0.86	0.87
1995–2001	1.11	0.81	0.18	0.73	0.65	0.98	0.43
			Productivity from IT Production				
1980–1989	0.23	0.14	0.23	0.29	0.28	0.32	0.15
1989–1995	0.23	0.14	0.32	0.29	0.43	0.38	0.20
1995–2001	0.48	0.17	0.82	0.56	0.65	0.68	0.46
			Productivity from Non-IT Production				
1980–1989	0.29	-0.08	0.11	0.03	-0.05	-0.68	1.00
1989–1995	0.03	-0.14	-0.43	-0.55	0.69	-0.01	0.84
1995–2001	0.06	0.41	0.09	0.04	-0.75	-1.17	0.29

Note: Percentage, contributions, Canadian data begin in 1981.

ALP, defined as output per hour worked, must be carefully distinguished from overall productivity, defined as output per unit of both capital and labour inputs. Output growth is the sum of growth in hours worked and growth in ALP. ALP growth depends on the contribution of capital deepening, the contribution of growth in labour quality, and productivity growth.

Capital deepening is the contribution of growth in capital input per hour worked and predominates over productivity as a source of ALP growth for the G7 nations. IT capital deepening predominates over Non-IT capital deepening in the US throughout the period 1980–2001 and in Canada after 1989, the UK and France after 1995. Finally, the contribution of labour quality is positive for all the G7 nations through the period.

6.4 ALTERNATIVE APPROACHES

Edward Denison's (1967) pathbreaking volume, *Why Growth Rates Differ*, compared differences in growth rates for national income net of capital consumption per capita for the period 1950–62 with differences of levels in 1960 for eight European countries and the US. The European countries were characterized by much more rapid growth and a lower level of national income per capita. However, this association did not hold for all comparisons between the individual countries and the US. Nonetheless, Denison concluded:[11]

> Aside from short-term aberrations Europe should be able to report higher growth rates, at least in national income per person employed, for a long time. Americans should expect this and not be disturbed by it.

Maddison (1987, 1991) constructed estimates of aggregate output, input, and productivity growth for France, Germany, Japan, The Netherlands, and the United Kingdom for the period 1870–1987. Maddison (1995) extended estimates for the US, the UK, and Japan backward to 1820 and forward to 1992. He defined output as gross of capital consumption throughout the period and constructed constant quality indices of labour input for the period 1913–1984, but not for 1870–1913.

Maddison employed capital stock as a measure of the input of capital, ignoring the changes in the composition of capital stock that are such an important source of growth for the G7 nations. This omission is especially critical in assessing the impact of investment in information technology. Finally, he reduced the growth rate of the price index for investment by one per cent per year for all countries and all time periods to correct for biases like those identified by Wyckoff (1995).

Comparisons without Growth Accounts

Kuznets (1971) provided elaborate comparisons of growth rates for fourteen industrialized countries. Unlike Denison (1967), he did not provide level comparisons. Maddison (1982) filled this lacuna by comparing levels of national product for sixteen countries. These comparisons used estimates of purchasing power parities by Irving Kravis, Alan Heston, and Robert Summers (1978).[12]

Maddison (1995) extended his long-term estimates of the growth of national product and population to 56 countries, covering the period 1820–1992. Maddison (2001) updated these estimates to 1998 in his magisterial volume, *The World Economy: A Millennial Perspective*. He provided estimates for 134 countries, as well as seven regions of the world – Western

Europe, Western Offshoots (Australia, Canada, New Zealand, and the United States), Eastern Europe, Former USSR, Latin America, Asia, and Africa.

Purchasing power parities have been updated by successive versions of the Penn World Table. A complete list of these tables through Mark 5 is given by Summers and Heston (1991). The current version of the Penn World Table is available on the Center for International Comparisons website at the University of Pennsylvania (CICUP). This covers 168 countries for the period 1950–2000 and represents one of the most significant achievements in economic measurement of the post-war period.[13]

Convergence

Data presented by Kuznets (1971), Maddison, and successive versions of the Penn World Table have made it possible to reconsider the issue of convergence raised by Denison (1967). Moses Abramovitz (1986) was the first to take up the challenge by analyzing convergence of output per capita among Maddison's sixteen countries. He found that convergence characterized the postwar period, while there was no tendency toward convergence before 1914 and during the interwar period. Baumol (1986) formalized these results by running a regression of growth rate of GDP per capita over the period 1870–1979 on the 1870 level of GDP per capita.[14]

In a highly innovative paper on 'Crazy Explanations for the Productivity Slowdown' Paul Romer (1987) derived Baumol's 'growth regression' from Solow's (1970) growth model with a Cobb-Douglas production function. Romer's empirical contribution was to extend the growth regressions from Maddison's (1982) sixteen advanced countries to the 115 countries in the Penn World Table (Mark 3). Romer's key finding was an estimate of the elasticity of output with respect to capital close to three-quarters. The share of capital in GNP implied by Solow's model was less than half as great.

Gregory Mankiw, David Romer, and David Weil (1992) defended the traditional framework of Kuznets (1971) and Solow (1970). The empirical part of their study is based on data for 98 countries from the Penn World Table (Mark 4). Like Paul Romer (1987), Mankiw, David Romer, and Weil derived a growth regression from the Solow (1970) model; however, they augmented this by allowing for investment in human capital.

The results of Mankiw, David Romer, and Weil (1992) provided empirical support for the augmented Solow model. There was clear evidence of the convergence predicted by the model; in addition, the estimated elasticity of output with respect to capital was in line with the share of capital in the value of output. The rate of convergence of output per capita was too slow to be consistent with the 1970 version of the Solow model, but supported the augmented version.

Modelling Productivity Differences

Finally, Islam (1995) exploited an important feature of the Penn World Table overlooked in prior studies. This panel data set contains benchmark comparisons of levels of the national product at five year intervals, beginning in 1960. This made it possible to test an assumption maintained in growth regressions. These regressions had assumed identical levels of productivity for all countries included in the Penn World Table.

Substantial differences in levels of productivity among countries have been documented by Denison (1967), by my papers with Christensen and Cummings (1981), Dougherty (1996, 1999), and Yip (2000) and in Section 6.2 above. By introducing econometric methods for panel data Islam (1995) was able to allow for these differences. He corroborated the finding of Mankiw, David Romer, and Weil (1992) that the elasticity of output with respect to capital input coincided with the share of capital in the value of output.

In addition, Islam (1995) found that the rate of convergence of output per capita among countries in the Penn World Table substantiated the unaugmented version of the Solow (1970) growth model. In short, 'crazy explanations' for the productivity slowdown, like those propounded by Paul Romer (1987), were unnecessary. Moreover, the model did not require augmentation by endogenous investment in human capital, as proposed by Mankiw, David Romer, and Weil (1992).

Islam concluded that differences in technology among countries must be included in econometric models of growth rates. This requires econometric techniques for panel data, like those originated by Gary Chamberlain (1984), rather than the regression methods of Baumol, Paul Romer, and Mankiw, David Romer, and Weil. Panel data techniques have now superseded regression methods in modelling differences in output per capita.

6.5 CONCLUSIONS

I conclude that a powerful surge in investment in information technology and equipment after 1995 characterizes all of the G7 economies. This accounts for a large portion of the resurgence in US economic growth, but contributes substantially to economic growth in the remaining G7 economies as well. Another significant source of the G7 growth resurgence after 1995 is a jump in productivity growth in IT-producing industries.

For Japan the dramatic upward leap in the impact of IT investment after 1995 was insufficient to overcome downward pressures from deficient growth of aggregate demand. This manifests itself in declining contributions of Non-

IT capital and labour inputs. Similar downturns are visible in Non-IT capital input in France, Germany, and especially the UK after 1995.

These findings are based on new data and new methodology for analyzing the sources of economic growth. Internationally harmonized prices for information technology equipment and software are essential for capturing differences among the G7 nations. Constant quality indices of capital and labour inputs are necessary to incorporate the impacts of investments in information technology and human capital.

Exploiting the new data and methodology, I have been able to show that investment in tangible assets is the most important source of economic growth in the G7 nations. The contribution of capital input exceeds that of productivity for all countries for all periods. The relative importance of productivity growth is far less than suggested by the traditional methodology of Kuznets (1971) and Solow (1970), which is now obsolete.

The conclusion from Islam's (1995) research is that the Solow (1970) model is appropriate for modelling the endogenous accumulation of tangible assets. It is unnecessary to endogenize human capital accumulation as well. The transition path to balanced growth equilibrium after a change in policies that affects investment in tangible assets requires decades, while the transition after a change affecting investment in human capital requires as much as a century.

NOTES

1. See Angus Maddison (2001) for 1998 data for world GDP and the GDP of each of the G7 countries.
2. See Dale Jorgenson and Kevin Stiroh (2000) and Stephen Oliner and Daniel Sichel (2000).
3. See Wyckoff (1995).
4. See Schreyer (2000). Alessandra Colecchia and Schreyer (2002) have employed these internationally harmonized prices in measuring the impact of IT investment.
5. See Jorgenson (2001).
6. See John Baldwin and Tarek Harchaoui (2002).
7. See Van Ark, Johanna Melka, Nanno Mulder, Marcel Timmer, and Gerard Ypma (2002).
8. See Jorgenson and Motohashi (2005).
9. See OECD (2002). Current data on purchasing power parities are available from the OECD website: http://www.sourceoecd.org.
10. The purchasing power parities for outputs are based on OECD (2002). Purchasing power parities for inputs follow the methodology described in detail by Jorgenson and Yip (2000).
11. See Denison (1967), especially Chapter 21, '*The Sources of Growth and the Contrast between Europe and the United States*', pp. 296-348.
12. For details see Maddison (1982), pp. 159-168.
13. See Heston, Summers and Aten (2002). The CICUP website is at: http://pwt.econ.upenn.edu/aboutpwt.html.
14. Baumol's 'growth regression' has spawned a vast literature, recently summarized by Steven Durlauf and Danny Quah (1999, Ellen McGrattan and James Schmitz (1999), and Islam (2003). Much of this literature is based on data from successive versions of the Penn World Table.

REFERENCES

Abramovitz, M. (1986), 'Catching Up, Forging Ahead, and Falling Behind', *Journal of Economic History*, **46** (2), 385–406.

Ark, B. van, J. Melka, N. Mulder, M. Timmer and G. Ypma (2002), *ICT Investment and Growth Accounts for the European Union, 1980–2000*, Brussels, European Commission, June.

Baldwin, J.R., and T.M. Harchaoui (2002), *Productivity Growth in Canada – 2002*, Ottawa, Statistics Canada.

Baumol, W.J. (1986), 'Productivity Growth, Convergence, and Welfare', *American Economic Review*, **76** (5), 1072–1085.

Chamberlain, G. (1984), 'Panel Data', in Zvi Griliches and Michael Intriligator, eds, *Handbook of Econometrics*, Vol. 2, 1247–1318.

Christensen, L.R., D. Cummings and D.W. Jorgenson (1980), 'Economic Growth, 1947–1973: An International Comparison', in John W. Kendrick and Beatrice Vaccara, eds, *New Developments in Productivity Measurement and Analysis*, Chicago, University of Chicago Press, 595–698.

Christensen, L.R., D. Cummings, and D.W. Jorgenson (1981), 'Relative Productivity Levels 1947–1973', *European Economic Review*, **16** (1), 61–94.

Colecchia, A. and P. Schreyer (2002), 'ICT Investment and Economic Growth in the 1990s: Is the United States a Unique Case? A Comparative Study of Nine OECD Countries', *Review of Economic Dynamics*, **5** (2), 408–442.

Denison, E.F. (1967), *Why Growth Rates Differ*, Washington, The Brookings Institution.

Dougherty, Ch. and D.W. Jorgenson (1996), 'International Comparisons of the Sources of Economic Growth', *American Economic Review*, **86** (2), 25–29.

Dougherty, Ch. and D.W. Jorgenson (1997), 'There Is No Silver Bullet: Investment and Growth in the G7', *National Institute Economic Review*, **162**, 57–74.

Durlauf, S.N. and D.T. Quah (1999), 'The New Empirics of Economic Growth', in Taylor and Woodford, eds, *Handbook of Macroeconomics*, Vol. 1A, 235–310, Amsterdam, North Holland.

Heston, A., R. Summers and B. Aten (2002), *Penn World Table Version 6.1*, Philadelphia, Center for International Comparisons at the University of Pennsylvania (CICUP), October.

Islam, N. (1995), 'Growth Empirics', *Quarterly Journal of Economics*, **110** (4), 1127–1170.

Islam, N. (2003), 'What Have We Learned from the Convergence Debate?', *Journal of Economic Surveys*, **17** (3), 309–362.

Jorgenson, D.W. (2001), 'Information Technology and the US Economy', *American Economic Review*, **91** (1), 1–32.

Jorgenson, D.W. (2003), 'Information Technology and the G7 Economies', *World Economics*, **4** (4), 139–170.

Jorgenson, D.W. and K. Motohashi (2005), 'Information Technology and the Japanese Economy', *Journal of the Japanese and International Economies*, **19** (4), forthcoming.

Jorgenson, D.W. and K.J. Stiroh (2000), 'Raising the Speed Limit: US Economic Growth in the Information Age', *Brookings Papers on Economic Activity* 1, 125–211.

Jorgenson, D.W. and E. Yip (2000), 'Whatever Happened to Productivity Growth?' in Charles R. Hulten, Edwin R. Dean, and Michael J. Harper, eds, *New Developments in Productivity Analysis*, Chicago, University of Chicago Press, 509–540.

Kravis, I.B., A. Heston, and R. Summers (1978), *International Comparisons of Real Product and Purchasing Power*, Baltimore, Johns Hopkins University Press.

Kuznets, S. (1971), *Economic Growth of Nations*, Cambridge, Harvard University Press.

Maddison, A. (1982), *Phases of Capitalist Development*, Oxford, Oxford University Press.

Maddison, A. (1987), 'Growth and Slowdown in Advanced Capitalist Economies: Techniques of Quantitative Assessment', *Journal of Economic Literature*, **25** (2), 649–698.

Maddison, A. (1991), *Dynamic Forces in Capitalist Development*, Oxford, Oxford University Press.

Maddison, A. (1995), Monitoring the World Economy, Paris, Organisation for Economic Co-operation and Development.

Maddison, A. (2001), The World Economy: A Millennial Perspective, Paris, Organisation for Economic Co-operation and Development.

Mankiw, N.G., D. Romer, and D. Weil (1992), 'A Contribution to the Empirics of Economic Growth', *Quarterly Journal of Economics*, **107** (2), 407–437.

McGrattan, E. and J. Schmitz (1999), 'Explaining Cross-Country Income Differences', in Taylor and Woodford, eds, *Handbook of Macroeconomics*, Vol. 1A, 669–737, Amsterdam, North Holland.

Oliner, S.D. and D.J. Sichel (2000), 'The Resurgence of Growth in the Late 1990s: Is Information Technology the Story?', *Journal of Economic Perspectives*, **14** (4), 3–22.

Organization for Economic Co-operation and Development (2002), *Purchasing Power Parities and Real Expenditures, 1999 Benchmark Year*, Paris, Organization for Economic Co-operation and Development.

Romer, P. (1987), 'Crazy Explanations for the Productivity Slowdown', in Stanley Fischer, ed., *NBER Macroeconomics Annual*, Cambridge, The MIT Press, 163–201.

Schreyer, P. (2000), *The Contribution of Information and Communication Technology to Output Growth: A Study of the G7 Countries*, Paris, Organization for Economic Co-operation and Development, May 23.

Solow, R.M. (1970), *Growth Theory: An Exposition*, New York, Oxford University Press.

Summers, R. and A. Heston (1991), 'The Penn World Table (Mark 5): An Expanded Set of International Comparisons, 1950–1988', *Quarterly Journal of Economics*, **106** (2), 327–368.

Triplett, J. (1996), 'High-Tech Industry Productivity and Hedonic Price Indices', in Organization for Economic Co-operation and Development (ed.), *Industry Productivity*, Paris, Organization for Economic Co-operation and Development, 119–142.

Wyckoff, A.W. (1995), 'The Impact of Computer Prices on International Comparisons of Productivity', *Economics of Innovation and New Technology*, **3** (3–4), 277–93.

7. Productivity, Innovation and ICT in Old and New Europe[1]

Bart van Ark and Marcin Piatkowski

7.1 SUMMARY

This chapter investigates the productivity performance of CEE countries vis-à-vis the EU-15 and the US during the 1990s and early 2000s to detect sources of convergence between the two regions. The paper shows that the joint trends of declining labour intensity in the CEE countries and a slight improvement in the EU-15 have been an important source of productivity convergence during the period. It is also found that despite lower income levels, ICT capital in the CEE countries has contributed as much to labour productivity growth as in the EU-15. Industry analysis shows that manufacturing industries that have invested heavily in ICT have been key to the restructuring process. As such ICT may therefore have been an important but probably temporary source of convergence. In the longer run the impact of ICT on growth will have to come primarily from its productive use in the services sector of the economy. The chapter includes a New Economy Indicator that reflects the existence of conducive environment for continued ICT investment and diffusion. It shows that further reforms are much needed for CEE countries to enter a second convergence phase in the coming decades.

7.2 INTRODUCTION

Following the collapse of the Berlin Wall and the transition of the economies of Central and Eastern Europe (CEE) from socialist centrally planned to a market economy, an important phase in the transition process, related to restructuring of the economy, has been completed in the eight CEE countries that acceded to the European Union in 2004. Three other CEE countries (Croatia, Bulgaria and Romania) are also making rapid progress on restructuring in order to be able enter the EU by the end of 2010.

As a result of these developments, comparisons of economic performance between the CEE countries and the present EU-15 as well as between the enlarged EU-25 and the US remain of great interest.[2] In this chapter our focus is on one important comparative aspect of economic performance, which is the impact of the rise in the production and use of information and communication technology (ICT) on the change in output, employment and productivity growth in CEE countries in comparison to EU-15 countries and the US.

The analysis in this chapter will be placed in the framework of the catch-up and convergence hypotheses. Irrespective of the motives of its messenger, the distinction between 'Old Europe' and 'New Europe' back in 2003 by the US secretary of defense, Donald Rumsfeld, appears quite useful from the perspective of analyzing ICT in the framework of catch up and convergence. Essentially we aim to shed light on which of the following hypotheses holds up best following the analysis in this paper:

(1)   The convergence (or even leapfrogging) hypothesis: 'The new economy in New Europe and the Old Economy in Old Europe'; or
(2)   The divergence (or falling behind) hypothesis: 'The old economy in New Europe and the new economy in Old Europe'.

At face value there are arguments in favour of both hypotheses. The convergence hypothesis would be supported by the 'advantages of backwardness'-literature, in particular Gerschenkron (1962) and Abramovitz (1986). In this light, CEE countries would benefit from the combination of rapid technology (ICT) diffusion and major restructuring of (in particular) the manufacturing sector. Indeed Central and Eastern Europe would then follow the path of East Asia over the past decades (van Ark and Timmer, 2003). The convergence hypothesis would be even more likely if the EU-15 countries get stuck on a 'low-productivity growth' track, partly due to insufficient effect from ICT investment on productivity growth, due to rigid product and labour markets, too much emphasis on cost competitiveness, failing innovation systems and lack of competition (Nicoletti and Scarpetta, 2003).

Alternatively the divergence hypothesis derives support from the development towards comparative advantages in CEE countries in low- and medium tech manufacturing industries (e.g. food manufacturing) on the basis of cost competitiveness, insufficient diffusion of new technologies from the foreign-dominated to the domestic part of the economy, and from manufacturing to services. Furthermore the EU-15 may ultimately succeed in exploiting the productivity potential from ICT, as there are clear indications that the ICT impact on productivity comes with some delay, in particular in the ICT-using sectors of the economy (Piatkowski and van Ark, 2005). This could mean that at least for the next decade or so, divergence in economic performance between CEE countries and the EU-15 would be more likely.

The chapter proceeds as follows. In Section 7.3 we show the convergence trends between CEE, EU-15 countries and the US in terms of average productivity and average per capita income since 1995.[3] The difference between the two measures indicates the impact of changes in labour intensity in the convergence process. Indeed a substantial part of the productivity recovery in CEE countries since the mid-1990s has been due to large cuts in employment and a decline in labour participation rates. In the EU-15, labour participation has significantly improved during the 1990s but at the same time productivity growth slowed. We investigate various indicators of labour intensity to assess whether differences between CEE countries and the EU-15 are likely to continue to be a source of convergence in the future.

In Section 7.4 we zoom in on the drivers of labour productivity growth, and use a growth accounting framework to establish the contributions from investment in capital, in particular ICT capital, and total factor productivity (TFP) growth. In particular we look at whether ICT capital, which is the main asset embodying new technology, has been a source of convergence or divergence between CEE countries and the EU-15.

In Section 7.5, the chapter adopts an industry perspective to show and explain the divergence in labour productivity growth rates between manufacturing and services in the CEE countries, the EU-15 and the US.

In Section 7.6 we broaden our analysis by comparing our results from Sections 7.4 and 7.5 with a 'New Economy Indicator' for each country, which reflects the development of institutional and economic infrastructure, trade openness and innovation (van Ark and Piatkowski, 2004). The relationships between the productivity results from ICT and the New Economy indicators provide an insight into how the economic environment can contribute to the realization of growth potential of the 'new economy' in both New and Old Europe.

Section 7.7 considers the characteristics of the convergence process up till now, and speculates on how – based on the observations hitherto as well as the comparative experience in Western Europe and the US – it may continue or change in nature during the coming period.

7.3 CONVERGENCE AND LABOUR INPUT DURING THE 1990s AND EARLY 2000s

Output and productivity growth in CEE countries has shown a U-turn since 1990. Between 1989 and 1992 output collapsed and per capita income fell by more than 20 per cent. Labour productivity declined somewhat less (by around 10 per cent) because the decline in output was to some extent offset by a rapid shakeout of unproductive activities (van Ark, 1999). Since 1992/1993 productivity growth has rapidly turned around as a result of a recovery in output growth and a continued decline in employment. The restructuring process has led to a continued process of shutting down of inefficient firms in CEE countries as well as to opening up new businesses with faster output growth compared to incumbent firms.

Table 7.1 shows that from 1995–2004 average annual GDP growth in CEE countries was 3.6 per cent on average, which was 1.5 percentage points higher than average GDP growth in the EU-15. On average, GDP growth in the enlarged European Union (EU-25) comes at 2.5 per cent.[4]

Table 7.1   Growth of real GDP, GDP per capita, labour productivity and working hours, 1995–2004 (Bai and Perron method)

	Real GDP	GDP per head of population	GDP per person employed	Employment
EU-15	2.3	2.0	1.1	1.2
CEE-10	3.6	3.7	4.2	-0.6
EU-25	2.4	2.2	1.5	0.9
United States	3.3	2.2	2.1	1.1

Note: For country detail, see www.ggdc.net/dseries/totecon.shtml

Source: Total Economy Database, Groningen Growth and Development Centre and The Conference Board; see www.ggdc.net/dseries/totecon.shtml

The difference in per capita income growth between the two regions is somewhat bigger than for real GDP. However, labour productivity growth, measured as output per person employed, differs by as much as 3.1 percentage points between the two regions. Whereas productivity growth in the EU-15 comes at no more than 1.1 per cent per year on average, CEE countries realized on average 4.2 per cent growth between 1995 and 2004.[5] High productivity growth coupled with a negative employment growth shows that the strong productivity convergence between the CEE-10 and the EU-15 has so far been mostly driven by job cuts.[6]

Table 7.2 shows that despite rapid productivity growth, the gap in productivity levels between CEE countries and the EU-15 is still quite large. Between 1995 and 2004 the productivity gap per capita between the two regions reduced by only 5.6 percentage points. Yet, due to job cuts, the productivity gap measured as GDP per employed decreased by 10.8 percentage points.

Nonetheless, in 2004 the average productivity level of the CEE-10 was still at only 44.5 per cent of the EU-15. Only Slovenia has productivity levels that are near those countries in the EU-15 with the lowest productivity levels, i.e. Portugal and Greece. Hence the period for catch-up to even the low-productivity echelon of the present EU-15, will still be considerable for large countries like Poland and Romania (see also Schadler and others, 2006).

Table 7.2   Relative levels of GDP per capita and GDP per person employed, 1995 and 2004

	GDP per head of poulation (EU-15 =100) 1995	GDP per person employed (EU-15 =100) 2004
EU-15	100.0	100.0
CEE-10	33.3	38.9
EU-25	90.2	91.7
United States	133.5	135.5

Note: For country detail, see www.ggdc.net/dseries/totecon.shtml

Source: Total Economy Database, Groningen Growth and Development Centre and The Conference Board; see www.ggdc.net/dseries/totecon.shtml

The per capita income and labour productivity measures can be analyzed in the light of the convergence hypothesis. This is done by combining Tables 7.1 and 7.2 through relating the relative levels for each country to the EU-15 average in the beginning year of the period (1995) to their subsequent growth rates from 1995 to 2004. Figure 7.1 shows that there is a slight negative relationship found for per capita income. For labour productivity a stronger negative relationship is found than for per capita income and the relationship is now statistically much stronger (Figure 7.2).[7]

The weaker relationship for per capita income vis-à-vis labour productivity is due to the fact that per capita income is not only affected by labour productivity, but also by labour intensity – more precisely by the employment to population ratio. Figure 7.3 shows that the change in the employment to population ratio is positively related to the level of labour productivity in the CEE-10 and the EU-15. Since 1995 the CEE-countries have generally shown negative or very small increases in the employment to population ratios. It has therefore strengthened labour productivity convergence, but weakened the relationship between average income level and per capita income growth. At lower income levels the 'cake' has been produced with an increasingly smaller number of people relative to the total population.

To establish whether labour saving will continue to be an important source for the productivity convergence process, Table 7.3 shows three measures of labour intensity. The first measure is the same as in Figure 7.3 and represents the ratio of employment to population for 1995 and 2004. This measure is directly obtained from the difference in the comparative levels of per capita income and GDP per person employed. The employment to population ratio shows an increase for the EU-15 and a slight decline in CEE-10 between 1995 and 2004. The level of employment to population is also considerably lower in CEE-10 than in EU-15, suggesting a divergence in the realization of labour potential in both regions.

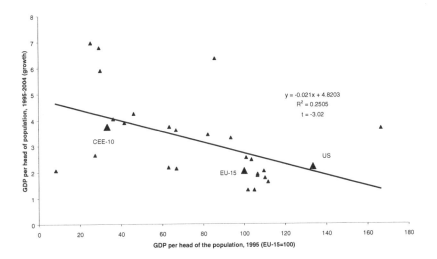

Note: For country detail, see www.ggdc.net/dseries/totecon.shtml; see also Table 7.2.

Source: Total Economy Database, Groningen Growth and Development Centre and The Conference Board (see www.ggdc.net/dseries/totecon.shtml).

Figure 7.1   Relationship between per capita income levels relative to
            EU-15 (1995) and per capita income growth

The second measure, which is the ratio of the labour force to the total population of working age (15–64 years), shows similar trends to the first measure. Whereas labour force participation in the CEE countries was roughly the same as in the EU-15 in 1995, it has fallen below the EU-15 level by 2004.[8]

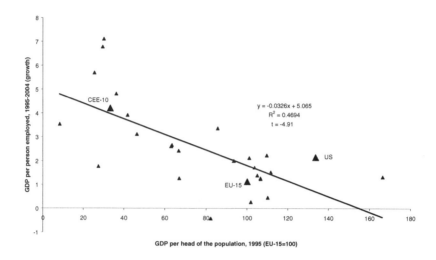

Note: For country detail, see www.ggdc.net/dseries/totecon.shtml; see also Table 7.2.

Source: Total economy database, Groningen Growth and Development Centre and The Con-ference Board (see www.ggdc.net/dseries/totecon.shtml).

Figure 7.2   Relationship between level of GDP per person employed rela-tive to EU-15 (1995) and growth of GDP per person employed (1995–2004)

The third measure in Table 7.3 indicates the degree to which the potential of labour has been realized. Potential labour intensity is derived from the product of the total working age population times 2,800 annual hours (which is equal to a 6-day working week at 9 hours per day).[9] Obviously the latter measure is not meant to formulate a target which countries should strive for. It merely serves as a benchmark against which the actual number of working hours can be compared. The estimates confirm that the realization of the la-bour potential in the EU-15 has improved since the mid-1990s, whereas it de-teriorated for CEE countries. Unlike the two other labour market indicators, the latter measure also suggests convergence rather than divergence of labour intensity, because the level in the CEE countries is still higher than for the EU-15.

From the perspective of convergence analysis, the measure of realized la-bour potential may be the most adequate measure of labour intensity. If one assumes that there is still scope for the EU-15 countries to increase labour in-tensity further, while labour intensity in the CEE countries may still decline somewhat further due to restructuring, these two processes will continue to

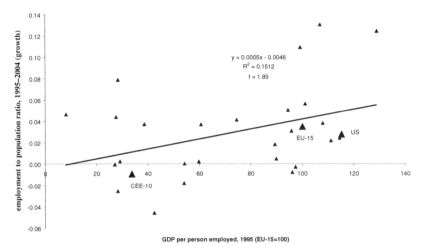

GDP per person employed, 1995 (EU-15=100)

Note: For country detail, see www.ggdc.net/dseries/totecon.shtml and Appendix Table 7.A1.

Source: Total Economy Database, Groningen Growth and Development Centre and The Conference Board (see www.ggdc.net/dseries/totecon.shtml).

Figure 7.3   Relationship between level of GDP per person employed relative to EU-15 (1995) and growth in employment to population ratio (1995–2004)

Table 7.3   Employment to population ratios, labour force participation rates and total hours to potential hours[a], 1995 and 2004

	Employment to Population ratios		Labour force to population 15–64 ratios		Total hours to potential hours ratios	
	1995	2004	1995	2004	1995	2004
EU-15	0.407	0.442	0.684	0.716	0.356	0.373
CEE-10[b]	0.397	0.388	0.685	0.660	0.419	0.387
EU-25[c]	0.405	0.433	0.684	0.708	0.377	0.386
United States	0.472	0.474	0.792	0.781	0.499	0.478

Notes:
For country detail, see Appendix Table 7.1.
[a] *Potential hours are based on working age population times 2,800 working hours per year.*
[b] *For the Labour Force to Population ratio and the Total Hours to Potential Hours ratio for the CEE-10 an aggregate of the Czech Republic, Hungary, Poland and the Slovak Republic is used, as Labour Force and Working Age Population data for the other CEE-10 countries is missing.*
[c] *As a result of the missing data for the CEE countries, the data for EU-25 is actually EU-15 plus the 4 CEE countries.*

Source: Groningen Growth and Development Centre (www.ggdc.net) and OECD Labour Force Statistics (various issues) and Eurostat, Employment in Europe (various issues).

drive part of the convergence process of labour productivity of CEE countries on the present EU-15 for the next decade or so. However, as employment growth has turned positive in various CEE countries since 2004, the main contribution to this convergence process will need to come from further increases in EU-15 hours input relative to potential hours, which seems feasible given the much higher levels in the United States.

7.4   THE CONTRIBUTION OF ICT CAPITAL TO GROWTH

An important question that arises from the previous section is how the labour saving process in Central and Eastern Europe has been translated into productivity growth between 1995 and 2003. Throughout the process of restructuring, productivity growth may have been driven by a rise in capital intensity but it may also have been supported by technical change. In particular when increased investment took place in new types of capital, such as ICT capital, technology may have been a major source of accelerated productivity growth. An important issue is to what extent ICT capital directly contributes to labour productivity growth, and to what extent it works indirectly through total factor productivity growth by industries that either produce or use ICT capital intensively. For example, during the 1990s and early 2000s, ICT capital has been a more important source of growth in the 'old' EU countries than ICT-related TFP growth.[10]

This issue is all the more important from the perspective of catch-up growth as has been discussed earlier in the light of East Asian growth during the past decades. For example, Krugman (1994) and Young (1995) indicated that most of the growth in Asia was driven by increases in capital intensity rather than by TFP growth. Unfortunately, detailed work on the role of ICT, using growth accounting techniques, for new and non-OECD countries is still limited, but the evidence available so far suggests a large impact from ICT capital although there is much variation.[11]

As far as the CEE countries are concerned, Piatkowski (2004) provides a detailed study of ICT and growth and productivity in seven CEE economies (Bulgaria, Czech Republic, Hungary, Poland, Romania, Slovakia and Slovenia) and Russia. In this section we update these results to cover 1995–2003. We then compare them with updated results from Timmer and van Ark (2005) for the EU-15 and the US.[12]

A detailed description of the methodology to measure the contribution of ICT to output and labour productivity growth is provided in several of the studies quoted above and can be summarized as follows. Gross domestic product (Y) is produced from aggregate factor input X, consisting of capital services (K) and labour services (L). Productivity is represented as Hicks-neutral augmentation of aggregate input (A). The aggregate production function takes the form:

$$Y = A \cdot X(L, K_n, K_{it}) \tag{7.1}$$

with subscript n indicating services from Non-IT capital and subscript $_{it}$ indicating services from information technology capital (including office and computing equipment, communication equipment and software). Under the assumption of competitive factor markets and constant returns to scale, growth accounting expresses the growth of output as a share weighted growth of inputs and total factor productivity, denoted by A, which is derived as a residual.

$$\Delta \ln Y = v_L \Delta \ln L + v_{Kn} \Delta \ln K_n + v_{it} \Delta \ln K_{it} + \Delta \ln A \tag{7.2}$$

where v denotes the average shares in total factor income and because of constant returns to scale: $v_L + v_{Kn} + v_{Kit} = 1$, and Δ refers to first differences. By rearranging equation (7.2) the results can be presented in terms of average labour productivity growth defined as $y = Y/L$, the ratio of output to employment, $k = K/L$, the ratio of capital services to persons employed and TFP:

$$\Delta \ln y = v_{Kn} \Delta \ln k_n + v_{it} \Delta \ln k_{it} + \Delta \ln A \tag{7.3}$$

Table 7.4 shows that between 1995 and 2003 the contribution of ICT capital to labour productivity growth ($v_{kit} \, \Delta \, \ln k_{it}$) in CEE countries in absolute terms was comparable to that in the EU-15, despite lower levels of productivity in the former (column 3). This relatively high contribution from ICT capital in the CEE countries has been due to a rapid acceleration in real quality-adjusted ICT investments, which were growing at an average rate exceeding 20 per cent a year between 1995 and 2003.

In both the CEE and EU countries high growth rates of ICT investment have been induced by rapidly falling prices of ICT products and services, which encouraged firms to substitute ICT for non-ICT capital. In the case of the CEE countries, the rapid build-up of the ICT capital stock was also driven by a large pent-up demand for ICT infrastructure. This was partly due to the legacy of a technological gap dating back to the socialist system and NATO-imposed restrictions on imports of technologically advanced equipment.[13] In addition, the restructuring process since transition created typical catch-up growth in ICT capital intensity.[14]

Table 7.4 ICT capital contribution to labour productivity growth (GDP per person employed) in CEE countries, EU-15 and the US, 1995–2003, in percentage points

	GDP per person employed (annual growth, %)	%-point contribution of:			ICT capital share in LP growth
		Non-ICT capital intensity	ICT capital intensity	Total factor producti-vity growth	
	(1)	(2)	(3)	(4)	(5)
CEE countries	**3.16**	**0.88**	**0.52**	**1.76**	**16%**
Bulgaria	2.28	0.35	0.46	1.48	20%
Czech Republic	2.55	1.19	0.64	0.73	25%
Hungary	2.82	0.31	0.60	1.91	21%
Poland	4.73	1.94	0.57	2.22	12%
Romania	2.58	0.76	0.35	1.47	14%
Slovakia	3.77	0.82	0.48	2.47	13%
Slovenia*	3.36	0.78	0.52	2.06	15%
Russia	3.47	-1.07	0.08	4.46	2%
EU-15	**0.99**	**0.23**	**0.49**	**0.27**	**50%**
Ireland	3.85	0.66	0.54	2.65	14%
Greece	3.08	0.67	0.40	2.01	13%
Austria	1.88	0.63	0.48	0.77	25%
Finland	2.26	-0.44	0.53	2.17	24%
Sweden	2.07	0.15	0.83	1.08	40%
Denmark	1.67	0.76	0.77	0.14	46%
UK	1.77	0.17	0.69	0.91	39%
Portugal	0.80	0.53	0.49	-0.23	62%
Belgium	1.21	-0.07	0.76	0.52	62%
Germany	1.19	0.25	0.42	0.52	35%
France	0.87	0.36	0.31	0.19	35%
Italy	0.31	0.44	0.42	-0.55	137%
Netherlands	0.35	-0.16	0.42	0.09	119%
Spain	-0.17	0.07	0.28	-0.53	-159%
United States	2.20	0.31	0.82	1.07	37%

*Note: *Slovenia 1995–2001 only. CEE represents an unweighted average.*

Source: CEE countries from van Ark and Piatkowski (2004), updated to 2003. Russia from Piatkowski (2004), updated to 2003; EU-15 and US from http://www.ggdc.net/ dseries/growth-accounting.shtml

Table 7.4 also shows that, within the CEE group, Bulgaria and Romania lagged behind the other five CEE countries. As argued by van Ark and Piat-kowski (2004), this seems to be mostly due to a slower pace of economic and institutional reforms in Bulgaria and Romania relative to the five new EU member states. Interestingly though, as shown in Figure 7.4, between 2000 and 2003 the ICT capital contribution to labour productivity growth in both countries practically caught up with the other five CEE countries. This seems to be related to the recent pick-up in structural and institutional reforms driven by EU accession. EBRD's (2004) transition indicators, which track progress in transition to a fully functioning market economy, for Bulgaria and Romania improved significantly in the recent period. The considerable increase in ICT capital contribution to labour productivity growth may suggest that benefiting from ICT investment requires a certain basic level of economic and institutional development. When this level is achieved, however, the contribution of ICT capital to growth slows, as was the case in the five leading CEE countries. The drastic decrease in the impact of ICT capital on labour productivity growth in the EU-15 and the US may in turn reflect diminishing returns to ICT investment (van Ark and Inklaar, 2005).

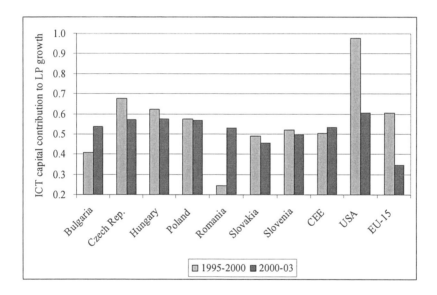

Source: Results from Piatkowski (2004) updated to 2003 and http://www.ggdc.net/dseries/growth-accounting.shtml

Figure 7.4   ICT capital contribution to labour productivity growth in CEE countries, EU-15 and the US, 1995–2000 and 2000–03, in percentage points

A glance at Figure 7.5, which relates the comparative level of GDP per person employed to the absolute ICT contribution to labour productivity growth, shows that ICT capital in itself has not been a direct source of convergence. However, lower labour productivity levels of the CEE countries also did not prevent them from benefiting from ICT capital to the same degree as the average for the EU, and it has therefore not been a cause for divergence either.[15]

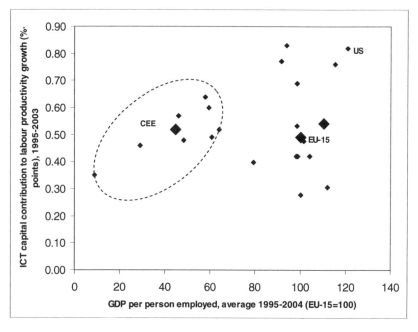

Note: CEE only for Bulgaria, Czech Republic, Hungary, Poland, Romania, Slovakia and Slovenia.

Source: Table 7.2 and Table 7.4.

*Figure 7.5   Contribution of ICT capital to labour productivity growth
(1995–2003) versus average GDP per person employed
(EU-15=100), 1995–2004*

The most important source of convergence between the CEE countries and the EU-15 comes from the higher contributions of total factor productivity in the former group (column 4 of Table 7.4). This result is in contrast to what was found for East Asia by Krugman (1994) and Young (1995), who suggested much slower TFP growth. Although the precise reasons for relatively high TFP growth are not known, these are likely to be strongly related to the effects of restructuring (privatization, emergence of new, more productive firms, liquidation of state-owned companies), technology transfer, higher capacity utilization, improvement in managerial and business skills, an increase in human capital and more entrenched macroeconomic stability. TFP growth may also have arisen from the productive exploitation of ICT capital, but its precise contribution cannot be directly determined. In any case it will then have been only one of the sources of convergence of productivity growth in CEE-countries relative to the average level of the EU-15.

While it is not possible to disentangle the productivity contribution from all factors, it can be argued that part of the rapid increase in labour productivity was driven by large scale privatization and liquidation of inefficient state-owned companies, a phenomenon mostly unique to countries transitioning from a centrally planned to a market economy.[16] Another part of the growth in labour productivity stemmed from a cyclical effect of higher capacity utilization as (after 1995) most CEE countries quickly recovered from the transitional recession, which shaved off 18 to 40 per cent of their GDP as of 1989 (Kolodko, 2000).

However, privatization and the surge in capacity utilization, which contributed to high labour productivity growth rates in the CEE countries, were mostly of a one-off nature. If these two factors could be disentangled from aggregate productivity growth, the relative contribution of ICT capital would most likely still be higher than in the EU-15 countries due to its own contribution to restructuring. Hence ICT can be seen as an important source of convergence between CEE countries and the EU-15 during the 1990s and early 2000s.

7.5   THE CONTRIBUTION OF ICT PRODUCTION AND ICT USE TO GROWTH

The estimates in Section 7.4 provide a useful perspective on the contribution of ICT investment to productivity growth at the country level. The estimates suggest that in absolute terms the contribution of ICT capital to labour productivity growth in CEE countries is comparable to that in the EU-15 despite lower levels of productivity. In addition ICT may have contributed to TFP growth, although the precise contribution of ICT to that residual cannot be easily quantified. Still, these facts may be interpreted as a sign of ICT playing an important role in the convergence process.

However, before we can settle on these conclusions, we require a perspective on the role of ICT at industry level. For example, ICT contributions in CEE countries may have been largest in those parts of the economy that opened up to international competition (mainly under the influence of foreign direct investment) but are declining in relative importance for the economy as a whole. This may be due to a restructuring process leading to massive closure of old firms and new entry of only a small number of modern and internationally competitive plants. In that case the higher ICT contribution to labour productivity growth may have been a temporary phenomenon and not a sustainable source of convergence. Alternatively, the ICT contributions may be largest in firms that have been surviving and that are able to expand market shares in an international competitive environment due to an improved quality-price mix.

The Taxonomy

Because of the lack of ICT investment series at the industry level, it is not possible to locate the industries in which ICT capital contributes most to productivity growth.[17] An alternative approach therefore is to look at the labour productivity growth rates for three main groups of industries, namely those that can typically be characterized as ICT-producing industries, those that make intensive use of ICT and those that use ICT less intensively ('non-ICT' industries) (see van Ark and Piatkowski, 2004 and Piatkowski, 2005a). However, it appears that such a distinction is quite sensitive to cross-country differences and the phase in which the technology has been diffused. In this paper we focus on a slightly cruder the distinction, that is between ICT producing industries, other good-producing industries (manufacturing and non-manufacturing) and market services. Van Ark and Inklaar (2005) show that the industry taxonomy used here is less sensitive to those factors.

The Data

For the analysis of productivity growth at industry level we make use of the 60 Industry Database of the Groningen Growth and Development Centre, which contains information on value added and employment in a wide range of OECD countries from 1979 to 2003.[18] For this paper we developed estimates for four CEE countries, namely Czech Republic, Hungary, Poland and Slovakia for the period from 1995 onwards. The point of departure is the new OECD STAN Database on national accounts on a common industrial classification.[19] To increase the level of industry detail, STAN was supplemented with national production surveys and services statistics covering production industries, distribution and services. In general the method employed was to use the additional data to divide the STAN aggregates into sub-industries.

The series are adjusted for two important measurement problems, which are the method of aggregation and the deflation of ICT goods output. At present, many countries still use fixed-weight (Laspeyres) indices to calculate aggregate value added at constant prices. This can lead to substitution bias if the structure of the economy is changing over time. To ensure consistency across countries, we use Törnqvist aggregation to calculate chain-weighted indices for the aggregated real output series. This means that our estimates for GDP will generally not conform to those from national statistical offices.

Another problem is the deflation of ICT goods. It is well known that the technical capabilities of computers have improved tremendously over the past few decades. Since consumers can buy computers with vastly more computing power at comparable prices, the price of computing power has declined continuously. However, traditional methods of sampling and quality adjustment in calculating price indices for these goods will almost certainly lead to an underestimation in the rate of the output price decline. At present there are only a few countries, like the US, Canada and some West European countries, that have an adequate system in place for measuring prices of computers and semiconductors. This means that measured productivity growth in ICT producing industries in all other countries is likely to be understated. For the EU-15 countries, we avoid this downward bias by applying a harmonisation procedure, which consists of applying the US deflators for each of the ICT producing manufacturing industries to all other countries after making a correction for the general inflation level.[20]

In the case of CEE countries, we have been more reluctant to make direct use of the US hedonic deflators for ICT-producing industries. It is clear that the composition of production in the ICT-producing industries in countries other than the US, and in particular in the CEE countries is quite different from that in the US. Especially ICT products at the high-tech end of the range, such as electronic computers and semiconductors, which show the fastest price declines, are hardly or even not at all represented in the ICT-producing industries of CEE countries. For the CEE countries we therefore present results based on national deflators. Although such alternatives have a significant impact on the output and productivity estimates of ICT-producing industries, they hardly affect the aggregate estimates for the total economy (see for instance van Ark and Piatkowski, 2004).

The Employment Share and Productivity Growth of ICT-Producing Industries

The main results are shown in Tables 7.5 to 7.7. Table 7.5 shows the shares of each industry group in total employment for the EU-15, the United States, and separately for the Czech Republic, Hungary, Poland and Slovakia in 1995 and 2003. The table shows that the employment shares of ICT-producing industries are quite small in all countries. Hungary has the largest ICT sector, while Poland has by far the smallest. This is due to a fair amount of foreign direct investment in particular in Hungary. However, most of the production in these industries does not represent ICT-products at the high-tech end, but rather components and assembly items, for example, television screens, computer monitors, other household electronic equipment and so on.

Indeed Table 7.6 shows that the labour productivity growth rates in ICT-producing manufacturing in the CEE countries are still high, reflecting the enormous overhaul in the ICT-producing sector of the CEE economies.[21] Table 7.7 shows that in Hungary and Slovakia ICT-producing manufacturing contributed less to aggregate productivity growth than in the US, but more than in the EU-15. In this respect it may be argued that these production activities, which largely rest on FDI and strategic alliances between foreign and national firms, have significantly contributed to accelerated productivity growth in both countries. In the Czech Republic and Poland the contribution of ICT-producing services is lower than in both the US and the EU-15. Piatkowski and van Ark (2005) argue that the differences in the growth of the ICT sector in CEE countries were due to inflows of FDI and privatization policies.

Despite its positive contribution, the ICT sector in CEE countries is simply too small (the share of the ICT sector in total value added in all CEE countries did not exceed 9 per cent in 2003) and the ICT-related spillover effects are too scant to drive the sustained convergence towards the EU-15 income levels. Hence, convergence will have to rely on productivity growth outside ICT producing industries.

The Employment Share and Productivity Growth of ICT-Using Industries

Table 7.5 shows that ICT-using industries, that is other production industries, in particular in manufacturing, and market services, account for a much larger share of total employment than ICT-producing industries. But it is useful to make a distinction between manufacturing industries and market services. With the possible exception of Poland (where agriculture – which is included under 'Other production: Non manufacturing' – is still a large sector with a share in total employment above 15 per cent in 2003), manufacturing industries are more important in terms of employment shares than in the EU-15 or the United States. Market services, though still smaller than in the EU-15 and in particular the US, also show an increasing employment share in CEE countries.

Table 7.6 shows productivity growth rates in manufacturing, non-manufacturing and services industries in four CEE countries, EU-15 and the US during 1995–2003.[22] It turns out that productivity growth rates in manufacturing in CEE countries were substantially higher than in the EU-15 and the US.[23] It provides evidence for the success of the 'first phase' restructuring of

Table 7.5 Employment (persons employed) by industry group as share of total employment, 1995 and 2003

	EU		US	
	1995	2003	1995	2003
ICT Production	3.8	4.1	4.9	4.7
Other Production: Manufacturing	19.0	16.7	14.8	11.5
Other Production: Non-manufacturing	6.7	5.1	3.4	2.9
Market Services	46.9	50.0	51.9	54.1
Non Market Services	23.6	24.1	25.0	26.9

	CZE		HUN		POL		SVK	
	1995	2003	1995	2003	1995	2003	1995	2003
ICT Production	3.7	4.2	4.7	5.0	2.4	2.7	4.3	4.5
Other Production: Manufacturing	25.4	27.0	22.1	21.2	20.2	18.4	26.2	23.5
Other Production: Non-manufacturing	9.5	6.5	12.1	8.0	31.4	22.0	12.0	7.0
Market Services	45.1	44.9	39.9	44.2	31.9	40.4	35.2	43.0
Non Market Services	16.3	17.3	21.3	21.6	14.1	16.4	22.4	21.9

Note: Real estate has been excluded.

Source: Groningen Growth and Development Centre, 60 Industry database, October 2005 version, www.ggdc.net

Table 7.6 Labour productivity growth (constant GDP per person engaged growth), 1995–2003

	EU-15	US	CZE	HUN	POL	SVK
ICT Production	7.91	10.78	4.91	10.98	8.80	10.50
Other Production: Manufacturing	1.65	2.14	4.06	3.43	7.50	3.72
Other Production: Non-Manufacturing	3.24	2.29	3.62	2.22	6.37	8.12
Market Services	0.50	3.02	0.76	0.71	2.04	0.58
Non Market Services	0.19	-0.49	1.11	2.13	1.51	8.71

Note: Real estate has been excluded from Market Services. Adjusted US hedonic deflators have been used for the EU-15, while national deflators have been used for CEE countries.

Source: Updated results from Piatkowski and van Ark (2005) based on the Groningen Growth and Development Centre, 60-Industry Database, October 2005.

Table 7.7   Contributions to total labour productivity growth (constant GDP per person engaged growth), 1995–2003

	EU-15	US	CZE	HUN	POL	SVK
ICT Production	0.48	0.87	0.42	0.78	0.39	0.66
Other Production: Manufacturing	0.34	0.33	1.00	0.76	1.50	0.87
Other Production: Non-Manufacturing	0.17	0.11	0.36	0.21	0.62	0.87
Market Services	0.23	1.44	0.33	0.29	1.02	0.23
Non Market Services	0.04	-0.11	0.14	0.38	0.25	1.30
Reallocation effect	-0.04	-0.22	-0.07	0.11	1.19	0.03

Note: As in Table 7.6.

Source: As in Table 7.6.

manufacturing industries in CEE countries. Thanks to the high productivity growth rates, manufacturing industries in the CEE countries contributed between 0.76 and 1.50 percentage points to aggregate labour productivity growth between 1995 and 2003, substantially more than in the EU-15 and the US (Table 7.6).

In market services, the employment share for CEE countries is considerably smaller than for the EU-15 and the US (Table 7.5). Productivity growth rates are much lower than in manufacturing. They are also much lower than in the US, but at or above the average performance of EU-15 countries (Table 7.6). The mixed picture of productivity growth in market services in the CEE countries, despite their generally intensive use of ICT, is also reflected in the contributions of this industry group to aggregate productivity growth, which range from 0.23 to 1.02 percentage points in CEE countries. This is higher than in the EU-15, but significantly lower than in the US.

As argued by Piatkowski and van Ark (2005), the differences in the productivity growth rates between CEE countries and the US are due to the much more conducive business environment in the US, which stems primarily from competitive products markets, flexible labour markets, organizational innovations, large investments in R&D, and availability of high-risk financing.

Piatkowski and van Ark (2005) also explain the stark differences in the productivity growth rates between manufacturing and market services in CEE countries. On the basis of a panel data analysis, they find that labour productivity growth in manufacturing is most closely correlated with basic fundamental reforms (quality of regulations and law enforcement, trade openness, macroeconomic stability, and financial system development). For market services, more sophisticated reforms (development of ICT infrastructure, human capital, and labour market and product market flexibility) seem to be more important for productivity growth.

These findings suggest that further convergence of CEE countries with the EU will especially require a more sophisticated deregulation of product markets, increased labour flexibility, better ICT infrastructure, organizational innovations in enterprises, improved management practices, access to financing and investment in a broader palette of human capital and ICT skills.[24] These structural reforms are especially important for CEE countries as the productivity effects from the 'restructuring' phase and simple post-transition growth reserves have been mostly exhausted, in particular in the most developed CEE countries (Piatkowski and van Ark, 2005; Schadler et al., 2006). These reforms, however, are much harder to achieve than those required during the restructuring phase.

Compared to the EU-15, CEE countries may or may not develop an advantage in achieving these structural reforms. Depending on whether the institutional environment can be improved, they may either follow the low-productivity path of the EU-15 or the high-productivity path of the US. Given the substantial differences in productivity growth rates between Europe and the US, particularly in services (Table 7.6), the institutional reform paths will have a significant impact on the pace of convergence of CEE countries with the EU-15 and the US.

Conclusions

Although there are differences between countries, which partly reflect differences in industry composition and partly measurement problems, three main conclusions can be derived from this analysis of labour productivity growth at industry level. Firstly, only in Hungary and Slovakia did the ICT sector contribute more to productivity growth than in the EU-15. In this respect, investment in the production of 'new economy' products cannot be seen as a major direct source of catch-up for CEE countries. Secondly, manufacturing industries have exploited a large catch-up potential, which may be largely related to significant restructuring. As manufacturing may become less important in terms of employment and GDP shares, it may only represent a temporary catch-up effect. Thirdly, sustained convergence with the EU will critically depend on the implementation of second-stage structural reforms, particularly in product and labour markets, and further improvement of human capital and ICT skills to support productivity growth in service industries.

7.6   DETERMINANTS OF ICT DIFFUSION AND THE CONVERGENCE PROCESS IN CEE COUNTRIES

The two previous sections presented contributions of ICT production and use to the catching-up process on the aggregate and industry-level in CEE and EU countries. We concluded that the evidence points in the direction of a role for ICT as a major source of growth in CEE countries, and in the manufacturing sector even as a (temporary) source of convergence. The more lasting contribution of ICT to growth, including total factor productivity, will more likely depend on the existence of a conducive environment for ICT investment in services and the adoption of productivity enhancing practices.

There is a relatively large literature analyzing the determinants of adoption and diffusion of ICT on both aggregate and industry-level in advanced countries.[25] These studies show that the low level of competition in product and labour markets coupled with limited innovation efforts, few ICT skills of the workforce and insufficient flexibility to reform business organizations negatively affects the pace of ICT diffusion as well as the productivity effects from the use of ICT.

Unfortunately, there are not many studies that focus on the determinants of ICT adoption in CEE countries. Piatkowski (2002) and van Ark and Piatkowski (2004) directly focus on the economic and institutional determinants of investment in ICT.[26] They construct a 'New Economy Indicator' aimed at measuring the capability of transition economies to exploit the potential of ICT to accelerate the long-term economic growth and catching-up with developed countries.

On the basis of the original New Economy Indicator for 2000, Slovenia scored the highest, followed by the Czech Republic, Hungary, Slovakia and Poland. Albania, Bosnia and Herzegovina, and FR Yugoslavia occupied the bottom of the table (Piatkowski, 2002). The ranking showed that the post-socialist countries which were most advanced in the transition process also received the highest scores. Since the level of development of the economic and institutional infrastructure is seen as crucial for innovation and technological change, Piatkowski (2002) argued that the most advanced CEE countries were also the most likely to benefit from the use of ICT and thus accelerate catching-up on the EU-15 countries.

For the purpose of the present chapter, and in order to analyze its relationship to the contribution of ICT capital to labour productivity growth, the New Economy Indicator has been updated, slightly reconstructed and extended to cover only CEE countries, EU-15 and the US. The New Economy Indicator comprises of ten variables, which are seen to be the most pertinent for diffusion of ICT and its profitable use. Table 7.8 shows the variables and sources of the components of the indicator.

Table 7.8 Variables and data sources for the New Economy Indicator

Factor	Variable	Source
1. Quality of regulations and contract enforcement	Sum of World Bank Regulatory Quality and Rule of Law Indicator	Kaufmann et al. (2005)
2. Infrastructure	Sum of total number of telephone lines (main and cellular) and PCs per 1 000 persons	WDI 2005
3. Trade openness	Share of trade in GDP (in %)	WDI 2005
4. Development of financial markets	Domestic credit to private sector (% of GDP)	WDI 2005
5. R&D spending	Annual R&D spending (% of GDP)	WDI 2005
6. Quality of human capital	Tertiary school enrollment (% gross)	WDI 2005
7. Labour market flexibility	Rigidity of Employment Index	World Bank (2005)
8. Product market flexibility	Product market regulation indicator	Conway et al. (2005)
9. Openness to foreign investment	Gross foreign direct investment (FDI in % of GDP)	WDI 2005
10. Macroeconomic stability	Inflation (CPI) (in %)	WDI 2005

Notes:
Indicators of Regulatory Quality and Rule of Law are available for 1996, 1998, 2000, 2002, and 2004. 1995 was assumed to equal 1996; 1997, 1999, 2001, and 2003 were calculated as averages of each corresponding two years. R&D spending for 1996–2002. Tertiary school enrollment for 1998–2001. Product market regulation indicator for 1998 and 2003. The indicator to Slovakia in 1988 is assumed to equal that of the Czech Republic, while Slovenia's score equals the value for Hungary. Indicators for Bulgaria, Romania and Slovenia for both years are based on the score for Poland multiplied by the ratio of the value of the EBRD's (2004) 'Competition Indicator' for each of the three countries to that of Poland. Rigidity of Employment Index for 2004 only.

Source: Based on van Ark and Piatkowski (2004).

Appendix Table 7.A2 shows the New Economy Indicator for each of the countries based on average scores for 1995–2003.[27] As could be expected, the value of the New Economy Indicator for the EU-15 is higher than for CEE countries. The US, Sweden, and Finland reported the highest values, whereas

Bulgaria, Russia and Romania ended at the bottom of the ranking. The difference in values reflects the much better developed institutions in the EU-15 and in the US, higher spending on R&D, higher level of liberalization of product markets and a more stable macroeconomic environment.

Relating the New Economy Indicator to the contribution of ICT capital to labour productivity growth suggests a clear distinction between CEE countries and EU-15 (Figure 7.6). Even at very low levels of the New Economy Indicator, the average absolute contribution of ICT capital to labour productivity growth in CEE countries is as high as for the EU-15. This might indicate that, despite a less well performing institutional environment, it did not prevent the process of restructuring. As argued above, much of the restructuring has taken place in manufacturing where ICT might have played an important role in strengthening downsizing and efficiency. Nevertheless, within the group of CEE countries, there was a clearly positive relationship between the New Economy Indicator and the ICT capital contribution.

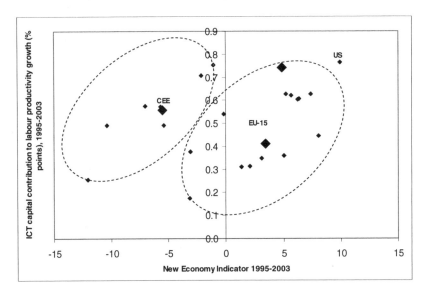

Source: New Economy Indicator, see Table 7.8 and Appendix Table 7.A2; ICT contribution to labour productivity growth, see Table 7.4.

Figure 7.6   New Economy Indicator and ICT capital contribution to labour productivity growth, 1995–2003

For the EU-15 countries, the relationship between the New Economy Indicator is also strongly positive. This is in contrast to the relationship between the productivity level and the ICT capital contribution as shown in Figure 7.5.

Combining the evidence from the two charts with the industry analysis in Section 7.5 suggests that the New Economy Indicator is in particular important from the perspective of ICT diffusion, especially in services, which is the key to growth in the EU-15.

Interestingly, various experiments by correlating individual indicators, such as R&D spending, FDI and product market regulation, to the ICT capital contribution (which in turn contributes to labour productivity growth) do not provide results, which are as strong as those for the New Economy Indicator. This suggests that there is a strong complementarity between the various factors, and that single-cause explanations are unlikely to provide strong effects on growth.

7.7 CONCLUSIONS

This chapter has investigated how the productivity performance of the CEE countries vis-à-vis the EU-15 and the US has evolved during the 1990s and early 2000s, and whether on the basis of the experience of the past decade, a process of convergence or divergence should be expected for the coming period. In Section 7.3 we showed that a continued decline in labour participation in the CEE countries and a rise in EU-15 countries may imply a further convergence of labour productivity in the near future. However, as employment growth in CEE countries has recently improved, a lot will depend on whether EU-15 countries will continue to increase their actual hours relative to potential hours. In Section 7.4 the role of ICT capital was highlighted as an important source of growth during the 1990s and early 2000s. We found that in absolute terms ICT capital in the CEE countries contributed as much to labour productivity growth as for the EU-15. This observation was further elaborated upon in Section 7.5, which identified ICT producing sector and manufacturing industries as key to the restructuring process and an important, but probably temporary source of convergence. We argue that sustained convergence with the EU will critically depend on increasing productivity in services. This will be dependent on the implementation of second-stage structural reforms, particularly in product and labour markets, and further improvement of human capital and ICT skills.

The New Economy Indicator in Section 7.6 suggests that competition, innovation and macroeconomic stability together provide a conducive environment for growth. Hence as such the New Economy Indicator provides an insight into how economic policy can contribute to the realization of growth potential of the 'new economy' in both the New and Old Europe. However, it should also be stressed that from the perspective of convergence analysis, many CEE countries were able to increase ICT intensity and raise the ICT contribution to productivity in spite of a much less developed economic, regulatory, and institutional environment than in the EU countries (with notable exceptions of Italy, Greece and Spain). This may be characteristic of the first phase of the transition and convergence during which restructuring (in particular in manufacturing) could take place even without the existence of such an environment. However, as the potential to realize productivity growth from ICT-investment in major using sectors, in particular in services, is still large, it is likely that these reforms are much more needed, as is also clear from comparisons between the traditional OECD countries (OECD, 2003, 2004).

Although our conclusions generally give more support to the convergence hypothesis than to the divergence hypothesis, we argue that the convergence process may slow as the productive implementation of ICT in services is more complicated and requires larger changes in the economic environments of CEE countries. Further income and productivity convergence of CEE countries with the EU will therefore depend on continued progress on the implementation of market-oriented policy reforms aimed at strengthening competition, increased innovation, improvements in the quality of the human capital and an enhancement of the comprehensiveness and effectiveness of regulations.

NOTES

1. We are grateful to Robert Inklaar, Gerard Ypma, and Edwin Stuivenwold for statistical assistance, and to various commentators on this chapter at seminars and workshops. We benefited in particular from comments by Bart Los and Marcel Timmer. The authors are solely responsible for the results presented and any remaining omissions. This chapter is an extended and updated version from an earlier article which was published under the same title in the *International Economics and Economic Policy*, Springer-Verlag, Volume 1, Special Issue No. 2+3, pp. 215–246.
2. A useful empirical review comparing productivity and competitiveness in CEE countries vis-à-vis the EU-15 can be found in European Commission (2004), Havlik (2003), and van Ark and Piatkowski (2004).
3. This relatively short period is used because the estimates for the first half of the 1990s are unreliable due to the immediate effects of the system shock in 1989/1990 and because of the substantial change in measurement methods of national accounts in CEE countries between 1991 and 1995. See http://www.ggdc.net/dseries/totecon.shtml for longer time series.
4. The EU-25 will consist of the present 15 EU member states, including the CEE-10 countries excluding Bulgaria and Romania, and including Cyprus and Malta.
5. On www.ggdc.net estimates are also shown in terms of output per hour worked. The hours estimates, however, are based on figures for a limited number of countries (Czech Republic, Hungary, Poland, and Slovakia). See also Table 7.3.
6. However, since 2004 this trend may be turning as employment in the more advanced CEE countries started to grow again. See Piatkowski and van Ark (2007).
7. All statistical tests include the United States.

8. Appendix Table 7.A2 shows a wide variation in labour force participation rates, with relatively low levels for Hungary and Romania and relatively high levels in the Baltic states in 2002.

9. See note 5 for a comment on the measure of working hours for the CEE countries. See van Ark, Frankema and Duteweerd (2004) for the concept of potential working hours.

10. See for example, Jorgenson (2004) for the G7, Colecchia and Schreyer (2001) for OECD, Daveri (2002) and Timmer et al. (2003) for the EU.

11. See, for example, Jorgenson and Vu (2005) global ICT growth accounting study and Lee and Kahtri (2003) for a study on Asia.

12. In contrast to Piatkowski (2004), the share of labour in total income was assumed to amount to 65 per cent for the Czech Republic, Hungary, Poland, Slovakia and Slovenia. It follows the approach taken by Doyle et al. (2001) and Crafts and Kaiser (2004). For Bulgaria and Romania, however, due to lower level of income per capita, the labour share was assumed at 60 per cent. Data on ICT investment is based on WITSA (2004) for 2000–03 and from WITSA (2002, 2000) for 1993–99. For 2000–03, the investment in office equipment was incorporated into computer hardware. Data on employment is based on GGDC total economy database available on http://www.ggdc.net/dseries/totecon.html

13. Until 1990/1991 imports of high-technology products to former socialist countries were restricted under the so-called COCOM (Coordinating Committee) restrictions enforced by NATO to prevent diffusion of dual use civilian-military high-tech equipment in the member countries of the Warsaw military pact.

14. For instance, the mainline telephone penetration in Poland in 1990 amounted to only 11 lines per 100 inhabitants. By the end of 2005, it increased to 33 mainlines and more than 60 mobile telephone lines (Polish Central Statistical Office, 2006).

15. The final column of Table 7.4 shows that the *relative* contributions of ICT capital to labour productivity growth were much lower for the CEE countries than for the EU-15 average (16 per cent and 50 per cent respectively) because of the higher growth rates of labour productivity in the CEE countries.

16. Between 1990 and 2003, the share of the private sector in GDP in CEE countries increased from less than 10 per cent to more than 60 per cent of the total (EBRD 2004). See also Schadler et al. (2006).

17. See, for example, Jorgenson, Ho and Stiroh (2003) for an industry analysis for the US; Inklaar, O'Mahony and Timmer (2005) for an industry analysis for France, Germany, the Netherlands and the United Kingdom. Some ICT-investment data by industry are also available for CEE countries, such as for example for Slovenia, but these have not yet been used for this study.

18. The underlying data material is described in more detail in van Ark, Inklaar and McGuckin (2002), but the estimates are updated for EU-15 and the US (see http://www.ggdc.net/dseries).

19. The STAN Database uses the international classification ISIC revision 3. This classification is very similar to the one European countries are using, but especially for the US much effort has been made to reconcile differences in industrial classification, see Appendix B of van Ark, Inklaar and McGuckin (2002).

20. See van Ark, Inklaar and McGuckin (2003) for details on this method, which was originally devised for deflation of ICT investment series by Schreyer (2002).

21. The productivity and employment growth rates for individual industries are available from www.ggdc.net

22. For a detailed classification of industries, please refer to van Ark and Inklaar (2005).

23. Given the scope of the paper, we will not analyze the non-manufacturing industries, which comprise agriculture, forestry, mining and quarrying, and fishing, and non-market services, which mostly relate to the public sector.

24. For a discussion of the importance of organizational changes in enterprises and improved management, please refer to Brynjolfsson and Hitt (2000) and Dorgan and Dowdy (2005).

25. See, for example, OECD (2003, 2004).

26. Muller and Salsas (2003, 2004) analyze the determinants of the Internet use among individuals and enterprises, while Clarke (2003) looks at the factors affecting firms' access to the Internet.

27. Following Piatkowski (2002), the aggregate New Economy Indicator is constructed in the following way: first, variables are selected, ensuring that each of them is either entirely positively or negatively related to the main concept; second, if variables are negatively correlated (like inflation), they are multiplied by -1 to ensure that always 'more is better'; third, the sample mean of values of all variables is subtracted from each number and then the result is divided by sample standard deviation. This implies a mean of zero and a standard deviation of one across countries in the sample. Hence, all results are comparable and can be aggregated. The final scores of the New Economy Indicator represent a sum of values of all ten variables for each country.

APPENDIX

Table 7.A1   Employment to population ratios, labour force participation rates and total hours to potential hours[a], 1995 and 2004

	Employment to population ratios		Labour force to population 15–64 ratios		Total hours to potential hours ratios	
	1995	2004	1995	2004	1995	2004
EU-15	0.407	0.442	0.684	0.716	0.356	0.373
Austria	0.464	0.456	0.720	0.718	0.384	0.364
Belgium	0.379	0.403	0.624	0.656	0.336	0.348
Denmark	0.505	0.510	0.801	0.813	0.406	0.414
Finland	0.403	0.453	0.727	0.743	0.363	0.399
France	0.390	0.412	0.673	0.696	0.334	0.324
Germany	0.438	0.435	0.710	0.735	0.350	0.339
Greece	0.364	0.405	0.620	0.677	0.387	0.416
Ireland	0.352	0.460	0.633	0.698	0.361	0.392
Italy	0.384	0.422	0.588	0.634	0.330	0.365
Luxembourg	0.526	0.651	0.606	0.648	0.439	0.526
Netherlands	0.443	0.500	0.706	0.762	0.318	0.361
Portugal	0.450	0.487	0.720	0.774	0.435	0.434
Spain	0.313	0.444	0.630	0.701	0.311	0.399
Sweden	0.460	0.478	0.808	0.799	0.423	0.419
United Kingdom	0.440	0.471	0.770	0.777	0.421	0.434
CEE-10[b]	0.397	0.388	0.685	0.660	0.419	0.387
Cyprus	0.388	0.467	n.a.	n.a.	n.a.	n.a.
Czech Republic	0.475	0.457	0.734	0.708	0.497	0.443
Estonia	0.427	0.427	n.a.	n.a.	n.a.	n.a.
Hungary	0.347	0.384	0.594	0.608	0.327	0.364
Latvia	0.385	0.431	n.a.	n.a.	n.a.	n.a.
Lithuania	0.448	0.402	n.a.	n.a.	n.a.	n.a.
Malta	0.373	0.375	n.a.	n.a.	n.a.	n.a.
Poland	0.383	0.358	0.694	0.655	0.420	0.376
Slovak Republic	0.400	0.400	0.696	0.699	0.432	0.400
Slovenia	0.432	0.476	n.a.	n.a.	n.a.	n.a.

Table 7.A1 continued

	Employment to population ratios		Labour force to population 15–64 ratios		Total hours to potential hours ratios	
	1995	2004	1995	2004	1995	2004
EU-25[c]	0.405	0.433	0.684	0.708	0.377	0.386
United States	0.472	0.474	0.792	0.781	0.499	0.478

Notes:
[a] *Potential hours are based on working age population times 2,800 working hours per year.*
[b] *For the Labour Force to Population ratio and the Total Hours to Potential Hours ratio for the CEE-10 an aggregate of the Czech Republic, Hungary, Poland and the Slovak Republic is used, as Labour Force and Working Age Population data for the other CEE-10 countries is missing.*
[c] *As a result of the missing data for the CEE countries, the data for EU-25 is actually EU-15 plus the 4 CEE countries.*

Source: Groningen Growth and Development Centre (www.ggdc.net) and OECD Labour Force Statistics (various issues) and Eurostat, Employment in Europe (various issues).

Table 7.A2   The New Economy Indicator for CEE countries, EU-15 and the US, 1995–2003 average

Country	Rank	Value 1995–2003	Regulations and law enforcement	Infra-structure	Trade openness	Financial system
United States	1	8.91	0.75	1.10	-1.60	2.87
Sweden	2	8.45	0.84	1.76	-0.15	0.36
Finland	3	6.91	1.09	1.15	-0.40	-0.38
UK	4	6.88	1.01	0.71	-0.73	1.04
Ireland	5	6.60	0.83	0.38	2.06	0.41
Netherlands	6	6.24	1.05	0.76	0.91	0.96
Denmark	6	6.24	0.95	1.42	-0.26	0.03
Belgium	8	5.79	0.35	0.17	1.81	0.06
Austria	9	3.15	0.90	0.44	0.19	0.55
Germany	10	2.18	0.75	0.59	-0.66	0.83
France	11	-0.17	0.22	0.36	-0.92	0.20
Portugal	12	-0.68	0.26	-0.19	-0.39	0.77
Czech Rep.	13	-1.73	-0.42	-0.58	0.91	-0.38
Spain	14	-1.79	0.23	-0.17	-0.78	0.34
Hungary	15	-2.33	-0.28	-0.83	1.05	-0.94
Slovenia	16	-2.53	-0.46	-0.14	0.83	-0.83
Italy	17	-3.23	-0.26	0.26	-0.89	-0.14
Slovakia	18	-3.98	-1.04	-1.03	1.35	-0.53
Greece	19	-4.79	-0.38	-0.12	-0.93	-0.61
Poland	20	-6.12	-0.70	-1.36	-0.79	-1.01
Bulgaria	21	-8.90	-1.38	-1.25	0.60	-1.06
Russia	22	-10.27	-2.56	-1.70	-0.72	-1.23
Romania	23	-14.82	-1.76	-1.73	-0.47	-1.32

Table 7.A2 continued

Country	R&D spending	Human Capital	Labour market flexibility	Product market flexibility	Openness to foreign investment
United States	1.23	1.49	2.16	1.03	-0.54
Sweden	2.49	1.14	-0.04	0.69	0.88
Finland	1.71	2.26	-0.09	0.52	0.58
UK	0.35	0.51	1.56	1.16	0.88
Ireland	-0.36	-0.40	0.51	0.90	2.02
Netherlands	0.47	0.04	-0.37	0.61	1.45
Denmark	0.71	0.38	1.39	0.90	0.30
Belgium	0.50	0.37	1.23	0.51	0.34
Austria	0.38	0.08	0.13	0.60	-0.57
Germany	0.96	-0.29	-0.70	0.53	-0.32
France	0.76	0.01	-1.30	0.12	-0.08
Portugal	-0.89	-0.29	-0.86	0.35	0.26
Czech Rep.	-0.44	-1.59	0.79	-0.14	-0.19
Spain	-0.71	0.24	-1.30	0.24	-0.19
Hungary	-0.85	-1.00	0.29	-0.07	0.52
Slovenia	-0.08	0.43	-1.19	-0.26	-0.73
Italy	-0.53	-0.28	-0.81	-0.11	-0.84
Slovakia	-0.85	-1.64	0.18	0.07	-0.37
Greece	-1.03	0.37	-1.30	-0.09	-0.93
Poland	-0.98	0.01	0.29	-1.13	-0.50
Bulgaria	-1.13	-0.83	-0.09	-2.15	-0.44
Russia	-0.54	0.91	0.68	-2.15	-0.82
Romania	-1.18	-1.92	-1.14	-2.15	-0.71

Source: Results from van Ark and Piatkowski (2004) updated to 2003.

BIBLIOGRAPHY

Abramovitz, M. (1986), 'Catching Up, Forging Ahead, and Falling Behind', *Journal of Economic History*, **46** (2), pp. 385–406.

Ark, B. van (1999), 'Economic Growth and Labour Productivity in Europe: Half a Century of East-West Comparisons', *Research Memorandum* GD-41, Groningen Growth and Development Centre. From http://www.eco.rug.nl/ggdc/pub/

Ark, B. van, E.H.P Frankema and H. Duteweerd (2004), 'Productivity and Employment Growth: An Empircal Review of Long And Medium Run Evidence', *Research Memorandum* GD-71, Groningen Growth and Development Centre, May. From http://www.ggdc.net/pub/gd71.pdf

Ark, B. van and R. Inklaar (2005), 'Catching Up or Getting Stuck? Europe's Troubles to Exploit ICT's Productivity Potential', *Research Memorandum* GD-79, Groningen Growth and Development Centre. From http://www.ggdc.net/pub/gd79.pdf

Ark, B. van, R. Inklaar and R.H. McGuckin (2002), 'Changing Gear': Productivity, ICT and Services: Europe and the United States', *Research Memorandum* GD-60, Groningen Growth and Development Centre. From http://www.eco.rug.nl/ggdc/pub/

Ark, B. van, R. Inklaar and R.H. McGuckin (2003), 'Changing Gear: Productivity, ICT and Service Industries in Europe and the United States', in J.F. Christensen and P. Maskell (eds), *The Industrial Dynamics of the New Digital Economy*, Cheltenham UK and Northampton, MA, USA: Edward Elgar, pp. 56–99.

Ark, B. van, R. Inklaar, R.H. McGuckin and M.P. Timmer (2003), 'The Employment Effects of the "new economy". A comparison of the European Union and the United States', *National Institute Economic Review*, **184**, April, pp. 86–98. From http://www.niesr.ac.uk/epke/bartrev.pdf

Ark, B. van and M. Piatkowski (2004), 'Productivity, Innovation and ICT in Old and New Europe', *International Economics and Economic Policy*, 1 (Special Issue No. 2+3), pp. 215–246.

Ark, B. van and M.P. Timmer (2003), 'Asia's Productivity Performance and Potential: The Contribution of Sectors and Structural Change', paper presented at RIETI-KEIO Conference on Japanese Economy: Leading East Asia in the 21st Century?, Tokyo, 30 May. From http://www.eco.rug.nl/medewerk/Ark/pdf/Asia Paper4.pdf

Brynjolfsson, E. and L.M. Hitt (2000), 'Beyond Computation: Information Technology, Organizational Transformation and Business Practices', *Journal of Economic Perspectives*, Vol. 14, No. 4, Fall, pp. 23–48. From http://ebusiness.mit.edu/erik/ JEP%20Beyond%20Computation%209-20.pdf

Clarke, G.R. (2001), 'Bridging the Digital Divide: How Enterprise Ownership and Foreign Competition Affect Internet Access in Eastern Europe and Central Asia', mimeo, World Bank.

Clarke, G.R. (2003), 'The Effect of Enterprise Ownership and Foreign Competition on Internet Diffusion in the Transition Economies'. International conference on The "New Economy" and Postsocialist Transition, *TIGER*, April 10–11, Warsaw. Conference materials. Available at www.tiger.edu.pl

Colecchia, A. and P. Schreyer (2001), 'ICT Investment and Economic Growth in the 1990s: Is the United States a Unique Case? A Comparative Study of Nine OECD Countries', *STI Working Paper*, 2001/7, OECD, Paris.

Conway, P., V. Janod and G. Nicoletti (2005), 'Product Market Regulation in OECD Countries, 1998 to 2003', *OECD Economics Department Working Paper*, 419, From www.oecd.org/eco/pmr

Crafts, N. and K. Kaiser (2004) 'Long-term growth prospects in transition economies: a reappraisal', *Structural Change and Economic Dynamics*, **15**, pp. 101–118.

Daveri, F. (2002), 'The New Economy in Europe, 1992–2001', *Oxford Review of Economic Policy*, **18** (3), pp. 345–362.

Dorgan, S.J. and J.J. Dowdy (2004), 'When IT lifts productivity', *McKinsey Quarterly*, *4*. From http://www.mckinseyquarterly.com/ ab_g.aspx? ar=1477&L 2=13 &L3=11

Doyle, P., L. Kuijs and G. Jiang (2001), 'Real Convergence to EU Income Levels: Central Europe from 1990 to the Long Term', *IMF Working Paper* WP/01/146, September. International Monetary Fund. From http://www.imf.org/external/ pubs/ ft/wp/2001/wp01146.pdf

EBRD (2004), *Transition Report 2004: Infrastructure*, European Bank of Reconstruction and Development, London.

European Commission (2004), *European Competitiveness Report 2004*, Commission Staff Working Paper SEC (2004)1397, November 8, Brussels. From http://europa.eu.int/comm/enterprise/enterprise_policy/competitiveness/doc/compr ep_2004_en.pdf

Gerschenkron, A. (1962), *Economic Backwardness in Historical Perspective*, Cambridge, MA: Belknap Press of Harvard University Press.

Havlik, P. (2003), 'Restructuring of Manufacturing Industry in the Central and East European Countries', *Prague Economic Papers*, 1, pp. 18–35.

Inklaar, R., M. O'Mahony and M.P. Timmer (2005), 'ICT and Europe's Productivity Performance: Industry-Level Growth Account Comparisons with the United States', *Review of Income and Wealth*, **51** (4), pp. 505–536.

Jorgenson, D.W. (2003), 'Information Technology and the G7 Economies', *World Economics*, **4** (4), pp. 139–170.

Jorgenson, D.W. (2004), 'Information Technology and the G7 Economies', Harvard University, mimeographed. From http://post.economics.harvard.edu/faculty/jorgenson/papers/handbook.extract03152004.pdf

Jorgenson, D.W. and K. Vu (2005) 'Information Technology and the World Economy', *Scandinavian Journal of Economics*, **107** (4), pp. 631–650.

Jorgenson, D.W., M.S. Ho, and K.J. Stiroh (2003), 'Growth of US Industries and Investments in Information Technology and Higher Education', *Economic Systems Research*, **155** (3), pp. 279 – 325.

Kaufmann, D., A. Kraay, and M. Mastruzzi (2005) 'Governance Matters IV: Governance Indicators for 1996–2004', *World Bank Policy Research Working Paper*, 3630, World Bank. From http://www.worldbank.org/wbi/governance/pubs/govmatters 4.html.

Kolodko, G.W. (2000), *From Shock to Therapy. The Political Economy of Postsocialist Transformation*, Oxford: Oxford University Press, pp.1–457.

Krugman, P. (1994), 'The Myth of Asia's Miracle', *Foreign Affairs*, November/December, pp. 62–78.

Lee, Il Houng and Y. Kahtri (2003), 'Information Technology and Productivity Growth in Asia', *IMF Working Paper*, WP/03/15, 2003, Washington D.C.

Muller, P. and P. Salsas (2003) 'Internet Use in Transition Countries Economic and Institutional Determinants', *TIGER Working Paper Series*, No. 44. From www.tiger.edu.pl.

Muller, P. and P. Salsas (2004) 'Internet Use by Businesses in Old and New EU Member Countries', *TIGER Working Paper Series*, No. 63. From www.tiger.edu.pl.

Nicoletti, G. and S. Scarpetta (2003), 'Regulation, Productivity and Growth: OECD Evidence', *OECD Economics Department Working Paper*, 347, January 2003.

OECD (2004), *The Economic Impact of ICT*, Organisation for Economic Co-operation and Development, Paris.

OECD (2003), *ICT and Economic Growth: Evidence from OECD Countries, Industries and Firms*, Organisation for Economic Co-operation and Development, Paris.

O'Mahony, M. and B. van Ark, (eds) (2003), *EU Productivity and Competitiveness: An Industry Perspective. Can Europe Resume the Catching-up Process?*, DG Enterprise, European Union, Luxembourg. From http://www.ggdc.net/pub/EU_productivity_and_competitiveness.pdf

Piatkowski, M. (2002), 'The "New Economy" and Economic Growth in Transition Economies. The Relevance of Institutional Infrastructure', *WIDER Discussion Paper 2002/62*, United Nations University World Institute for Development Economics Research (UNU/WIDER).

Piatkowski, M. (2004), 'The Impact of ICT on Growth in Transition Economies', *TIGER Working Paper Series*, No. 59. From http://www.tiger.edu.pl/publikacje/TWPNo59.pdf

Piatkowski, M. and B. van Ark (2005), 'ICT and Productivity Growth in Transition Economies: Two-Phase Convergence and Structural Reforms', *TIGER Working Paper Series* No. 72.

Piatkowski, M. (2005a), 'Can ICT Make a Difference?', *Information Technologies and International Development*, **3** (1), Fall, forthcoming.

Piatkowski, M. (2005b), *Information Society in Poland. A Prospective Analysis*, Warsaw: Leon Kozminski Academy Publishing House, pp. 1–206.

Piatkowski, M. and B. van Ark (2007), 'Productivity Growth, Technology and Structural Reforms in Transition Economies: A Two-Phase Convergence Process' in Krzysztof Piech (ed.) *Knowledge and innovation processes in Central and East European economies,* Instytute of Knowledge and Innovation, Warsaw, forthcoming.

Polish Central Statistical Office (2006), *Annual Statistics 2006*, Warsaw: Central Statistical Office.

Schadler, S., A. Mody, A. Abiad, and D. Leigh (2006), 'Growth in the Central and Eastern European Countries of the European Union: A Regional Review', *IMF Occasional Paper*, forthcoming.

Schreyer, P. (2002), 'Computer Price Indices and International Growth and Productivity Comparisons', *Review of Income and Wealth,* **48** (1), pp. 15–31.

Timmer, M.P., G. Ypma and B. van Ark (2003), 'IT in the European Union: Driving Productivity Divergence?', *Research Memorandum GD-67*, Groningen Growth and Development Centre, Groningen, October. Updated June 2005. Available at http://www.ggdc.net/pub/gd67.pdf

Timmer, M.P. and B. van Ark (2005), 'IT in the European Union: A driver of productivity divergence?', *Oxford Economic Papers,* **57** (4), pp. 693–716.

Triplett, J.E. and B. Bosworth (2004), *Productivity in the US Services Sector. New Sources of Economic Growth*, Washington D.C.: Brookings Institution Press, pp. 1–401.

Young, A. (1995), 'The Tyranny of Numbers: Confronting the Statistical Realities of the East Asian Growth Experience', *Quarterly Journal of Economics,* **110**, pp. 641–680.

WITSA (2004, 2002, 2000), *Digital Planet: The Global Information Economy*, World Information Technology and Services Alliance.

World Bank (2005), 'Doing Business 2005. Removing Obstacles to Growth', Database. From http://www.doingbusiness.org/

8. Information Technology and the Japanese Economy

Dale W. Jorgenson and Kazuyuki Motohashi

8.1 ABSTRACT

In this chapter we compare sources of economic growth in Japan and the United States from 1975 through 2003, focusing on the role of information technology (IT). We have adjusted Japanese data to conform to US definitions in order to provide a rigorous comparison between the two economies. The adjusted data show that the share of the Japanese gross domestic product devoted to investment in computers, telecommunications equipment, and software rose sharply after 1995. The contribution of total factor productivity growth from the IT sector in Japan also increased, while the contributions of labour input and productivity growth from the Non-IT sector lagged far behind the United States. Our projection of potential economic growth in Japan for the next decade is substantially below that in the United States, mainly due to slower growth of labour input. Our projections of labour productivity growth in the two economies are much more similar.

8.2 INTRODUCTION

Jorgenson (2002b) has shown that a substantial part of the American growth resurgence after 1995 can be attributed to information technology (IT). The rapid growth in US labour productivity during the boom of the 1990s, the economic slowdown that began in 2001, and the subsequent recovery suggest that the potential growth of the US economy has been considerably enhanced.[1] By contrast, the Japanese economy appears to be mired in the slump that followed the collapse of the 'bubble economy' of the 1980s. This leads to the question, has the Japanese economy failed to benefit from advances in information technology?

There are many examples of cutting-edge businesses in the US, such as Dell and Wal-Mart, that produce and use information technology effectively.

While it is often argued that major Japanese businesses do not fully utilize information systems, research conducted in Japan shows that the burgeoning levels of IT investment by businesses during the last half of the 1990s did contribute substantially to increased labour productivity growth.[2] It is clear that the impact of investment in IT on both the Japanese and US economies has been very sizable. But how does the impact of this investment differ between the two countries?

In order to compare the relationships between investment in information technology equipment and software and productivity growth in Japan and the United States, it is essential to lessen the differences in the treatment of IT in the official statistics. Under the United Nations System of National Accounts of 1993 (SNA93)[3] software is recognized as an investment in both countries, but the definitions are different. Second, prices of equipment and software must be measured in a consistent way, reflecting advances in information technology.

We have adopted the framework of Jorgenson (2002a) for analyzing the relationship between investment in IT and economic growth, encompassing the impact of IT investment by household and government sectors as well as the business sector. An important objective of this paper is to develop data for Japan that are comparable to the US National Income and Product Accounts (NIPA). We have constructed new data on software investment for Japan and new IT price data to mitigate possible biases present in the Japanese national accounts. Exploiting this new information, we have constructed growth accounts for Japan between 1975 and 2003, and developed growth projections for the next 10 years.

In the following section we present an analytical framework introduced by Jorgenson (1995c), based on the production possibility frontier.[4] In Section 8.4 we describe the data on investment in information technology equipment and software for Japan and the US and address possible upward biases in the official IT price data for Japan. In Section 8.5 we present the results of our analysis of the role of information technology in the growth of the Japanese and US economies. Section 8.6 is devoted to economic growth projections from 2003 to 2013. Finally, we summarize our conclusions and outline the agenda for future research.

8.3   THEORETICAL FRAMEWORK

Role of Information Technology in Economic Growth

Moore's Law states that the density of semiconductor chips doubles every 18–24 months. Doubling in 18 months is equivalent to increasing the density of chips by 100 times every 10 years. The staggering rate of technical progress in the IT-producing industries – semiconductors, computers, software, and telecommunications equipment – has led to a very rapid decline in IT prices. This price decline has stimulated a rapidly rising flow of investment into IT equipment and software by the IT-using industries in Japan and the United States.

For example, in 1990 a typical personal computer (PC) used Intel's 386 microprocessor with a clock speed of 20 megahertz (MHz) for the central processing unit. Intel's Pentium 4 processor, used in today's PCs, has a clock speed of 2.8 gigahertz (GHz) – 140 times as fast. However, the price of a personal computer in Japan has changed very little, varying within a range of 200,000–500,000 yen. The technological progress in PCs can be observed in the rapid improvements in performance, rather than a decline in the price of a typical machine.

The key to capturing the rapid development of information technology is the construction of a price index for IT equipment and software that holds performance constant. Economic statisticians in Japan and the United States have used prices for matched models of IT products in overlapping time periods, as well as hedonic models of IT prices, to construct constant-quality price indexes. However, the methodology for price statistics differs between the two countries, making international comparisons problematical. We will return to this issue in the section on price data for Japan and the United States.

Production Possibility Frontier

In order to capture the rapid pace of decline of IT prices, we employ the production possibility frontier introduced by Jorgenson (1995c).

$$Y\left(I_n, I_c, I_s, I_t, C_n, C_c\right) = A \cdot X\left(K_n, K_c, K_s, K_t, L\right). \qquad (8.1)$$

Aggregate output Y consists of Non-IT investment goods I_n, computer investment I_c, software investment I_s, investment in communications equipment I_t, consumption of Non-IT goods and services C_n, and consumption of IT capital services by governments and house-holds C_c. Aggregate input X consists of Non-IT capital services K_n, computer services K_c, software services K_s, communications equipment services K_t, and labour services L. Total factor productivity (TFP) or output per unit of input is denoted A.

The major advantage of this approach is the explicit role it provides for modelling the impacts of relative price changes on IT and Non-IT outputs and inputs. For example, a constant-quality price index for computers is used in constructing computer investment data on the output side. In addition, the computer price index is included in the rental price of computer capital services on the input side and computer investment is incorporated into the estimate of the stock of computers used in production. These data are used in modelling the substitution between computers and other outputs, as well as the substitution between the services of computers and other productive inputs.

Since the production possibility frontier describes efficient combinations of outputs and inputs for the economy as a whole, external costs of adjustment in outputs and inputs are fully reflected in prices. For this reason the production possibility frontier is preferable to the principal competing methodology, the aggregate production function. The production function fails to treat relative price differences in outputs explicitly and does not incorporate costs of adjustment.[5]

Under the assumption that product and factor markets are competitive, producer equilibrium implies that the share-weighted growth of outputs is the sum of the share-weighted growth of inputs and total factor productivity growth:

$$\overline{w}_{I,n}\Delta\ln I_n + \overline{w}_{I,c}\Delta\ln I_c + \overline{w}_{I,s}\Delta\ln I_s + \overline{w}_{I,t}\Delta\ln I_t + \overline{w}_{C,n}\Delta\ln C_n + \overline{w}_{C,c}\Delta\ln C_c$$

$$= \overline{v}_{K,n}\Delta\ln K_n + \overline{v}_{K,c}\Delta\ln K_c + \overline{v}_{K,s}\Delta\ln K_s + \overline{v}_{K,t}\Delta\ln K_t$$

$$+ \overline{v}_L\Delta\ln L + \Delta\ln A, \tag{8.2}$$

where $\overline{w}$ and $\overline{v}$ denote average value shares of outputs and inputs, respectively, in adjacent time periods.

The shares of outputs and inputs add to one under the assumption of constant returns:

$$\overline{w}_{I,n} + \overline{w}_{I,c} + \overline{w}_{I,s} + \overline{w}_{I,t} + \overline{w}_{C,n} + \overline{w}_{C,c} = \overline{v}_{K,n} + \overline{v}_{K,c} + \overline{v}_{K,s} + \overline{v}_{K,t} + \overline{v}_L \tag{8.3}$$

In (8.2), the growth rate of outputs is a weighted average of growth rate of investments and consumption goods outputs. Similarly, the growth rate of inputs is a weighted average of growth rates of capital and labour services inputs. The contribution of TFP is derived as the difference between growth rates of output and input.

Theory of Capital Service Inputs

Data on output and labour input can be collected directly from transactions in product and labour markets. By contrast data for capital stock and capital service prices must be imputed from market transactions in investment goods. We next review the measurement of capital stock and capital service prices.[6]

Since capital stock in the current time period K_t is comprised of capital goods acquired in previous time periods $A_{t-\tau}$ and the efficiency of capital services $d\tau$ varies with the vintage t of capital goods, K_t may be expressed as follows:

$$K_t = \sum_0^\infty d_\tau A_{t-\tau} \tag{8.4}$$

If we define the mortality rate m_τ as the rate of decline in efficiency d_τ for each vintage, the difference in capital stock between two adjacent periods is:

$$K_t - K_{t-1} = A_t + \sum_{\tau=1}^\infty (d_\tau - d_{\tau-1})A_{t-\tau} = A_t - \sum_{\tau=1}^\infty m_\tau A_{t-\tau} = A_t - R_t, \tag{8.5}$$

where R_t represents the replacement requirement or the decrease in capital stock due to mortality. If, in addition, efficiency declines at a constant rate d, capital stock takes the form:

$$K_t = A_t + K_{t-1} - R_t = A_t + (1-\delta)K_{t-1}. \tag{8.6}$$

Similarly, the price of capital services or the rental price of using a unit of capital stock for one time period is derived from the following capital-market non-arbitrage condition: the price of capital goods is the sum of future capital rentals. The price of capital goods can be expressed by the following formula:[7]

$$q_{A,t} = \sum_{\tau=0}^\infty d_\tau q_{K,t+\tau+1} \tag{8.7}$$

where $q_{A,t}$ and $q_{K,t+\tau+1}$ are discounted prices for capital goods and capital services, respectively. Evaluating this expression at the current prices for capital goods and capital services, $p_{A,t}$ and $p_{K,t+\tau+1}$, and denoting the discount rate by r:

$$q_{K,t+\tau+1} = \left(\prod_{s=1}^{\tau+1} \frac{1}{1+r_{s+t}} \right) p_{K,t+\tau+1} \tag{8.8}$$

We can use formula (8.7) to express the differences in acquisition prices for capital goods over time:

$$q_{A,t} - q_{A,t-1} = -q_{K,t} - \sum_{\tau=1}^\infty (d_\tau - d_{\tau-1}) q_{K,t+\tau+1}$$

$$= -q_{K,t} - \sum_{\tau=1}^\infty m_t q_{K,t+\tau+1} = -q_{K,t} + q_{D,t} \tag{8.9}$$

where $q_{D,t}$ represents the discounted price of depreciation of capital goods. If we express depreciation in terms of current prices, we obtain the following:

$$p_{K,t} = r_t p_{A,t-1} + p_{D,t} - \left(p_{A,t} - p_{A,t-1}\right) \qquad (8.10)$$

The capital rental price $p_{K,t}$ is the sum of the cost of capital $r_t p_{A,t-1}$ and depreciation $p_{D,t}$, less capital gains on the capital good $p_{A,t}$ -$p_{A,t-1}$. This is the non-arbitrage condition for the value of investment in capital goods and the rental value of capital services.

When the rate of depreciation on capital is constant ($p_{D,t}/p_{A,t-1} = d$), the rental price reduces to:

$$p_{K,t} = \left(r_t + \delta + \tfrac{p_{A,t} - p_{A,t-1}}{p_{A,t-1}} \right) p_{A,t-1} \qquad (8.11)$$

A higher rate of depreciation requires the recovery of investment over a shorter period of time and the capital rental cost increases. Similarly, if the price of a capital good is decreasing more rapidly, a greater future capital loss must be anticipated and the rental cost increases.

Even if the prices of two capital goods are the same, the rates of depreciation and rates of change in the prices of capital goods may differ, leading to different capital rental costs. Equation (8.11) is the formula we use for imputing the rental prices of capital services from the prices of investment goods. However, this formula must be modified to incorporate taxes, as shown by Jorgenson and Yun (2001). The formulas used in this study will be described in a later section.

8.4 DATA

Output Data

The data for Japan used in our analysis are comparable to the US data presented in Jorgenson (2002b). We distinguish three sectors of the Japanese economy – businesses, governments, and households. The data structure is presented in Table 8.1.

Output data are based on official estimates of the gross domestic product (GDP), published by the Economic and Social Research Institute (ESRI) of the Cabinet of Office of the Japanese Government.

In 2000 the Japanese System of National Accounts was revised to comply with United Nations (1993) *System of National Accounts* (SNA93). The major points of revision of the nominal value of GDP were

(1) adding custom-made software to private and public investments, and
(2) adding depreciation of public infrastructure to government consumption.
     ESRI estimated that the impact of these accounting changes led to a 2.0

per cent upward shift in the level of GDP in 1995 and an upward shift of 0.2 per cent in the annual growth rate GDP in constant prices in 1998 and 1999.

Table 8.1   Variables used in growth factor analysis

	Business sector	Public sector	Household sector
Output	93SNA Official GDP + software adjustments	93SNA Official GDP + software adjustments	93SNA Official GDP + capital service from household
Capital Input	*Depreciable assets* Based on investment series by 62 types of asset (5 types of IT), capital stock and capital service are estimated.		Based on investment series by 20 types of asset (3 types of IT), capital stock and capital service are estimated.
	Land Based on land stock data by 5 types of its category, consistent with SNA data.		
	Inventory Use SNA base aggregated inventory stock and price to estimate capital service.		
Labour	Number of workers, hours worked and per hour wage data by sex, age and education category.		

Note: Refer to Motohashi (2002) for details in depreciable asset data.

Our study uses the SNA93 current price GDP for Japan as a point of departure.[8] We adjust these data to achieve comparability with US data from the US National Income and Product Accounts (NIPA). One major difference between the Japanese SNA93 and NIPA is in the treatment of software. The Japanese SNA93 treats custom software as an investment, while the US NIPA also includes prepackaged and own-account software in investment. Therefore, we have estimated investment in prepackaged and own-account software in Japan and added this to the official Japanese GDP.

Since households are included in the production sector, the capital service flow from consumer durables must be treated as both an output and an input of households. In the Japanese SNA and the US NIPA only capital services from owner-occupied housing are imputed and included in the GDP. We have treated other types of consumer durables, including information technology equipment and software, in the same way as housing. We have imputed the value of capital services for households and added this to GDP for Japan and the US, following Jorgenson (2002b).

The government is also included in the production sector, so that the capital services from government capital must be treated as an output and an input of governments. In the Japanese SNA and the US NIPA only depreciation from government capital is included in the GDP. However, depreciation is only one component of the price of capital services (8.11), so that we must add the cost of capital and capital losses due to declines in asset prices to the value of government capital services. This makes the treatment of government capital symmetrical to business and household capital.

Table 8.2 compares output data for Japan in current prices of 2000 used in this study with the official Japanese GDP. The value of GDP in this study is about 534 trillion yen in 2000, which is about 23 trillion yen greater than the official GDP based on SNA93. About four trillion yen comes from adding prepackaged and own-account software investment in business, government, and household sectors and about 19 trillion yen comes from the capital service flow from consumer durables and government capital stock.

Table 8.2   Comparing current price output in 2000 (in billion yen)

Official GDP: 93 SNA	511 462
+ Software adjustment	3 704
+ Consumer durables adjustment	19 049
Adjusted output data	534 215
Official GDP: 68 SNA (reference)	490 518

We also note the differences between methods for deflating the current value of GDP to obtain GDP in constant prices in the Japanese SNA and the US NIPA. In Japan, ESRI has recently published a chain weighted GDP index, as well as historical series back to 1994. We have to rely on fixed weight GDP index in Japan before 1993. By contrast the US NIPA has incorporated a chain-weighted index for historical data on output and prices for some time. Since the share of information technology equipment and software in GDP is increasing rapidly, the role of IT investment in the Japanese economy will be under-estimated, relative to the US. In order to achieve greater comparability with US data, we estimate IT and Non-IT components separately for Japan and apply a flexible weighting scheme to estimate the rate of growth of output.

Input Data

Investment in IT equipment and software

In order to make comparisons of the impact of investment in IT equipment and software between the two countries, it is important to use a common definition of IT. The US NIPA publishes both nominal and real values of investment by category of capital goods. Jorgenson (2002b) used the following categories of IT-related investment: computers and equipment, software, and communication equipment. In this study, we have defined IT investment for Japan in the same way.[9]

We have generated data on investment in IT equipment for Japan that is comparable to the US NIPA by using Japanese input-output tables. However, as discussed in the previous section, the definition of software in the Japanese SNA is different from the US definition. Japanese GDP data, based on SNA93, includes only custom-made software; prepackaged and own-account software are excluded. Therefore, we have estimated the software investments in these two categories in order to match the US definition.

Although ESRI treats only custom-made software as an investment, the benchmark IO table for 2000, published by Japanese Statistical Bureau, has estimated the amount of prepackaged software to be treated as an investment. According to this table, the ratio of investment to total expenditure on pre-packaged software is about 40 per cent. Since the data are available only in 2000, we use this ratio for prepackaged software to adjust the annual expenditure data to generate an investment series. The Ministry of Economy, Trade and Industry's (METI) Survey on Selected Service Industries provides annual data on investment in prepackaged and custom-made software. Therefore, we use this information as well as the benchmark input-output tables published every five years to estimate investment in custom-made and prepackaged software.

Neither Japan's input-output tables nor METI's Survey of Selected Service Industries includes investment in own-account software. We have estimated this investment using methods similar to those used for the US NIPA, de-scribed in Parker and Grimm (2000). Specifically, we have estimated labour expenses for software development by employees in industries other than the IT sector, which produces custom-made and prepackaged software.

Finally, Jorgenson (2002b) used expenditures on computers and software from Private Consumption Expenditure (PCE) in NIPA to estimate invest-ment in IT equipment and software in the household sector.[10] Similarly, gov-ernment expenditures on IT equipment and software were taken from NIPA. We have employed data from the Survey of Selected Service Industries as well as household and government consumption of software in the Japanese benchmark input-output tables to estimate investment in IT equipment and software in the household and government sectors.

Capital services

In order to estimate capital services as precisely as possible, we have esti-mated capital stock and capital service prices by detailed category of investment goods. This enables us to take into account changes in the composition of capital stock. We have captured the improvement in the quality of capital associated with the substitution of investment goods with high marginal products, such as IT equipment and software, for goods with lower marginal products, such as Non-IT investment goods.

Based on Japan's benchmark input-output tables, compiled every five years, as well as METI's annual extension tables with more than 500 commodity categories, we have estimated investment by 62 commodity groups for business and government sectors and 20 commodity groups for the household sector from 1970 to 2003. We have deflated this current price investment by the Wholesale Price Index constructed by the Bank of Japan for business and government investment and by the Consumer Price Index constructed by the Japanese Statistical Bureau for household durables.[11]

We have estimated capital stocks by the perpetual inventory method. Initial values of capital stock for 1973 are estimated by assuming that the real investment for each type of capital goods increased continuously in the past by the same growth rate as that for the period 1970–1973.[12] We have used US NIPA depreciation rates for each type of capital goods presented by Fraumeni (1997).

In imputing capital service prices, Eq. (8.11) has to be modified to incorporate the taxation of capital income for each type of investment good in each sector. For example, there is a special acquisition tax for automobiles and there is no corporate tax in government and household sectors. Nomura (2004) took these features of the Japanese tax system into account, as well as many others. In this paper, we have applied the formulas for capital service prices used by Nomura (2004) for business, government and household sectors, separately.[13]

Labour input

Our estimates of labour input for Japan are taken from the ICPA project of RIETI,[14] originally derived from KEIO database (Keio Economic Observatory, 1996). This is calculated by using the data of the number of workers, hours worked, and hourly wage rates, cross-classified by sex, age and education. As with data for capital services, the change in the quality of labour input associated with upgrading of the labour force can be captured by comparing the growth of hours worked with the growth of the labour input index.

Prices for investment in IT equipment and software

We employ the production possibility frontier (1), explicitly measuring both outputs and inputs, so that prices of IT equipment and software affect both sides of our growth accounts. Since technological advances are so rapid and quality changes are so dramatic, a small change in methodology for measuring prices may result in significant differences in growth accounting. We find that there is a considerable divergence between Japanese and US IT prices, even after controlling for relative price differences in the two economies, as shown in Table 8.3.

Table 8.3   Comparison of IT prices

	WPI Laspeyres index (%)		US BEA price (%)		Price index for this study (%)	
	1975–1995	1995–2003	1975–1995	1995–2003	1975–1995	1995–2003
Computer	-6.4	-12.0	-16.3	-21.2	-6.4	-15.5
Comm. equipment	-1.4	-5.1	1.5	-3.4	-1.6	-9.3
Software	4.2	-0.2	-1.1	-0.9	-2.9	-1.5

Although price indexes for computers in both countries are based on hedonic methods, a substantial difference can be found in movements of the price index for computers and peripherals. This index is a composite of personal computers, large-scale computers, and various kinds of computer peripherals. The differences can be explained by price differences at the commodity level, as well as the index number methodology. A major factor behind the price differences is that the Bank of Japan's (BOJ) WPI/CGPI is based on a fixed-weight Laspeyres index with a base that is changed only every five years, while BEA employs a chain-weighted index.

Nomura and Samuels (2004) have found substantial fixed-weight bias in the Japanese WPI in the late 1990s because personal computers with faster price declines gained output share. BOJ has recognized this problem and published chain-weighted price indexes as a reference series. We use the BOJ chain-weighted index for computers and peripherals from 1995 to 2003, instead of the fixed-weight Laspeyres price index employed in the Japanese national accounts. No chain-weighted price index for Japan is available before 1995, but differences between the two countries in the early 1990s can be partly explained by NEC's domination of the PC market condition in Japan, according to Nomura and Samuels.

For communications equipment the rate of price decline is slightly higher in the Bank of Japan's WPI/CGPI than in the US NIPA index. Although both indexes use matched models, Japan's WPI is based on a more detailed list of items and may be more accurate. We use BOJ's chain-weighted price index for communications equipment, beginning in 1995. Since detailed commodity-level price information is available for 1985 to 1995, we employ a chain-weighted index for this period, as well.

Finally, the BOJ's price index for custom-made software by CSPI (company service price index) uses an estimate of costs that assumes no increase in labour productivity, while the US NIPA price index uses a weighted average of costs for custom software and a hedonic price index for packaged software. BOJ publishes prepackaged software prices by CSPI after the 2000 benchmark year revision, so that we use them for 2000–2003 data. Before 2000, only the custom-made software price is available. Since it is unrealistic to assume no productivity growth in Japanese software industry, 'internationally harmonized' prices, based on US price indexes, are used for prepackaged software before 2000.

The basic idea of an internationally harmonized price index is to use US prices of IT products relative to Non-IT products to estimate prices of IT products relative to Non-IT products in Japan. This approach was introduced in a series of OECD studies, for example, Colecchia and Schreyer (2002), and has been used in international comparisons by Van Ark et al. (2002). We use CGPI's price series for custom-made software as well as own-account software.[15] The adjusted price index used in this study is presented in Table 8.3.

8.5 RESULTS

Information Technology and Economic Growth in Japan and the United States

Table 8.4 gives our estimates of the contribution of information technology to output and input of the Japanese economy, together with the corresponding results for the US, based on an update of Jorgenson (2002b). It is possible to compare the results between the two countries from the middle 1970s. The results from 1980 are also displayed for Japan, since capital stock data in the 1970s may be less reliable. The contribution of information technology to Gross Domestic Product (GDP) includes investments in computers, software and communication equipment by business, government, and household sectors. Capital service flows from IT equipment and software in government and household sectors are included in 'contribution of Non-IT', since they are output contributions from government or household sectors, instead of the IT sectors.

The growth rate of GDP in Japan dropped from about 4 per cent in the 1980s to less than 2 per cent in the 1990s. The contribution of IT to output growth in Japan after 1995 was 0.5 per cent, which is comparable to that in the US. About two thirds of Japanese output growth from 1995 to 2003 can be attributed to IT production. The last half of the 1990s was the era of American growth resurgence. While IT played a significant role in this resurgence, about five sixths of output growth can be explained by the contributions of Non-IT goods and services.

Table 8.4 Sources of gross domestic products

Japan	1975–1980	1980–1990	1990–1995	1995–2003
		Outputs		
Gross domestic product	4.03	3.97	1.64	1.28
Contribution of information technology	0.43	0.55	0.22	0.47
Computers	0.22	0.29	0.11	0.19
Software	0.13	0.18	0.08	0.22
Communications equipment	0.08	0.09	0.03	0.06
Contribution of non-information technology	3.61	3.42	1.41	0.81
		Inputs		
Gross domestic income	2.46	2.71	0.84	0.83
Contrib. of info. tech. capital services	0.36	0.44	0.29	0.54
Computers	0.18	0.21	0.13	0.22
Software	0.12	0.16	0.12	0.20
Communications equipment	0.07	0.07	0.04	0.11
Contrib. of non-info. tech. capital services	1.01	1.08	0.77	0.62
Contribution of labour services	1.09	1.19	-0.22	-0.32
Total factor productivity	1.57	1.25	0.80	0.45

US	1948–1973	1973–1989	1989–1995	1995–2003
		Outputs		
Gross domestic product	4.00	2.99	2.43	3.56
Contribution of information technology	0.11	0.35	0.37	0.59
Computers	0.03	0.18	0.15	0.32
Software	0.02	0.08	0.15	0.17
Communications equipment	0.07	0.09	0.08	0.09
Contribution of non-information technology	3.88	2.64	2.06	2.97
		Inputs		
Gross domestic income	3.07	2.68	2.13	2.56
Contrib. of info. tech. capital services	0.16	0.38	0.49	0.88
Computers	0.04	0.20	0.22	0.49
Software	0.02	0.07	0.16	0.22
Communications equipment	0.09	0.11	0.10	0.17
Contrib. of non-info. tech. capital services	1.80	1.11	0.71	1.01
Contribution of labour services	1.11	1.18	0.93	0.67
Total factor productivity	0.93	0.31	0.31	0.99

Note: Average annual percentage rates of growth. The contribution of an output or input is the rate of growth, multiplied by the value share.

Table 8.4 presents the sources of growth in the two countries. The growth rate of gross domestic income can be decomposed among the contributions of IT capital, Non-IT capital, and labour services. The difference in growth rates between GDI and GDP is equal to the growth rate of total factor productivity (TFP). Our most striking finding on the sources of Japanese economic growth is the surge in the contribution of capital services from IT equipment and software from 1995, reflecting the sharp rise of IT investment.

The contribution of IT capital services in the US rose steadily throughout the period 1973–2003. The contribution of IT capital in Japan declined during the first half of the 1990s, but rebounded strongly after 1995. The contribution of IT capital in Japan during this period was 0.54 per cent per year, while the corresponding figure for the US was 0.88 per cent. Investment in IT capital rose rapidly in both countries.

Our second finding is that the TFP growth rate in Japan fell after 1995, due to the slowdown of growth in TFP in the Non-IT sector. The TFP growth rate in Japan from 1995 to 2003 is about half of that of the US. However, it is important to note that the growth rate of TFP in Japan substantially exceeded that of the US throughout the period 1973–2000.

An important part of the slowdown in economic growth in Japan during the 1990s is attributable to the drastic decline in the contribution of labour input analyzed by Hayashi and Prescott (2002). The labour input contribution dropped from 0.88 per cent per year before 1990 to negative rate of -0.22 per cent before 1995 and declined further to -0.32 per cent after 1995. However, the contribution of Non-IT capital services also declined during the first half of the 1990s and continued to sink during the last half of the 1990s. The contribution of labour input in the US fell only modestly during the first half of the 1990s and after 1995.

The Japanese economy grew at annual rates in the 3–5 per cent range throughout the late 1970s and 1980s. In the 1990s growth rates dropped to the 1 per cent range. Although more than 10 years have elapsed since the bursting of the 'bubble economy', there is no sign of revival in the official statistics. Our estimates show that the contribution of IT to economic growth becomes larger throughout the period of economic slowdown.

TFP Decomposition Between IT and Non-IT

Jorgenson et al. (1987) provide a model for tracing aggregate productivity growth to its sources at the level of individual industries. Productivity growth for each industry is weighted by the ratio of the gross output of the industry to GDP to obtain the industry's contribution to aggregate TFP growth. The price or 'dual approach' to productivity measurement employed by Jorgenson (2002b) identifies productivity growth in different sectors from differences between output and input price changes.[16] Since the price of output falls rapidly in the IT-producing industries, the change in IT prices relative to the aggregate price index can be used as a proxy for the TFP growth rate.[17] While an important part of the decline in IT prices can be attributed to the rapid de-

Table 8.5   Decomposition of TFP growth

Japan	1975–1990	1990–1995	1995–2003
Total factor productivity growth	1.57	0.80	0.45
Contributions to TFP growth			
Information technology	0.23	0.32	0.36
Computers	0.13	0.18	0.23
Software	0.05	0.10	0.04
Communications equipment	0.05	0.04	0.09
Non-information technology	1.35	0.48	0.10
Relative price changes			
Information technology	-9.18	-8.51	-7.35
Computers	-12.37	-10.21	-16.52
Software	-4.79	-8.59	-2.45
Communications equipment	-7.52	-4.41	-9.40
Non-information technology	-1.31	-0.47	-0.09
Average nominal shares			
Information technology	2.31	3.59	4.25
Computers	1.10	1.65	1.44
Software	0.58	1.16	1.92
Communications equipment	0.63	0.78	0.90
Non-information technology	97.69	96.41	95.75

US	1948–1973	1973–1989	1989–1995	1995–2003
Total factor productivity growth	0.93	0.31	0.31	0.99
Contributions to TFP growth				
Information technology	0.05	0.20	0.23	0.46
Computers	0.02	0.13	0.13	0.31
Software	0.00	0.03	0.06	0.06
Communications equipment	0.03	0.05	0.04	0.08
Non-information technology	0.88	0.11	0.08	0.53
Relative price changes				
Information technology	-4.3	-9.1	-7.5	-11.5
Computers	-21.9	-21.5	-15.2	-31.3
Software	-5.0	-5.1	-5.3	-3.9
Communications equipment	-3.1	-4.7	-3.9	-6.7
Non-information technology	-0.9	-0.1	-0.1	-0.6
Average nominal shares				
Information technology	0.91	2.20	3.04	4.04
Computers	0.10	0.64	0.83	0.97
Software	0.07	0.49	1.12	1.78
Communications equipment	0.74	1.07	1.08	1.28
Non-information technology	99.09	97.80	96.96	95.96

cline of constant-quality prices for semiconductors, most semiconductors are used in the production of information technology equipment and other products. Accordingly, semi-conductors appear as both an input and an output at the industry level and productivity growth in semiconductor production cancels out.

Table 8.5 shows the contribution of TFP in IT-production to TFP growth in Japan using the dual method, compared to the contribution for the US. The nominal share of IT production in GDP in the late 1990s was nearly the same for the two countries, a little more than 4 per cent, and the IT contribution to the TFP growth rate was also very similar. The share of computers was higher in Japan than in the US. The relative price of computers fell faster than the prices of software or communication equipment in Japan, pushing up the contribution of IT to TFP growth.

It should be noted that contribution of IT to total TFP growth increased after 1995, while the Non-IT contribution fell sharply. Compared to the US, the TFP growth rate in the Non-IT sector is greater in Japan for all periods except 1995 to 2003. As an explanation of this finding, Jorgenson (2003) has suggested that both Japan and the US are close to the technology frontier in IT, while the level of Japanese technology continues to lag outside the IT-producing sectors. Investment in IT equipment and software has resulted in convergence of productivity toward US levels.[18] However, the rate of convergence will gradually slow.

Discussion

Sensitivity of data adjustments

It is useful to compare our estimates of output in Japan with the official GDP data. As described at the start of Section 8.4, we have made adjustments in the scope of the official Japanese GDP data to achieve comparability with the US. The nominal value of GDP is adjusted by adding pre-packaged and own-account software, excluded from the Japanese SNA93 concept of GDP, as well as rental services from consumer durables. In addition, we have adjusted IT prices in Japan in order to assess the impact of IT in the two countries.

Table 8.6 presents the same data as in Table 8.4 (Sources of Gross Domestic Products), using the official statistics for Japan. The price changes have significant impacts on both output and input data. This discrepancy becomes wider in recent years, due to the growing importance of IT in the Japanese economy. The annual growth rate of output after 1995 falls by 0.14 per cent; the largest difference comes from computers and software.

Table 8.6   Sources of GDP by using official price data in Japan

	1975–1990	1980–1990	1990–1995	1995–2003
Gross domestic product	3.98	3.89	1.55	1.14
Contribution of information technology	0.37	0.47	0.14	0.34
Computers	0.22	0.29	0.11	0.14
Software	0.07	0.10	0.00	0.19
Communications equipment	0.08	0.09	0.03	0.02
Contribution of non-info. technology	3.61	3.42	1.41	0.80
Gross domestic income	2.40	2.64	0.73	0.69
Contrib. of info. tech. capital services	0.30	0.36	0.18	0.40
Computers	0.18	0.21	0.13	0.17
Software	0.06	0.09	0.01	0.16
Communications equipment	0.07	0.07	0.04	0.07
Contrib. of non-info. tech. capital services	1.01	1.08	0.77	0.62
Contribution of labour services	1.09	1.19	-0.22	-0.32
Total factor productivity	1.57	1.25	0.82	0.45

Note: Average annual percentage rates of growth. The contribution of an output or input is the rate of growth, multiplied by the value share.

Table 8.7   Comparison of output with official GDP in Japan (%)

	1975–1990	1990–1995	1995–2003
Official statistics (93 SNA)	4.03	1.53	0.95
+ IT price adjustment	0.05	0.09	0.14
+ CD and GOV adjustment	-0.05	0.02	0.19
Final GDP growth rate	4.03	1.64	1.28

Slower growth of input results from a lower pace of price decline, since the growth rate of capital stock decreases. In addition, since the capital service price falls with a lower rate of price decline in Eq. (8.11), the share of IT capital services also decreases. These effects are revealed in the fall of the contribution of IT capital services in Table 8.6. Slower growth in outputs and inputs cancels out, so that the effect on the TFP growth rate is small. The TFP growth rate in the late 1990s does not change.

The difference in the GDP growth rates in the 1990s comes from capital services from consumer durables and government capital, which are not included in the official GDP. Table 8.7 shows the differences between official GDP and our estimates. As the share of the IT sector increases, the impact of IT prices becomes larger. As for consumer durables and the government capital adjustment (CD and GOV), the contribution in the period 1975–1990 is negative, since the growth rate of official GDP is larger than that of CD and GOV, while it becomes positive after 1990.

Other issues in TFP estimation

Our TFP growth rate in the 1990s is very high by comparison with the Economic Research and Social Institute (2003) and Hayashi and Prescott (2002). Since these studies are based on the official price statistics, this is not surprising. In addition, we include land as a capital input, using six types of land data to take quality change into account, while the total volume of land is constant. Only capital services from depreciable assets are counted as capital inputs in the other studies. Including land in growth accounts reduces the positive contribution of capital services to GDP and pushes up the TFP growth rate. The shares of land rentals for periods 1975–1990, 1990–1995, and 1995–2003 are 23.2, 45.9, and 31.6 per cent, respectively. If we eliminated land stock from our estimation, the annual TFP growth for each period would become smaller – by 1.14, 0.44, and 0.37 per cent, respectively.

Another issue is a level of classification of capital and labour inputs. In this study, capital and labour inputs are estimated from Divisia indexes incorporating detailed data, classified by type. Labour input has a larger share and a greater impact on the TFP estimate. The contributions of quality changes to economic growth are 0.93, 0.58, and 0.56 per cent for periods 1975–1990, 1990–1995 and 1995–2003, respectively. If we eliminated these quality changes, estimated TFP would become larger – by 2.68, 1.14, and 0.76 per cent, respectively.

Finally, TFP is derived as a residual between the growth of output and the growth of input. Basu (1996) observes that TFP moves in the same direction as output and is pro-cyclical in the US. He attributes this to the effects of market distortions. Since the Japanese economy experienced an economic surge in the late 1980s and a sharp decline in the beginning of 1990s, some caution is needed in interpreting the TFP growth rate in these periods. In this sense, TFP slowdown after 1995 may be partly explained by this business cycle effect.

8.6 POTENTIAL OUTPUT GROWTH IN JAPAN AND THE US

Table 8.8 gives growth projections for the US, using the methodology developed by Jorgenson et al. (2004). The key assumptions are, first, that hours worked grows at the same rate as the working age population for the next decade, plus 0.1 per cent per year to allow for elimination of slack in the labour market. The second key assumption is that reproducible capital stock – plant, equipment and software, and inventories – rises at the same rate as output. Land remains fixed in supply. These assumptions characterize growth in the US over periods longer than a typical business cycle.

Table 8.8   Growth projections from 2003 to 2013 in the United States

	Projections		
	Pessimistic	Base case	Optimistic
Projections			
Output growth	1.73	2.93	3.55
ALP growth	1.01	2.21	2.83
Effective capital stock	1.46	2.48	3.00
Common assumptions			
Hours growth	0.723	0.723	0.723
Labour quality growth	0.087	0.087	0.087
Capital share	0.410	0.410	0.410
IT output share	0.039	0.039	0.039
Reproducible capital stock share	0.846	0.846	0.846
Alternative assumptions			
TFP growth in IT	8.67	10.02	11.51
Implied IT-related TFP contribution	0.21	0.37	0.45
Other TFP contribution	0.10	0.38	0.54
Capital quality growth	0.84	1.66	2.08
Implied capital deepening contribution	0.65	1.40	1.79

Notes:
In all projections, hours growth and labour quality growth are from internal projections, capital share and reproducible capital stock shares are 1959–2003 averages, and IT output shares are for 1995–2003. Pessimistic case uses 1973–1995 average growth of capital quality, IT-related TFP growth, and Non-IT TFP contribution. Base case uses 1990–2003 averages and optimistic cases uses 1995–2003 averages.

We present three alternative growth scenarios for the US – a base case, an optimistic case, and a pessimistic case. These three scenarios use a common set of assumptions for the growth of hours, the growth of labour quality, the share of capital in the national income, the share of IT output in the GDP, and the proportion of capital stock that is reproducible. The scenarios differ in assumptions about total factor productivity (TFP) growth in the IT-producing industries and the Non-IT industries. They also differ in assumptions about the growth of capital quality, defined as capital input per unit of capital stock. This reflects shifts in the composition of capital toward less durable assets like IT hardware and software.

The base case projection of potential output for the US uses 1990–2003 averages of growth rates in IT and Non-IT total factor productivity and capital quality. This reflects the experience of the last half of the 1990s, dominated by the acceleration in TFP growth in the IT-producing industries, as well as the first half of the 1990s, before the acceleration took place. This is consistent with the International Technology Roadmap for Semiconductors (2004), which projects a continuation of a two-year product cycle through 2007 and resumption of the three-year cycle after that.

The optimistic case for the US uses 1995–2003 averages of growth in productivity and capital quality for the decade 2003–2013. Jorgenson et al. (2004) have shown that this is in line with productivity growth in the US, since the recession of 2001. Even if this trend were to continue, US growth would fall short of the historical growth rate of 4.05 per cent per year during the period 1995–2000, when growth of hours worked of 1.99 per cent was almost double the rate of labour force growth. For the US the pessimistic case involves reversion to trends in productivity before 1995. This would imply a substantial slowdown in capital quality growth, reflecting the reduced impact of IT investment.

The base case projection of US labour productivity growth is 2.21 per cent per year. The drop in the projected growth of hours worked from 1.16 per cent per year to 0.72 per cent reduces the base case projection of US GDP growth to 2.67 per cent per year, well below the growth of 3.56 per cent during 1995–2003. Output growth would be 3.55 per cent per year in the optimistic case, essentially the same as the 1995–2003 growth rate. Finally, productivity growth in the pessimistic case would be only 1.01 per cent per year, well below the level before 1995. The corresponding rate of growth of GDP would be only 1.73 per cent per year.

Table 8.9 presents our projections of Japanese economic growth for the decade 2003–2013. We use the same methodology as for the US. However, hours are projected to decline at the same rate as the working age population -0.63 per cent per year, partly offset by a rise of 0.15 per cent to allow for a decline in unemployment. Our base case for Japan uses 1990–2003 averages for IT and Non-IT productivity growth and the growth of capital quality. This was a period of very rapid productivity growth outside of the IT-producing industries and reflects Japan's continuing success in closing the productivity gap with other industrialized countries. However, Jorgenson (2003) shows that Japanese productivity was the lowest among the G7 nations in 2000, so that a sizable gap remains.

Our optimistic case for Japan is based on the productivity averages of 1995–2003 for the IT-producing industries, just as for the US. These averages are combined with growth of Non-IT productivity and capital quality at the more rapid rates of 1990–1995. Finally, our pessimistic case is based on 1990–1995 averages for IT-producing industries – the beginning of the so-called 'lost decade'. These are combined with Non-IT productivity and capital quality growth at the slower rates of 1995–2003.

Table 8.9   Growth projections from 2003 to 2013 in Japan

	Projections		
	Pessimistic	Base case	Optimistic
Projections			
Output growth	0.84	1.48	1.88
ALP growth	1.32	1.97	2.37
Effective capital stock	0.56	1.00	1.27
Common assumptions			
Hours growth	-0.483	-0.483	-0.483
Labour quality growth	0.430	0.430	0.430
Capital share	0.393	0.393	0.393
IT output share	0.043	0.043	0.043
Reproducible capital stock share	0.674	0.674	0.674
Alternative assumptions			
TFP growth in IT	7.53	8.11	8.47
Implied IT-related TFP contribution	0.32	0.34	0.36
Other TFP contribution	0.10	0.33	0.48
Capital quality growth	0.58	1.13	1.47
Implied capital deepening contribution	0.64	1.03	1.27

Notes:
Hours growth is from the Institute for Population and Social Security. Labour quality growth is from internal projections. Capital share and reproducible capital stock shares are 1975–2003 averages. IT output shares are for 1995–2003. Pessimistic case uses 1990–1995 average growth IT-related TFP growth, and 1995–2003 average Non-IT TFP contribution and capital quality growth. Base case uses 1990–2003 averages for all of them. Optimistic cases uses 1995–2003 averages for IT-related TFP growth and 1990–1995 Non-IT TFP contribution and capital quality growth.

Our base projection of Japanese labour productivity is 1.97 per cent per year, somewhat below the US projection of 2.21 per cent. The decline of hours worked in Japan will provide opportunities for capital deepening. In addition, the growth of TFP in IT-production and the Non-IT sector will remain lower in Japan than in the US. On the other hand, labour quality growth in Japan will continue at growth rates well above the US rates. These three components, together with elimination of the unemployment gap, will enable Japanese productivity growth to maintain the levels of the 1990s. Our optimistic projection of Japanese labour productivity growth is 2.37 per cent per year, also below the US projection of 2.83 per cent per year. On the other hand, our pessimistic projection for Japan is 1.32 per cent per year, above the projected US growth rate of 1.01 per cent.

We conclude that Japanese economic growth will continue to lag behind the US. This is implied by the projected decline in the working age population in Japan, even with a reduction in the unemployment rate and continued improvements in labour quality. Our optimistic growth projection for Japan is 1.88 per cent per year for the period 2003–2013, substantially below the projection for the US of 3.55 per cent. Our pessimistic projection for Japan for the same period is 0.84 per cent, also below the US projection. Finally, our base case projection of Japanese GDP growth is 1.48 per cent per year, well below the projected US growth rate of 2.93 per cent.

8.7 CONCLUSIONS

We have analyzed aggregate economic data for Japan and the US to determine whether the increase in the rate of economic growth from surging IT investment in the US in the late 1990s can also be observed in Japan. We have adjusted estimates of IT investments in Japan to achieve comparability with the US estimates by Jorgenson (2002b). In order to make a rigorous comparison, we have constructed similar price deflators to IT investment in Japan. We have also used the Japanese official statistics to assess the robustness of our results.

We have shown that the expansion of investment in IT equipment and software in the US during the last half of the 1990s, accompanied by rising growth of TFP in the IT-producing sector, has a precise parallel in Japan. While this combination contributed to a sharp rise in the rate of economic growth in the US, it encountered a severely depressed economic environment in Japan. Growth rates of labour input plummeted in Japan during the 1990s, dragging down the rate of economic growth. However, the rising contribution of TFP in the IT sector after 1995 suggests that long-term prospects for the Japanese economy are less dismal than suggested by the official statistics.

The top priority for future research is to analyze relative levels of productivity in Japan and the US, following Jorgenson and Kuroda (1995) and Jorgenson and Nishimizu (1995). We believe that level comparisons will show that productivity in the IT-producing industries is similar in Japan and the United States. We anticipate that the IT-using industries in Japan lag behind their US counterparts in the use of IT equipment and software, but will converge to US levels. However, substantial parts of the Japanese economy are impervious to changes resulting from the adoption of IT and will continue to languish.

For economic policy it is very important whether TFP growth is concentrated in the IT-producing industries, as our results for the United States suggest. We have decomposed TFP growth in Japan between IT and Non-IT sectors, using the decline in IT prices as a proxy for TFP growth in the IT-producing sectors. The growth of TFP in IT-using industries has been relatively strong in all periods except 1995–2003, which is consistent with persistence of opportunities to 'catch up' to US levels of technology in these industries.

In the analysis of individual industries, the effects of statistical issues arising from productivity measurements will be greater. For example, although productivity growth in service industries has been considered to be lower than that in manufacturing industries, this may be related to deficiencies in price deflators for service industry outputs. For example, the financial services industry shows particularly higher rates of investment in IT-related equipment and software,[19] but the output of this industry may be difficult to measure.

To avoid some of the statistical issues associated with the analysis of individual industries, analysis can also be conducted at a firm level. This would permit comparisons of the relationships of IT and productivity among businesses in the same industry. Brynjolffson and Hitt (1995) conducted one of the first studies of the relationship between IT and productivity on a company level. More recently, the effects of IT investment on business organization have been explored by Brynjolffson and Hitt (2000). Finally, IT investment covers a wide range of different situations – from applications of CAD/CAM technology in manufacturing to applications of ERP in business services. Motohashi (2003) has shown that the effects on productivity vary by application.

As illustrated by these examples, the economic analysis of investment in IT has made important progress in many areas. However, the rapid pace of technological advance is constantly generating new questions. It is vital that microeconomic analysis on a company level and macroeconomic analysis for the economy as a whole be properly aligned in order to clarify the mechanisms that underlie the structural changes resulting from the IT investments.

NOTES

1. Jorgenson et al. (2004) have analyzed the potential growth of the US economy.
2. See Economic Research Institute, Economic Planning Agency (2000).
3. See United Nations (1993).
4. This framework is used by Jorgenson and Stiroh (2002), Jorgenson (2002a), and Jorgenson et al. (2005).
5. See Jorgenson et al. (2005) for more detail on this point.
6. Description of this section is based on the duality between investment and capital service prices developed by Jorgenson (1996).
7. We first present the benchmark case with no taxation. The empirical estimates are based on a model that also takes into account the effects of taxation on capital income.
8. ESRI published historical SNA93 data back to 1980. Prior to 1980 only SNA68 data are available. Therefore, we extend SNA93 data backward by using growth rates of SNA68 data.
9. Specifically, the categories for computers (1995 IO category: 3311011) and computer peripherals (3311021) correspond to 'computers and equipment', and television and radio (3211021), video (3211031), cable communications devices (3321011), and wireless communications devices (3321021) correspond to 'communications equipment'.
10. The corresponding sectors of the Japanese input–output tables are those for computers (1995 IO category: 3311011), computer peripherals (3311021), cable communications devices (3321011), wireless communications devices (3321021), and software (8512011).

11. The Japanese WPI and CPI are Laspeyres price indexes, with new benchmarks every five years. We constructed similar deflators for the period of our analysis. After the 2000 benchmark the WPI will be renamed as the CGPI (Corporate Goods Price Index).

12. In Japan, large-scale National Wealth Surveys were conducted several times prior to 1970. Although the results of these surveys are valuable for some purposes, for example, estimating wartime damages, they do not include detailed stock data on each type of investment good. For this reason, we have used the method described in the text to estimate initial values.

13. Detailed formulas can be found in Appendix 3 of Motohashi (2002).

14. Refer to RIETI (2004) for the ICPA project as well as classifications for this data set.

15. In US national accounts, the deflator for custom-made software was formerly derived as a weighted average price of prepackaged and own-account software. However, after the 2002 benchmark revision of US national accounts, the same price index is used for custom and own-account software.

16. The dual approach must be carefully distinguished from aggregation over sectors. Jorgenson and Nomura (2005) have presented estimates based on aggregation over sectors. We rely on expenditure data from the Japanese national accounts, rather than data for individual industries. A detailed comparison of these alternative methodologies is presented by Jorgenson et al. (2005).

17. In an industry with rapid productivity growth, output price falls rapidly relative to the input price. TFP growth can be measured from relative change of the input price to the output price. In this sense, we assume differences of factor price changes between IT and Non-IT sector are negligible as compared to output price changes.

18. This is consistent with the findings of the studies in Jorgenson (1995b), including the study of Jorgenson and Kuroda (1995).

19. Griliches (1994) discusses statistical issues in the measurement of service sector output as a source of underestimation of the impact of IT investment.

REFERENCES

Ark, B. van, J. Melka, N. Mulder, M. Timmer, G. Ypma (2002), 'ICT investments and growth accounts for the European Union 1980–2000', Research memorandum. Groningen University.

Basu, S. (1996), 'Procyclical productivity: Increasing returns or cyclical utilization?', *Quarterly Journal of Economics*, **111** (3), 719–751.

Brynjolffson, E., L. Hitt (1995), 'Information technology as a factor of production, the role of differences among firms', *Economics of Innovation and New Technology*, **3**, 183–199.

Brynjolffson, E., L. Hitt (2000), 'Beyond computation: Information technology, organizational transformation and business performance', *Journal of Economic Perspectives*, **14** (4), 23–48.

Colecchia, A., P. Schreyer (2002), 'ICT investment and economic growth in the 1990s: Is the United States a unique case? A comparative study of nine OECD countries', *Review of Economic Dynamics*, **5** (2), 408–442.

Economic Research and Social Institute (2003), 'Industrial Productivity and Economic Growth; 1970–98', Japan's Cabinet Office, Tokyo (in Japanese).

Economic Research Institute, Economic Planning Agency (2000) 'The effect of information and technology on productivity: In search of Japan's "New Economy"' (in Japanese), *Seisaku Koka Repoto* (Report on Policies and Effects), No. 4, October.

Fraumeni, B. (1997), 'The measurement of depreciation in the US national income and product accounts', *Survey of Current Business,* **77** (7), 7–23.

Griliches, Z. (1994), 'Productivity, R&D, and the data constraint', *American Economic Review*, **84** (1), 1–23.

Hayashi, F., E. Prescott (2002), 'The 1990s in Japan: A lost decade', *Review of Economic Dynamics*, **5** (1), 206–235.

Jorgenson, D.W. (1995a), *Postwar US Economic* Growth, MIT Press, Cambridge.

Jorgenson, D.W. (1995b), *International Comparisons of Economic Growth*, MIT Press, Cambridge.

Jorgenson, D.W. (1995c), 'The embodiment hypothesis', Chapter 2 in Jorgenson (1995a), 25–50.

Jorgenson, D.W. (1996). 'The economic theory of replacement and depreciation', Chapter 5 in Jorgenson, D.W. (Ed.), *Tax Policy and the Cost of Capital*, MIT Press, Cambridge, 125–156.

Jorgenson, D.W. (2002a), *Economic Growth in the Information Age*, MIT Press, Cambridge.

Jorgenson, D.W. (2002b), 'Information technology and the US economy', Chapter 1 in Jorgenson (2002a), 1–42.

Jorgenson, D.W. (2003), Information technology and the G7 economies, *World Economy*, **4** (3).

Jorgenson, D.W., F.M. Gollop, B.M. Fraumeni (1987), *Productivity and US Economic Growth*, Harvard Univ. Press, Cambridge.

Jorgenson, D.W., M.S. Ho, K. Stiroh (2004), 'Will the US productivity resurgence continue?', *Current Issues in Economics and Finance*, **10** (13), 1–7.

Jorgenson, D.W., M.S. Ho, K. Stiroh (2005), *Information Technology and the American Growth Resurgence*, MIT Press, Cambridge.

Jorgenson, D.W., M. Kuroda (1995) 'Productivity and international competitiveness in Japan and the United States, 1960–1985', Chapter 9 in Jorgenson (1995b), 387–418.

Jorgenson, D.W., M. Nishimizu (1995), 'US and Japanese economic growth, 1952–1974: An international comparison', Chapter 3 in Jorgenson (1995b), 179–202.

Jorgenson, D.W., K. Nomura (2005), 'The industry origins of Japanese economic growth', *Journal of the Japanese and International Economies*.

Jorgenson, D.W., K. Stiroh (2002) 'Raising the speed limit: US economic growth in the information age', Chapter 3 in Jorgenson (2002a), 71–150.

Jorgenson, D.W., K.-Y. Yun (2001), *Lifting the Burden: Tax Reform, the Cost of Capital and US Economic Growth*, MIT Press, Cambridge.

Keio University Institute for Economic and Industry Studies (Keio Economic Observatory) (1996), *KEO Database*, Keio Economic Observatory Monograph Series, No. 8.

Motohashi, K. (2002), 'IT investment and productivity growth of Japanese economy and comparison to the United States' (in Japanese), *RIETI Discussion Paper Series*, 02-J-018.

Motohashi, K. (2003), 'Firm level analysis of information network use and productivity in Japan', *RIETI Discussion Paper Series*, 03-E-021.

Nomura, K. (2004), *Measuring Capital and Productivity in Japan* (in Japanese), Keio Univ. Press.

Nomura, K., J. Samuels (2004), *Can we go back to data? Reconsideration of US harmonized computer price in Japan*, Program on Technology and Economic Policy, Harvard University.

Parker, R., B. Grimm (2000), *Recognition of business and government expenditures for software as investment: Methodology and quantitative impacts, 1959–98*, BEA, US Department of Commerce.

RIETI (2004), 'International comparison of productivity among Asian countries (ICPA) Project', report, March 2004, Research Institute of Economy, Trade and Industry, Tokyo, Japan. http://www.rieti.go.jp/jp/database/data/icpa-description.pdf

United Nations (1993), *System of National Accounts 1993*, United Nations, New York.

9. Outsourcing and Productivity Growth: Sectoral Evidence from Germany

Theo Eicher, Thomas Fuchs and Hans-Günther Vieweg

9.1 ABSTRACT

We examine the determinants of German sectoral productivity growth in the 1990s. To establish the importance of outsourcing across industries and time, we compare and contrast alternative productivity measures. The new *Ifo Productivity Database* now allows interindustry and intertemporal comparisons between gross value and value added measures of productivity growth, to highlight the effects of changing intermediate input shares in German production.

By constructing the gross output productivity measure for Germany we find that output (productivity) growth is significantly understated (overstated) by the value added measure over time and across industries. We also provide preliminary evidence that many sectors do not satisfy the assumptions to allow value added to proxy for gross output measures.

In terms of the sources of economic growth, we find that, true to the theory, outsourcing is the key variant between the two productivity measures, and that apparently most of this outsourcing has its origin in increased German imports. Most strikingly, the factor that drives productivity growth in Germany between 1993 and 2001 is intermediates and here high intermediate growth also translated not only into high output growth but also high sectoral TFP growth.

9.2 INTRODUCTION

Productivity statistics are collected to document the driving forces of economic growth and per capita income. Productivity measures themselves are, however, only as good as the data and the methods that they are based upon. In this chapter we utilize a new dataset to contrast two different methods of analyzing German sectoral productivity growth. The purpose is not only to contrast the two measures, but to highlight the effect of outsourcing on German productivity growth.

Our two measures of productivity growth are based on value added and on gross output. The former excludes the contribution of intermediate inputs (materials, energy and services in sectoral production) while the latter includes all inputs into production. The two measures thus differ roughly by the degree to which changes in intermediates are underreported and counted as productivity changes in the value added measure.

Higher levels of sectoral aggregation diminish the differences between the two output measures; however, even at the national level the measures differ to the extent that intermediate inputs are sourced from imports (Schreyer 2001, p. 42). We can thus utilize the differential between value-added productivity and gross output productivity to provide inferences about the changing outsourcing shares across German sectors.

Gross output or the value-added measures have been used extensively to characterize total factor productivity (TFP) growth. Value-added productivity reports capital-labour TFP while gross-output productivity reports capital-labour-intermediate TFP is reflected by the gross output measure (see OECD 2001, p. 10). The new Ifo Productivity database allows us to break aggregate sectoral performance into its components of capital, labour and intermediate goods and hence establish the first gross output productivity measures for Germany during the information technology boom. In addition, the Ifo Productivity Database contains assembled capital stocks and capital services flows data that more accurately reflect the contributions of factor inputs in sectoral and aggregate growth accounting exercises than most other studies. Our resulting productivity measures are important benchmarks for comparisons with long established value-added productivity measures in the literature.

The significance of intermediates in production varies across countries and industries. For the case of Germany, the median ratio of intermediates over gross output across sectors is 60.5 per cent in 2001. This statistic emphasizes how dramatically changes in the intermediate intensity in production will affect output and productivity; an effect that is documented extensively below. The large share of intermediates in output at the German sectoral level also highlights the importance of considering intermediate inputs in productivity growth accounting.

All productivity measures are inherently sensitive to substitution between factor inputs (including intermediate inputs) and outsourcing (of intermediate services); the question is how this sensitivity is reflected in the productivity statistic. The value-added productivity measure will be shown to exaggerate productivity since it implicitly includes changes in the structure of intermediates inputs. There are several theoretical reasons to prefer the gross output productivity measure, particularly at the sectoral level. First, the measure does not ignore improvements in the price-efficiency ratio of intermediate inputs, second, it allows for an adequate account of intersectoral production spillover effects, and finally the gross output productivity measure does not neglect intermediates-input-embodied technological change. The disadvantage of the gross output based measure is, however, that it is not a reliable representation of a sector's contribution towards aggregate TFP trends. To calculate this contribution correctly, the sectoral productivities must be combined with Domar weights.

While the German Statistical Office does not provide gross output productivity measures, these figures are reported by the US Bureau of Labor Statistics for manufacturing industries. Previous authors that have examined gross output TFP at the sectoral level are Jorgensen et al. (1987), Gullickson and Harper (1999b) and (2002), Baldwin et al. (2001) for the US, Oulton and O'Mahony (1994) for the UK, Gu and Ho (2001) and Gu, Lee and Tang (2001) for Canada. Aside from Crafts and Mills (2001), who compare the UK and West Germany until 1996, to our knowledge there exists no gross output productivity measure for Unified Germany.

Value-added productivity measures are popular in comparative analyses: they lower the data requirements and thus facilitate cross country comparisons. For example Van Ark and Pilat (1993) and Bernard and Jones (1996a,b) use the measure in an OECD intercountry approach, Harris and Trainor (1997) for the regional UK. In Spain, Hernando and Nuñez (2002) use a value-added approach for regional comparisons of productivity.

There are also a number of studies that compare sectoral productivity growth rates according to value-added and gross output-based estimates. Oulton and O'Mahony (1994) provided estimates of aggregate manufacturing TFP for the period 1953–1986 based on both methods. Van der Wiel (1999) has estimated labour productivity and TFP according to both approaches for Dutch manufacturing and service industries, and Sichel (2001) provided a comparison for the US communication sector. Harchaoui et al. (2001) provide estimates of industry TFP in Canada according to several different output measures. Oulton (2000) obtained gross output-based estimates of TFP growth for UK industry sectors by using the ratio of value added to gross output to convert value-added based TFP estimates. Goerlich and Orts (1994, 1996) underline differences in sectoral TFP estimates at the aggregate level for the Spanish economy. In all cases the empirics confirm the analytical results we review below in that the value-added productivity measure consistently exceeds the gross output estimates TFP growth by a factor equal to the ratio of gross output to value-added.

By constructing the gross output productivity measure we find that, for the case of Germany, output productivity growth is significantly understated by the value-added measure, while TFP growth is significantly overstated if gross output is not taken into account. These results are similar to those obtained by Oulton and O'Mahony (1994) for the UK. We also provide preliminary evidence that many sectors do not satisfy the assumptions to allow value added to proxy for gross output measures.

In terms of the sources of economic growth, we find that, true to the theory, outsourcing is a key variant between the two measures, and that apparently most of this outsourcing has its origin in increased German imports. Most striking is that the factor which drove productivity growth in Germany between 1993 and 2001 is intermediates and here high intermediate growth also translated not only into high output growth but also high sectoral TFP growth. These results are reminiscent of Jorgenson et al. (1987) and Jorgenson and Stiroh (2001) for the case of the US.

The structure of the chapter is as follows. First we outline the differences, advantages and disadvantages of the gross and value-added productivity measures. Then we describe the novel dataset that has been assembled at the IFO Institute. Finally we compare the performance of the value-added and gross output measures with special emphasis on the contributions of intermediates and outsourcing to sectoral productivity. Section 9.6 concludes.

9.3   METHODOLOGY: VALUE-ADDED VS. GROSS OUTPUT MEASURES

There exist two standard concepts in the economics literature to establish 'output'. Gross output is the total value of sales and operating receipts, while value added subtracts from gross output the value of goods and services purchased from other sectors as intermediate inputs. The differences between the measures are both practical and conceptual.

Value added is attractive because of its relative simplicity; dollar income, or payments to capital and labour are readily available from tax data. Time series data also requires, however, the use of separate deflators for sales and inputs. Gross output is closer to the ordinary notion of productivity as it represents sales per employee. As gross output deals explicitly with intermediate goods it is not subject to distortions when the primary and intermediate input mix changes.

The value-added productivity concept is widely used for international comparisons because the data are more readily available from countries' national accounts whereas sectoral gross output requires more detailed and disaggregated data and is therefore less easily available. Hence, while the US

Bureau of Labor statistics has determined that gross output is the correct basis for US measures of productivity, it acknowledges that there are other considerations that may make value added a better concept for international comparisons such as differences among countries in the extent of vertical integration of industries. We commence with a brief review of the issues related to gross and value-added output productivity measures and then examine their performance in Germany.

Gross Output

The most natural measure of productivity is directly related to the volume changes in output. The gross output productivity measure is a natural analog to the model of Hicks neutral technical change. Here technological change could be R&D or learning-by-doing. The productivity increase is disembodied technical change because it is the residual output change that is not physically tied to any factor of production.

The basic growth accounting equation using the gross output concept is:

$$\Delta \ln Y_{it} = \overline{v}_{it}^{L} \Delta \ln L_{it} + \overline{v}_{it}^{K} \Delta \ln K_{it} + \overline{v}_{it}^{M} \Delta \ln M_{it} + \Delta \ln TFP_{Yi}, \quad (9.1)$$

with Y_{it} as gross output in industry i during period t, L is the flow of labour inputs, K are capital service flows, M are intermediate inputs, and TFP$_Y$ is gross output total factor productivity. v_{it} represents the input shares in gross output, under constant returns they fulfill the condition: $\overline{v}_{it}^{L} + \overline{v}_{it}^{K} + \overline{v}_{it}^{M} = 1$.

In a perfect world, the gross output concept is, as highlighted by Jorgenson and Stiroh (2001), the appropriate concept for industry-level growth accounting studies. However, the measure has several shortcomings. Sichel (2001, p.7) reviews the literature and highlights that in practice, gross output TFP measures also reflect a number of additional influences including changes in efficiency, economies of scale, capacity utilization, market structure and measurement error. Under the assumption of competitive markets and constant returns to scale, these factors are assumed to be constant and to have no effect on TFP.

The value-added productivity measure is, however, subject to the same criticism. The advantage of the gross output-based productivity measure is that it accounts for intermediate inputs as a source of industry growth and hence appropriately considers differences in the input mix as explanations for output and TFP growth. Some argue that this renders a more complete representation of the production process (Sichel 2001, p. 7). Jorgenson and Stiroh (2001) have provided an example of the importance of intermediate input growth in the analysis of TFP, when they showed that productivity improvements reduced semi-conductor prices and increased their flow as intermediate inputs to other industries. A full account of the contribution of these inputs appropriately reduces biases of the attributed productivity contribution to primary inputs (capital/labour) and TFP across sectors.

By correctly accounting for the quantity and quality of intermediate inputs, the gross output concept allows aggregate TFP gains to be better allocated among industries (Jorgenson and Stiroh 2001, p. 53). The method of aggregation is crucial (Gullickson 1995, p. 15). Aggregate outputs and inputs are not simple sums of their sectoral counterparts and inconsistencies can arise between the productivity estimates. Aggregate output and input measures exclude all intermediate transactions between domestic industries to avoid double counting and to capture movements in inputs and outputs resulting from technological change and other efficiency changes. However, industry inputs include purchases from other industries and industry outputs include sales to other industries as well as sales to final demand. As a result, aggregate productivity growth cannot be obtained as an average using a set of weights that sum to one (Gullickson and Harper 1999a, p. 51).

Consistency between aggregate and sectoral estimates of TFP based on gross output is enhanced by the exclusion of intra-industry inputs and by the adoption of a sectoral productivity weighting system to derive aggregate estimates. As the sector size increases, the proportion of all transactions that are intra-sector tends to rise and the ratio of intermediate inputs to value added tends to fall. Equivalently, as the level of sectoral aggregation increases, the difference between gross output-based estimates of TFP growth and value-added based estimates tends to decrease. In the case of a closed economy, sectoral output at the most aggregate level is identical to total value added (OECD 2001, p. 91).

Domar (1961) proposed that TFP growth at the aggregate level should be measured as a weighted sum of industry-level TFP growth rates (see Oulton and O'Mahony 1994, pp. 13–14 and pp. 118–21). The industry productivity growth rates are estimated using gross output and incorporate intermediate inputs from other sectors. The 'Domar' weight is the ratio of the value of gross output of an industry/sector to the sum of value added in all industries/sectors. This weighting scheme can be adapted to different aggregates, whether a sectoral aggregate or the market economy.

The effect of weighting industry growth rates is to scale the industry TFP estimates by their relative importance to permit reconciliation with aggregate estimates. These weights reflect the direct contribution of sectoral productivity change to economic growth through deliveries to final demand and the indirect contribution through deliveries to intermediate demand (Jorgenson et al. 1987, p. 7). This weighting methodology implies that economy-wide TFP growth can grow faster than productivity in any single industry, since productivity gains are magnified as they work their way through the production process (Jorgenson and Stiroh 2001, p. 53).

Table 9.1 Industry output growth and average contributions 1993–2001

	ΔY	ΔK^n	ΔK^{ICT}	ΔLH	ΔLQ	ΔM	TFP_Y
Communications	13.31	0.25	0.06	-0.88	-0.03	7.49	6.41
Transport Equipment	3.99	0.26	-0.02	0.26	0.15	4.13	-0.79
Financial Intermediation	3.71	0.19	0.15	0.22	1.04	2.16	-0.04
Real Estate Activ. & Bus. Services	3.49	2.42	0.10	0.80	0.46	0.71	-1.01
Chemicals	3.48	0.43	0.03	-0.55	0.07	2.86	0.65
Transport	3.39	0.84	0.10	-0.11	0.09	1.91	0.57
Elec. and Electron. Equip. Instr.	3.29	0.09	-0.07	-0.44	0.08	3.77	-0.13
Rubber & Plastics	2.42	0.33	0.04	-0.01	0.11	1.85	0.10
Electricity, Gas and Water Supply	2.41	1.30	0.07	-0.69	0.29	1.36	0.08
Wood & Pro. of Wood and Cork	1.77	0.32	0.03	-0.75	0.33	1.84	0.01
Basic Metals & Fab.Metal Products	1.77	0.22	0.00	-0.27	-0.04	1.59	0.27
Agriculture, Forestry and Fishing	1.45	0.80	0.00	-0.61	0.41	0.69	0.16
Non-Market Services	1.44	0.73	0.05	0.09	0.60	0.49	-0.51
Other Services	0.77	0.61	0.13	0.98	0.38	0.01	-1.33
Food, Drink & Tobacco	0.77	0.14	-0.04	-0.06	0.08	0.52	0.13
Non-Metallic Mineral Products	0.74	0.44	-0.01	-0.61	0.31	0.84	-0.22
Repairs and wholesale trade	0.41	0.35	-0.02	-0.08	0.50	0.28	-0.62
Retail trade	0.38	0.36	0.04	0.02	0.50	-0.24	-0.29
Mechanical Engineering	0.24	0.15	-0.04	-0.36	0.05	0.57	-0.13
Construction	-0.37	-0.03	-0.01	-0.93	0.19	0.37	0.04
Pulp, & Paper Prod.; Print. & Publ.	-0.40	0.34	0.02	-0.63	0.03	0.21	-0.37
Furniture, Misc. Manuf.; recycling	-2.52	0.24	0.01	-0.66	0.19	-0.80	-1.50
Hotels & Catering	-2.68	0.30	0.00	0.68	0.31	-2.02	-1.95
Text., Leather, Footwear & Clothing	-3.47	0.04	-0.03	-1.22	-0.11	-1.72	-0.42
Mineral Oil Ref., Coke & Nuclear	-4.03	0.21	0.01	-0.08	0.00	-4.75	0.59
Mining and Quarrying	-9.62	0.00	0.00	-1.56	-0.38	-5.13	-2.56

Note: Percentage Points, ΔY: Output Growth; ΔK^n: non-ICT capital contribution, ΔK^{ICT}: ICT capital contribution, ΔLH: contribution of total hours worked, ΔLQ: contribution of labour quality changes, ΔM: contribution of intermediate input consumption, TFP: total factor productivity.

Source: Ifo Productivity Database.

The Domar aggregation of gross output-based TFP measures across industries provides an accurate picture of the contributions of industries to aggregate TFP change. However, there are significant data problems associated with input-output tables and their consistency with national accounts. This issue is discussed below. One cost of this approach is that sectoral productivity growth rates cannot be compared with the aggregate because the aggregate is built up as weighted sums, but not averages, from its components. In contrast, as noted earlier, value-added based productivity measures of aggregates are weighted averages of their components and can be compared across levels of aggregation because the weights add to unity.

Table 9.1 represents the average gross output growth between 1993 and 2001 and the contributions of various inputs to the average output growth. Table 9.1 indicates that, for example in the case of the communications sector 7.49 per cent of the 13.31 per cent productivity growth is derived from intermediates. TFP growth contributed 6.41 per cent to the average growth rate in between 1993 and 2001.

The top 5 sectors in terms of average growth rates are Communications, Transportation Equipment, Financial Intermediation, Real Estate and Chemicals. Most of the growth in these sectors is derived via growth in intermediates (except in the case of real estate where capital accumulation dominated). The same is true for the 5 biggest losing sectors, Mining, Minerals, Textiles, Hotel, and Furniture, where most of the contraction is derived from reductions in intermediates. Hence their gross output measure highlights the importance of German growth in the 1990s being driven by changes in outsourcing or intermediates.

Note that TFP contributes positively in only 11 of the 26 sectors. Most interesting is that the correlation between the TFP contribution to output growth and the intermediates contribution to output growth is 0.66, suggesting that those sectors that had large expansions (contractions) in intermediate growth also experienced large TFP contributions to output growth. Only the correlation between TFP and output growth is higher with 0.77, clearly indicating the important relationship between total factor productivity and output performance.

Value Added

The value-added productivity measure possesses two strong advantages. First, it can be derived with relatively low data requirements, as it abstracts from inter-sectoral good and service flows. Secondly, the approach provides a simple link between sectoral and aggregate TFP growth (see OECD 2001, p. 30). Sectoral value added can also be simply aggregated using weights that represent each sector's current price share in total value added. This implies that value-added productivity can be easily compared across sectors or industries, and that sectoral productivity growth can be compared to the national average.

The basic value-added growth accounting equation is:

$$\Delta \ln VA_{it} = \tilde{v}_{it}^{L} \Delta \ln L_{it} + \tilde{v}_{it}^{K} \Delta \ln K_{it} + \Delta \ln TFP_{VA_i}, \qquad (9.2)$$

where *VA* is value added, and TFP_{VA} is value-added total factor productivity. $\tilde{v}_{it}$ represent the input shares of labour and capital for value added; they fulfill the condition: $\tilde{v}_{it}^L + \tilde{v}_{it}^K = 1$.

This conveniently implementable and comparable methodology comes at a price. Value-added productivity is at times criticized as providing at best an ambiguous picture of the actual productivity, due to its abstraction from intermediates, and due to the fact no real world analog to value added is actually produced by plants (Sudit and Finger 1981, p. 14; Oulton and O'Mahony 1994, p. 33; Hulten 2000, p. 58).

Since value added is the difference between separately deflated gross output, *Y*, and intermediate inputs, *M*, the concept requires an additively separable production function of the type *Y* = *VA* + *M*. Such a function imposes strong restrictions on generality and the role of technological change (see Gollop 1979, p. 320; Bruno 1980; Diewert 1980). Empirical testing suggests, for example, that there exists no separability between the value-added function and intermediate inputs. Jorgenson et al. (1987) find that the conditions necessary and sufficient for the existence of a sectoral value-added function did not exist in forty out of forty-five US industries analyzed.

An additional simplification of the value-added measure is that it abstracts from substitution between capital/labour and intermediate inputs. This assumption is especially problematic in countries with rigid labour markets where downsizing limits introduce friction and slack into sectoral employment. One might argue that in this respect, Germany is a good candidate for establishing gross output productivities.

Price changes in intermediate inputs, potentially significant drivers of sectoral productivity growth, are assumed not to affect the relative usage of other inputs (Jorgenson et al. 1987, p. 9; Dean and Harper 2000, p. 48). The value-added concept thus assumes that prices of intermediates always rise at the same rate as those of all other factors. Finally, technological change is assumed to affect only capital and labour, since intermediate usage is, by assumption, not affected by the improvements in productivity (Gollop 1979, p. 322 and Gullickson 1995, p. 17). Hence a country that experiences rapid productivity growth through outsourcing and a shift of sectoral production towards higher productivity intermediate goods will find such changes attributed to capital and labour in the value-added measure.

Value-added productivity estimates can thus be expected to be higher than gross output-based estimates, since value-added productivity reflects implicit changes in intermediate inputs. Following Diewert (2001, p. 18), gross output productivity can be written as $Y/(M+L+K)$ and value-added productivity is then defined as $VA/(L+K) = (Y-M)/(L+K)$. In real terms, a productivity improvement of $\Delta \tilde{Y}$ that cannot be attributed to changes in *M, L, K,* yields a gross output productivity growth rate of

$$\hat{TFP}_Y = \frac{Y + \Delta\tilde{Y}}{M + L + K} \bigg/ \frac{Y}{M + L + K} = 1 + \frac{\Delta\tilde{Y}}{Y} \qquad (9.3)$$

which is less than the real value-added productivity growth rate given by

$$\hat{TFP}_{VA} = \frac{Y + \Delta\tilde{Y} - M}{L + K} \bigg/ \frac{Y - M}{L + K} = 1 + \frac{\Delta\tilde{Y}}{Y - M} \qquad (9.4)$$

The smaller denominator in the value-added TFP measure translates into larger TFP growth measure for value added. Comparing the two growth rates, it follows that

$$\hat{TFP}_{VA} = (Y / VA)\hat{TFP}_Y \qquad (9.5)$$

Which clearly highlights that value-added productivity is expected to exceed TFP productivity.

Comparisons of gross output and value-added measures of sectoral TFP growth in Germany, confirm this observation:

Table 9.2 highlights several important factors. Interestingly in 18 out of 26 sectors the value-added concept over represents actual output growth. In addition, value-added TFP growth indeed significantly exceeds the gross output productivity measure (in 22 of 26 cases), however, not uniformly so. The last two columns of Table 9.2 indicate the existence of significant differences between the expected ratios of TFP_{VA}/TFP_Y and the estimated ones using the gross output and value-added concept. There exist large differences between the two ratios in just about all sectors. In 17 out of 26 industries the ratio is smaller than one and in nine out of these thirteen industries the ratio becomes even negative, which clearly contradicts the result proposed by the theory in equation (9.5). The two columns provide the first evidence that the assumptions necessary to derive qualitatively (and sometimes even quantitatively) valid statements of industry-level TFP using the value-added concept are too restrictive for the case of Germany. Below we present some analyses for a sample sector to indicate how the omission of intermediate inputs can cause the above described distortions in the value-added concept.

A caveat that must be added to Table 9.2 is, however, that intersectoral comparisons of productivity growth may be distorted because two sectors may share the same productivity growth on a gross output basis, but different rates of productivity growth on a value-added basis. As discussed above, this may occur because the proportion of intermediate inputs in total costs differs in these two sectors. This possibility is demonstrated for several Dutch industries by van der Wiel 1999 and in our data this is highlighted by, for example the German Electrical and Electronic sector and Mechanical Engineering. Both sectors share identical gross output productivities, but differ in their value-added productivity.

Table 9.2   Comparison of gross output and value-added measures, Germany 1993–2001

	Average 1993–2000						
	ΔY	ΔVA	TFP_Y	TFP_{VA}	Y/VA	TFP_{VA}/TFP_Y	$(TFP_{VA}/TFP_Y)/(Y/VA)$
Communications	13.31	9.75	6.41	10.91	3.00	1.70	0.57
Transport Equipment	3.99	0.53	-0.79	-0.02	1.32	0.03	0.02
Financial Intermediation	3.71	2.89	-0.04	3.98	2.69	-99.50	-36.99
Real Estate Activ. and Business Services	3.49	3.81	-1.01	-0.86	1.62	0.85	0.53
Chemicals	3.48	1.84	0.65	3.32	3.53	5.11	1.45
Transport	3.39	3.52	0.57	2.23	1.36	3.91	2.88
Electrical and Electronic Equipment; Instr.	3.29	-0.67	-0.13	1.66	2.44	-12.77	-5.23
Rubber & Plastics	2.42	1.61	0.10	1.67	1.37	16.70	12.19
Electricity, Gas and Water Supply	2.41	1.78	0.08	0.89	7.28	11.13	1.53
Wood & Products of Wood and Cork	1.77	-0.10	0.01	1.47	1.41	147.00	104.26
Basic Metals & Fabricated Metal Products	1.77	0.65	0.27	2.00	2.55	7.41	2.90
Agriculture, Forestry and Fishing	1.45	1.63	0.16	1.89	2.05	11.81	5.76
Non-Market Services	1.44	1.35	-0.51	0.10	2.55	-0.20	-0.08
Other Services	0.77	1.01	-1.33	-1.26	2.20	0.95	0.43
Food, Drink & Tobacco	0.77	1.01	0.13	1.10	2.42	8.46	3.50
Non-Metallic Mineral Products	0.74	-0.18	-0.22	0.76	1.84	-3.45	-1.88
Repairs and wholesale trade	0.41	0.30	-0.62	0.08	2.41	-0.13	-0.05
Retail trade	0.38	1.01	-0.29	0.21	2.35	-0.72	-0.31
Mechanical Engineering	0.24	-0.58	-0.13	1.80	2.41	-13.85	-5.75
Construction	-0.37	-1.61	0.04	0.02	2.67	0.50	0.19
Pulp, Paper & Paper Prod.; Print. & Publ..	-0.40	-1.37	-0.37	0.13	1.62	-0.35	-0.22
Furniture, Miscellaneous Manuf.; recycling	-2.52	-4.16	-1.50	-2.24	2.36	1.49	0.63
Hotels & Catering	-2.68	-1.65	-1.95	-4.31	2.63	2.21	0.84
Textiles, Leather, Footwear & Clothing	-3.47	-4.98	-0.42	0.74	1.82	-1.76	-0.97
Mineral Oil Refin., Coke & Nuclear Fuel	-4.03	4.58	0.59	5.11	2.50	8.66	3.46
Mining and Quarrying	-9.62	-11.16	-2.56	-4.82	3.27	1.88	0.58

Source: Authors' calculations using the Ifo Productivity Database.

Differences in Intertemporal Productivity Trends

The ratio of gross output to value added may vary dramatically according to the characteristics of a sector. This implies that not only average TFP growth rates may differ, but also that intertemporal comparisons of productivity are distorted (Gullickson and Harper 1999b, p. 19). The measures differ intertemporally because the value-added share in gross output changes as the composition between intermediates and capital/labour is altered. This composition is largely affected by outsourcing, as demonstrated by Gullickson and Harper (1999b, p. 18) who emphasized the role of outsourced production abroad by rewriting the relation between TFP$_{VA}$ growth and TFP$_G$ growth in equation (9.5) above as

$$T\hat{F}P_{VA} = (1 + M/VA)T\hat{F}P_Y \qquad (9.5')$$

If sectors increasingly outsource parts of the production process, and intermediate inputs account for an ever increasing share of value added in that sector, value-added productivity will grow ever faster than gross output productivity as a consequence of the outsourcing. Hence on an aggregate level, the differential between value-added productivity and gross output productivity can be seen as a rough measure of outsourcing activity. This outsourcing might be international or domestic. However, in Germany it is tempting to search for effects of outsourcing that are driven largely by international factors.

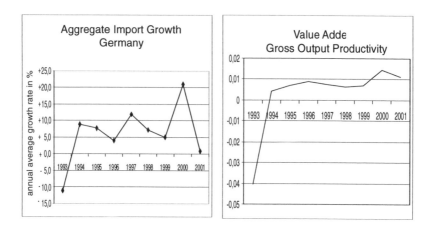

Figure 9.1   Comparison imports and TFP$_{VA}$/TFP$_Y$, 1993–2001

The graphs in Figure 9.1 nicely highlight the differences between the value-added and gross output productivity measures. First, the ratio of the two measures reflects the upward trends in imports between 1993 and 2000 in Germany. As outsourcing falls after 2000 (value-added TFP actually drops below aggregate TFP in 2001) possibly due to the large contraction of the construction industry, which constitutes a large share in German output, imports followed suit.

Figure 9.1 also shows that the intertemporal rate at which value-added productivity overestimates gross output productivity is largely stable; around one per cent on the aggregate level. This stability coincides with a tie of relatively stable import growth between 1994 and 2000. However, variations in imports are immediately reflected also in the amount by which value-added TFP overstates gross output productivity, as seen in 1994 and 2001.

Finally it is the contribution of any given factor to growth that is most severely distorted by the value-added measures. If we abstract from intermediates in the study of productivity growth, all improvements in productivity growth that actually arise through outsourcing or intermediate productivity growth are instead attributed to capital and labour. Several sectors, such as finance and computer services, rely heavily on the growth of intermediate inputs' efficiency. Indeed the entire R&D based literature has generated a cottage industry of models that rely on productivity increases generated by the intermediate inputs. In addition, any improvements in productivity in intermediate supplying industries may contribute to improvements in productivity in the downstream sector in several ways. Suppliers might increase output quality without changing inputs used and downstream firms might benefit from such quality improvement in the form of increased productivity (presuming the changed quality is not fully compensated for by price changes).

For the US, Jorgenson et al. (1987) and Jorgenson and Stiroh (2001) show that intermediate inputs are the predominant source of output growth at the sectoral level, exceeding both productivity growth and the contributions of capital and labour in the large majority of industries. The estimates prepared by Oulton and O'Mahony (1994) for the UK show that input growth explains a much higher proportion of productivity growth according to the gross output estimates than in the case of the value-added estimates. The same is true in the German data here.

9.4 THE IFO PRODUCTIVITY DATABASE

Our data is derived from the German Productivity Database that is currently being assembled at the Ifo Institute. At this point the database covers 52 sectors between 1991 and 2001, the associated capital stocks, asset types, prices, depreciation rates and labour, in 1995 and current prices. Currently this database is being expanded to cover 1960–2001. The Ifo Productivity Database allows for sector- and asset-specific price deflators in a growth accounting study for Germany.

Primary data on real and nominal output, value added and intermediates input data is obtained from the National Accounts statistics of the German Statistical office. The German Statistical Office classifies this data according to a 'Systematik der Wirtschaftszweige' (WZ 93) system, which is based on the NACE Industry Classification.[1] The source of the capital stock data is the *Ifo Investorenrechnung Database*, which augments German Statistical Office investment-series with Ifo survey data for 52 sectors and eleven investment assets/services.[2] The great advantage of the capital stock data in the Ifo Productivity Database is thus its reliance on sectoral capital stock and sectoral investment distributions data. Depreciation rates are survey based Germany-specific, industry-specific and asset-specific and are, according to our knowledge, unique and for the first time employed in a growth accounting study for Germany.

The capital stock is then calculated using the perpetual inventory method:

$$S_{i,j,t} = S_{i,j,t-1} + \left(1 - \delta_{i,j}\right)I_{i,j,t} \tag{9.6}$$

where S is the capital stock, I is investment, δ is a constant depreciation rate, and the subscript j, refers to the asset type.[3] The Ifo Investorenrechnung Database permits the calculation of capital stock data for each investment type in each sector without restricting assumptions regarding investment distributions (e.g. a uniform distribution across industries and investment types) that are usually necessary in the literature.

Investment data is also taken from the Ifo Investorenrechnung Database, which recalculates data from the German Statistical Office using Ifo survey data, and the Ifo Investitionstest. The Ifo Investorenrechnung Database thus provides industry-specific investment distributions that establish a unique link between the economic use of an investment asset and its statistical classification.[4]

The Ifo Productivity Database employs the Jorgenson and Stiroh (2001) method of calculating the capital services flow over a given period, rather than the capital stock in this period. Capital services flows are assumed to be proportional to the average capital stock available at the beginning and end of a given period:

$$K_{i,j,t} = q_{i,j} \frac{\left(S_{i,j,t} + S_{i,j,t-1}\right)}{2}, \tag{9.7}$$

where q denotes a constant of proportionality. The aggregate capital flow data is based on disaggregated sectoral data for each asset.

Currently the investment price deflators used to value the capital stock are obtained from the German Statistical Office. However, the Ifo Productivity Database is currently expanded to include quality changes based on the US Bureau of Labor Statistic hedonic price indices. Preliminary calculations using the US hedonic price deflators for ICT-investment indicate that the differences resulting from the use of hedonic price deflators are small.

The quantity of the capital services flow over a given period is given by a rental price formula

$$\left(1 + r_t\right)P_{i,j,t-1} = c_{i,j,t} + \left(1 - \delta_{i,j}\right)P_{i,j,t} \tag{9.8}$$

which assumes investors are indifferent between a rental fee *c,* and a return on the capital market with nominal interest rate r_t.[5] In order to decrease the impact of cyclical fluctuations in the calculations of the capital services flow, we employ a 5-year moving-average smoothing method.

The rental arbitrage equation yields the familiar cost of capital equation:

$$c_{i,j,t} = \left(r_t - \pi_{i,j,t} \right) P_{i,j,t} + \delta_{i,j} P_{i,j,t} \qquad (9.9)$$

where the industry and asset-specific capital gains are given by

$$\pi_{i,j,t} = \left(P_{i,j,t} - P_{i,j,t-1} \right) / P_{i,j,t-1} \qquad (9.10)$$

The cost of capital equation includes expected capital gains of assets, which may differ across industries. The specification allows for both industry and asset specific price differences. The advantage of industry and asset specific investment pricing is that this method restricts investment-price-deflators to a lesser degree and hence delivers more realistic and appropriate results compared to other methods.

The Ifo Productivity data also contains data on labour inputs derived using the Jorgenson and Stiroh (2001) methodology (which is similar to the capital stock methodology). Labour input data are obtained from the German Statistical Office data, which contains information on wages and total hours worked.[6] For now the dataset includes labour quality data from the Groningen Growth and Development Data.[7]

Labour services flows are assumed to be proportional to total hours worked:

$$L_{i,t} = q_{i,t} H_{i,t} \qquad (9.11)$$

where $H_{i,t}$ are total hours worked in industry *i* in period *t* and $q_{i,t}$ is a constant of proportionality. This methodology is similar to the one implied by Steindel and Stiroh (2001) and assures comparability with other growth accounting studies for Germany.

9.5 EXPLANATION OF KEY INDUSTRIES

A prime example of the differences between the value-added and gross productivity measures is the manufacture of vehicles (the transport equipment sector), which has always been uniquely dependent on complex subcontracting networks. Since the introduction of lean-management and just-in-time production the mid-1980s, the industry has created structures of legally independent companies that are closely related along the value-added chain. First-tier system-suppliers are know-how driven companies with a direct access to the major auto manufacturers. Then follow several layers of part and component suppliers that may or may not reside in the sector's classification.

During the second half of the 1990s, the dissemination of ICT technologies provided an additional stimulus to specialize production among subcontracting companies. E-business has become particularly important in this sector, although mostly for commodities and not for key car parts and components. The impact of the automotive production networks on growth and on productivity can be discussed on two levels. We can examine first the rise of efficiency as a result of specialization and subsequent reduction of transaction costs in addition to the reduction of labour costs due to outsourcing; and secondly, the scope of R&D in the growth and productivity of the automotive industry. The latter point is key to the understanding of the differences in the TFP concepts.

Value added in the automotive industry as defined by the European nomenclature group 34 (NACE Rev. 1) comprises the manufacture of engines, car bodies, drive trains etc. However, a number of parts that are destined to be assembled (such as wind-screens, plugs etc.) have never been part of the automotive industry production. These products are intermediates that are taken into account only in TFP_Y but not in the TFP_{VA} concept. As long as there are no changes in the automotive industry structure, technology and its upstream linkages within the production network, both concepts should provide intertemporally comparable results that differ only in levels.

Two major developments have, however, affected upstream linkages: innovation and outsourcing. Both activities induced a reduction of the manufacturing penetration. As measured by the share of value added on total gross-output, manufacturing penetration contracted dramatically between 1993 and 2001.

Technological progress led to the development of a broad range of new components that are indispensable in the modern car. Most of these elements are not manufactured by the automotive industry, e.g. anti-blocking systems and traction control (ABS, ASR), air bags, air-conditioning. These intermediate inputs receive an ever higher share in the total value of a car and have become important to the continued growth in the demand for vehicles. Gross-output has been stimulated by this development, whereas the value added cannot account for this increase over the period under investigation.

Outsourcing to subcontractors has long been a priority in the automotive industry. This trend has been driven by economies-of-scope and price differentials in factor inputs. Beyond the opportunities provided by the advanced ICT, the creation of the Single Market and the accession of CEE countries have also contributed to cross-border outsourcing. Generally speaking, these activities induce cost reductions based on automotive companies' decisions to make-or-buy. In real terms, the relocation has, *ceteris paribus,* the same impact on the TFP_Y and TFP_{VA} whenever companies shift abroad their capacities without friction. If factor markets are not perfectly flexible, however, TFP will be a negative during the adjustment period. This negative dip will be more pronounced for the TFP_{VA} concept.

9.6 CONCLUSIONS

The OECD Productivity Manual (2001, p. 10) states that the choice between productivity measures depends in part on the purpose of the productivity measure. In principle, the value-added and gross output-based measures are measures of two different concepts. We construct and employ a novel Ifo Productivity Database construct to allow the analysis of gross output productivity in Germany. We then compare sectoral productivities with exiting value-added measures in the literature.

The OECD (2001, p. 27) concludes that each measure has its place, depending on the standpoint adopted. Our results suggest that gross output and value-added based TFP measures are useful complements. Both follow roughly the same trend on the aggregate, although they do diverge significantly on the sectoral level. When technical progress affects all factors of production proportionally, the value-added measure is the simpler measure of technical change. Generally, the gross output-based TFP measure is less sensitive to situations of outsourcing, i.e., to changes in the degree of vertical integration between sectors. Value-added based TFP measures are contaminated by changes in outsourcing and provide an indication of the importance of the productivity improvement for the economy as a whole.

NOTES

1. For a small part of the output and intermediates real sample data is not available. In these cases the Ifo Productivity Database estimates real values using value-added data and the available data on the next higher aggregated level. This is the case for some manufacturing and service sectors. The estimation method guarantees consistent estimates of the sectoral and aggregate TFP. The estimates are also checked against current price data to avoid estimation biases.
2. The Ifo Productivity Database follows the procedures of the German Statistical Office to account for German reunification.
3. The depreciation rates refer to their economic use and not to tax-based depreciation rates.
4. The Investorenrechnung is less prone to misclassifications on the industry level due its use of an ownership-based statistical classification concept rather than an economic usage-based concept. The main difference between these concepts is that assets and investments of leas-

ing or other financial companies, not involved in the production process, are classified to the industry which has the economic use of the asset.
5. The use of the nominal interest rate rather than the ex-post rate of return is based on Steindel and Stiroh (2001).
6. Total hours worked over time are disaggregated data whenever possible. For 29 industries, only an aggregate data on the next higher industry level was available, so that the industry-specific total hours were estimated. Here it was assumed that sub-industries had the same change in hours as the lowest available industry level classification.
7. The Ifo Productivity Database is currently being expanded to include Jorgenson and Stiroh (2001) labour quality data. Please refer to www.ggdc.net for more information on the calculation of labour quality.

BIBLIOGRAPHY

Ark, B. van and D. Pilat (eds. 1993), *Explaining Economic Growth: Essays in Honour of Angus Maddison*, North-Holland, Amsterdam.
Baily, M.N., C. Hulten and D. Campbell (1992), 'The distribution of productivity in manufacturing plants', *Brookings Papers on Economic Activity: Microeconomics*, pp. 187–249.
Baldwin, J.R., T.M. Harchaoui and J.-P. Maynard (2001), 'Productivity growth in Canada and the United States', in J.R. Baldwin, D. Beckstead, N. Dhaliwal, R. Durand, V. Gaudreault, T.M. Harchaoui, J. Hosein, M. Kaci, and J.-P. Maynard, *Productivity Growth in Canada*, Statistics Canada, Ottawa, pp. 51–60.
Barnes, M. and J. Haskel (2000), 'Productivity in the 1990s: evidence from British plants', Queen Mary, University of London, http://www.qmw.ac.uk/~ugte153/.
Bartelsman, E.J. and M. Doms (2000), 'Understanding productivity: Lessons from longitudinal microdata', *Journal of Economic Literature*, **38** (3), pp. 569–94.
Bernard, A. and C.I. Jones (1996a), 'Productivity and Convergence Across US States and Industries', *Empirical Economics,* **21**, pp. 113–135.
Bernard, A. and C.I. Jones (1996b), 'Productivity Across Industries and Countries: Time Series Theory and Evidence', *Review of Economics and Statistics,* **78** (1), pp. 135–146.
Berndt, E.R. and D.O. Wood (1975), 'Technology, prices and the derived demand for energy', *Review of Economics and Statistics*, **57**, pp. 259–68.
Bruno, M. (1980), 'Duality, intermediate inputs and value-added', in Fuss, M. and McFadden, D. (eds), *Production Economics: A Dual Approach to Theory and Applications,* Vol. 2, North-Holland, Amsterdam, pp. 3–16.
Crafts, N. and T. Mills (2001), 'TFP Growth In British and German Manufacturing 1950–1996', *CEPR discussion paper* 3078.
Dean, E.R. and M. J. Harper (2000), 'The BLS Productivity Measurement Program', US Bureau of Labor Statistics, Washington.
Dean, E.R., M.J. Harper and M.S. Sherwood (1996), 'Productivity measurement with changing-weight indexes of outputs and inputs', in OECD, *Industry Productivity: International Comparisons and Measurement Issues*, OECD, Paris, pp. 183–215.
Diewert, E.W. (1980), 'Hicks' aggregation theorem and the existence of a real value-added function', in M. Fuss and D. McFadden (eds), *Production Economics: A Dual Approach to Theory and Applications,* Vol. 2, North-Holland, Amsterdam, pp. 17–51.

Diewert, E.W. (2001), 'Productivity trends and determinants in Canada', Discussion Paper no. 01–15, Department of Economics, University of British Columbia, http://www.econ.ubc.ca/discpapers/dp0115.pdf

Diewert, E.W. and A.O. Nakamura (1998), 'A survey of empirical methods of productivity measurement', http://lily.spc.uchicago.edu/~klmjenni/london/Papers/diewnak.pdf

Domar, E.D. 1961, 'On the measurement of technological change', *Economic Journal*, **71**, pp. 709–29.

Flaig, G. and V. Steiner (1993), 'Searching for the productivity slowdown: some surprising findings from West German Manufacturing', *Review of Economics and Statistics*, **75**, pp. 57–65

Goerlich, F.J. and V. Orts (1994), 'Margen precio-coste marginal and economías de escala en la industria española: 1964–1989', *Revista de Economía Aplicada*, **6** (2), pp. 29–53.

Goerlich, F.J. and V. Orts (1996), 'Economías de escala, externalidades and atesoramiento de trabajo en la industria española, 1964–1989', *Revista de Economía Aplicada*, **11** (4), pp. 151–166.

Gollop, F.M. (1979), 'Accounting for intermediate input: The link between sectoral and aggregate measures of productivity growth', in National Research Council, *Measurement and Interpretation of Productivity*, National Academy of Sciences, Washington, pp. 318–33.

Gollop, F.M. and M.J. Roberts (1981), 'Imported intermediate input: Its impact on sectoral productivity in US manufacturing', in Dogramaci, A. and Adam, N.R. (eds), *Aggregate and Industry-Level Productivity Analysis*, Martinus Nijhoff Publishing, Boston, pp. 149–86.

Gretton, P.K., J. Gali and D. Parham (2002), 'Uptake and impacts of ICTs in the Australian economy: Evidence from aggregate, sectoral and firm levels', Paper prepared for the Workshop on ICT and Business Performance, OECD, Paris, 9 December.

Gu, W. and M. S. Ho (2001), 'A comparison of productivity growth in manufacturing between Canada and the United States, 1961–9', in Jorgenson, D.W. and Lee, F.C. (eds), *Industry-level Productivity and International Competitiveness Between Canada and the United States, Industry Canada*, Ottawa, pp. 121–154, http://strategis.ic.gc.ca/sc_ecnmy/mera/engdoc/02.html.

Gu, W., F.C. Lee and J. Tang (2001), 'Economic and productivity growth in Canadian industries', in Jorgenson, D.W. and Lee, F.C. (eds), *Industry-level Productivity and International Competitiveness Between Canada and the United States*, Industry Canada, Ottawa, pp. 77–120, http://strategis.ic.gc.ca/sc_ecnmy/mera/engdoc/02.html.

Gullickson, W. (1995), 'Measurement of productivity growth in US manufacturing', *Monthly Labor Review*, pp. 13–28.

Gullickson, W. and M. Harper (1999a), 'Possible measurement bias in aggregate productivity growth', *Monthly Labor Review*, pp. 47–67.

Gullickson, W. and M. Harper (1999b), 'Production Functions, Input-Output Tables, and the Relationship between Industry and Aggregate Productivity Measures', Bureau of Labor Statistics, Washington, February.

Gullickson, W. and M. Harper (2002), 'Bias in aggregate productivity trends revisited', *Monthly Labor Review*, pp. 32–40.

Harchaoui, T.M., M. Kaci and J.-P. Maynard (2001), 'The Statistics Canada productivity program: concepts and methods', in J.R Baldwin, D. Beckstead, N. Dhaliwal, R. Durand, V. Gaudreault,, T.M. Harchaoui, J. Hosein, M. Kaci and J.-P. Maynard, *Productivity Growth in Canada*, Statistics Canada, Ottawa, pp. 143–76.

Harris, R. and M. Trainor (1997), 'Productivity and Growth in UK Regions, 1968–91', *Oxford Bulletin of Economics and Statistics*, **59** (4), pp. 485–510.

Hernando, I. and S. Nuñez (2002), 'The Contribution of ICT to Economic Activity: A Growth Accounting Exercise With Spanish Firm Level Data', Banco de España, Research Department, MA.

Hulten, C.R. 2000, 'Total Factor Productivity: A Short Bibliography', *National Bureau of Economic ResearchWorking Paper*, 7471, NBER, Cambridge, MA.

Jorgenson, D.W., F.M. Gollop and B.M. Fraumeni (1987), *Productivity and US Economic Growth*, Harvard University Press, Cambridge, MA.

Jorgenson, D.W and K. Stiroh (2001), 'Raising the speed limit: US economic growth in the information age', in D.W. Jorgenson and F.C. Lee (eds), *Industry-Level Productivity and International Competitiveness Between Canada and the United States*, Industry Canada, Ottawa, pp. 2–75.

Lum, S.K.S., B.C. Moyer and R. E. Yuskavage (2000), 'Improved estimates of gross product by industry for 1947–98', *Survey of Current Business*, June, pp. 23–54.

OECD (Organisation for Economic Co-operation and Development, 2001), *Productivity Manual: A Guide to the Measurement of Industry-level and Aggregate Productivity Growth*, OECD, Paris.

Oulton, N. (1998), 'Competition and the dispersion of labour productivity amongst UK companies', *Oxford Economic Papers,* **50** (1), pp. 23–38.

Oulton, N. (2000), 'Must Growth Rates Decline? Baumol's Unbalanced Growth Revisited', *Bank of England Working Paper,* 107, January, www.bankofengland.co.uk/workingpapers/wp107.pdf

Oulton, N. and M. O'Mahony (1994), *Productivity and Growth*, Cambridge University Press, Cambridge.

Schreyer, P. (2001), 'The OECD productivity manual: A guide to the measurement of industry-level and aggregate productivity', *International Productivity Monitor*, Spring, pp. 37–51.

Sichel, D.E. (2001), 'Productivity in the communications sector: an overview', Paper presented to Workshop on Communications Output and Productivity at the Brookings Institute, 23 February, http://www.brook.edu/es/research/projects/productivity/workshops/20010223/20010223.html.

Smolny, W. (2000), 'Sources of productivity growth – An empirical analysis with German sectoral data', *Applied Economics,* **32**, p. 305–314.

Sorenson, A. and M. Fosgerau (2000), 'Decomposition of Economic and Productivity Growth in Denmark', *Working Paper*, 2000–2, Centre for Economic and Business Research, Ministry of Trade and Industry, Copenhagen, http://www.cebr.dk/.

Steindel, C. and K. J. Stiroh (2001), 'Productivity: What is it, and Why do we Care About it?', Staff Report no. 122, Federal Reserve Bank of New York, April, http://www.newyorkfed.org/rmaghome/staff_rp/2001/sr122.html.

Sudit, E. and N. Finger (1981), 'Methodological issues in aggregate productivity analysis', in A. Dogramaci and N.R. Adam (eds), *Aggregate and Industry-Level Productivity Analysis*, Martinus Nijhoff Publishing, Boston, pp. 7–30.

van der Wiel, H.P. (1999), 'Sectoral Labour Productivity Growth', *Research Memorandum* No. 158, CPB Netherlands Bureau for Economic Policy Analysis, The Hague, September, http://www.cpb.nl/eng/pub/onderzoek/.

Zheng, S., I. Bobbin, S. Zhao and K. Tallis (2002), 'Deriving industry total factor productivity from the I-O system', Paper presented to the 14th International Conference on Input-Output Techniques, Montreal, October.

10. Determinants of Productivity per Employee: an Empirical Estimation Using Panel Data

Nicolas Belorgey, Rémy Lecat and Tristan-Pierre Maury

10.1 ABSTRACT

Two different approaches are used in this chapter to study productivity per employee: the determinants of its growth rate in the 1990s are first examined, and then the determinants of its level, using a more structural approach. ICT are shown to have a positive and significant effect on both growth rates and levels of productivity. This result is consistent with that of Gust and Marquez (2002), although the sample of countries is larger and GMM are used. In both sections of the chapter, the employment rate and productivity exhibit a significant negative relationship, arising from the concentration of employment on the most productive members of the workforce. Indicators of financial depth and price stability are found to be significant.

10.2 INTRODUCTION

Growth decomposition analyses attribute a large share of labour productivity growth to 'technical progress'. To make this blurry concept clearer, various articles have highlighted the role played by research and development (R&D) (Greenan, Mairesse and Topiol-Bensaid, 2001; Scarpetta and Tressel, 2002; Guellec and de la Potterie, 2001), the level of education (Lucas, 1988), public infrastructure (Aschauer, 1989) and the age of the capital stock. At the close of the 1990s, the economic debate expanded beyond these traditional determinants to include information and communication technologies (ICT), usually considered to comprise IT hardware, software and communications equipment.

ICT are believed to have played a part in productivity trends in the 1990s. In particular, several analyses suggest that the surge in the average productivity growth rate in the United States in the second half of 1990s can be largely ascribed to the production and utilisation of these new technologies. ICT are thought to have influenced labour productivity through three channels:

- A major contribution to productivity growth from ICT-producing sectors. Despite the small size of these sectors (7.3 per cent of GDP),[1] their robust productivity gains are estimated to account for 40 per cent of the acceleration in US labour productivity since 1995, according to Oliner and Sichel (2002). The falling cost of computing power – 18 per cent a year over the last four decades – mainly owing to enhanced processor performances, has amplified the strong expansion in volumes produced by these sectors. As a result, labour productivity has raced ahead in these sectors, boosting their GDP share and hence their contribution to growth in the industrialised countries.
- ICT investment, which has soared as new-technology performances improved. The rise in investment has increased the stock of capital available per employee, or capital deepening, leading to a faster pace of equipment renewal. This appears to have had a positive impact on labour productivity. Oliner and Sichel (2002) estimate that ICT investment could be responsible for almost 60 per cent of the pick-up in US productivity.
- There is still some debate about the third channel, through which ICT are said to have increased the total factor productivity (TFP) of sectors that are heavy users of ICT, such as insurance, finance, retail and aeronautics. In particular, by enhancing the co-ordination of those involved in the production process, ICT enabled inputs to be used more efficiently. The US retail sector, for example, recorded hefty productivity gains. Some authors have attributed this to utilisation of ICT, which is estimated to have improved management of inventories, the supply chain and warehouse logistics.[2,3]

Thus far, research into the impact of ICT has mainly yielded growth decomposition analyses of individual countries. In the United States, several papers, notably Jorgenson and Stiroh (2000) and Oliner and Sichel (2000), have shed light on the contribution of ICT-producing sectors to TFP growth and the contribution of ICT investment to growth in apparent labour productivity.

There are fewer cross-country comparisons of productivity determinants, however. Gust and Marquez (2002) carry out just such an analysis for 13 countries. They conclude that differences in productivity between the beginning and end of the 1990s are linked to the production and utilisation of ICT, as well as to changes in the employment rate. They also find that the following all have an indirect impact on productivity via their effect on ICT: the degree of regulation of goods and labour markets; the level of education; and the percentage of employment in the services sector. The diffusion of ICT may therefore be impeded by regulatory constraints that prevent companies from reorganising their workforce as well as by barriers to entry on certain markets. This last finding is shared by Scarpetta and Tressel (2002). Pilat and Lee (2001) also explore the relationship between ICT investment and the cost of ICT or telecommunications, which may differ across countries because of regulatory distortions.

In this analysis, the determinants of productivity are examined first by focusing on the 1990s, then by comparing productivity levels via a more structural approach.

The first section of the chapter investigates the relationship of annual productivity growth to its determinants from 1992 to 2000 across a panel of 25 countries. Unlike Gust and Marquez (2002), who use the ordinary or generalised least squares approach (OLS), the generalised method of moments (GMM) is employed here, which allows examination of the possibility that certain determinants may have a diffusion effect on productivity. More importantly, it enables us to deal with most endogeneity and simultaneity issues. The results are quantitatively different from those of Gust and Marquez (2002), but qualitatively similar. For instance, statistical confirmation is obtained that ICT production and expenditures are significant determinants of labour productivity. In addition, the impact on productivity of the capacity utilisation rate and the investment ratio is demonstrated.

The second section, which focuses on the long term, looks at the determinants of labour productivity levels in 2000 across a large number of countries: 77 without ICT spending and 49 with. These findings confirm that the level of development of public infrastructure, the education system and the banking system all have a positive impact on the productivity level. Evidence of the positive role played by price stability as well as of the inverse relationship between the employment rate and the productivity level is also obtained. The investigation of a 49-country sub-sample demonstrates that ICT do have a significant impact on productivity.

10.3   DETERMINANTS OF THE GROWTH RATE OF APPARENT LABOUR PRODUCTIVITY IN THE 1990s

Baseline Equation, Methodology and Data Sources

Baseline equation

This study is seeking to identify the main determinants of the growth rate of apparent labour productivity (here, GDP per employee). The baseline equation that is estimated takes the form:

$$\Delta Y_{i,t} = a.\Delta Y_{i,t-1} + b.ITP_{i,t} + c.ITS_{i,t} + d.\Delta H_{i,t} + e.\Delta TE_{i,t}\eta_t + \varepsilon_{i,t}$$

$$+ g.INV_{i,t} + f.\Delta TUC_{i,t} + u_i + \eta_t + \varepsilon_{i,t} \tag{10.1}$$

where $i = 1,...,N$ (where N is the number of countries) and $t = 1992, 1993,...,$ 2000. Y denotes the apparent productivity of labour, measured here as GDP over employment; ITP is the GDP share of ICT production; ITS is the GDP share of ICT spending; H denotes hours worked; TE is the employment rate; INV is the GDP share of investment and TUC is the capacity utilisation rate. ΔY is the log difference of Y (the same applies to all other variables in differences). ITS, ITP and INV are in logs. The usual country-specific effect, u, is included. η is a time dummy. ε is disturbance.

An autoregressive term is included in the baseline equation. In doing so, the possibility that the independent variables may have an ongoing impact on productivity is taken account of. For instance, a rise in ICT production or spending could have an effect on per capita productivity spread over several years.

One goal of this study is to assess the impact of ICT. In the introduction, several theoretical channels of transmission from ICT to per capita productivity that the literature has identified were recalled. These channels concern ICT-producing and ICT-using sectors alike. Accordingly, ICT production and ICT spending are included in the baseline equation, as do Gust and Marquez (2002). ICT production captures the impact on per capita productivity of TFP in ICT-producing sectors, while ICT spending captures effects of substitution by ICT products in user sectors.

The employment rate is also likely to be a key determinant of apparent labour productivity. Indeed, Gust and Marquez (2002) identify a negative relationship between changes in the employment rate and productivity growth. The authors link this effect to the fact that a rise in the employment rate is accompanied by the arrival of lower-skilled workers in the workforce, which crimps per capita productivity.

Working time is also included as one of the determinants in the baseline equation. This is a vital inclusion because the endogenous variable is per capita productivity, not hourly productivity. The ratio of investment in physical capital is also one of the independent variables. The impact of this variable as a proxy for the effect of overall capital deepening on per capita productivity is assessed. Lastly, the capacity utilisation rate is added to take into account the business cycle's effect on productivity.

The significance of other independent variables is tested. It is explained in the Findings section why they were not retained.

Methodology

The baseline equation poses a problem: all the independent variables are contemporaneous with the endogenous variable. This creates the possibility of reverse causality, i.e. of productivity impacting the independent variables. For this reason, the baseline equation cannot be estimated with the usual techniques. These issues are dealt with by using a GMM approach, which is designed to at least partially correct biases in estimates arising from the above-mentioned problems.

The generalised method of moments (GMM) for dynamic panel data models was developed by Holtz-Eakin, Newey and Rosen (1988), and Arellano and Bond (1991). Arellano and Bond (1991) propose first differencing the equation:

$$\Delta Y_{i,t} - \Delta Y_{i,t-1} = a.\left(\Delta Y_{i,t-1} - \Delta Y_{i,t-2}\right)$$

$$+ \beta'.\left(X_{i,t} - X_{i,t-1}\right) + \left(\varepsilon_{i,t} - \varepsilon_{i,t-1}\right) \qquad (10.2)$$

where the matrix X contains the set of independent variables other than the lagged endogenous variable (including time dummies). β is the vector of parameters other than a. While differencing eliminates the country-specific effect, a new problem is created: by construction, the term $\varepsilon_{i,t}\text{-}\varepsilon_{i,t-1}$ is correlated with the lagged endogenous variable $y_{i,t-1}\text{-}y_{i,t-2}$.

Under the assumptions that (i) the error term, ε, is not serially correlated, and (ii) the independent variables, X, are weakly exogenous, i.e. they are uncorrelated with future realisations of the error term, Arellano and Bond (1991) propose the following moment conditions:

$$E\left[\Delta Y_{i,t-s}.\left(\varepsilon_{i,t} - \varepsilon_{i,t-1}\right)\right] = 0$$
$$E\left[X_{i,t-s}.\left(\varepsilon_{i,t} - \varepsilon_{i,t-1}\right)\right] = 0 \qquad (10.3)$$

for $s > 1$ and $t = 3, ..., T$. This technique thus consists in using the lagged levels of variables as instruments for estimating the baseline equation in differences. The authors show that this method is far more accurate than previous techniques (Chamberlain's matrix, OLS in levels, within groups, and so forth). Moreover, following Arellano and Bond's approach (1991), the variables included in the matrix of instruments are multiplied by a time dummy. This technique cannot be applied to all the variables in the matrix because this would considerably increase the number of instruments. It is applied only in the case of the lagged endogenous variable and the ICT variables, i.e. the three variables that are suspected most strongly of endogeneity. The remaining lagged independent variables are included in the matrix of instruments without being multiplied by a time dummy. s is supposed to be $2<s<3$ in equation (10.3) above to restrict the number of instruments (data are available on just 25 countries).

While using the GMM approach for the equation in differences yields far more accurate estimates than do traditional techniques, the utilisation of lagged variables in levels is not always adequate. Alonso-Borrego and Arellano (1999), and Blundell and Bond (1998) have shown that, on small samples, coefficients can be seriously biased if the independent variables in levels are strongly autocorrelated. For this reason, Arellano and Bover (1995) and Blundell and Bond (1998) propose complementing the GMM on the equation in differences with a GMM on the baseline equation in levels with lagged independent variables in differences as instruments

$$
\begin{aligned}
E\big[\big(\Delta Y_{i,t-s} - \Delta Y_{i,t-s-1}\big)\big(u_i + \varepsilon_{i,t}\big)\big] &= 0 \\
E\big[\big(X_{i,t-s} - X_{i,t-s-1}\big)\big(u_i + \varepsilon_{i,t}\big)\big] &= 0
\end{aligned}
\tag{10.4}
$$

for $s=1$. These new conditions are valid under the additional assumption of stationarity of the independent variables, i.e. that there is no correlation between the country-specific effect and the independent variables in differences.

The combination of these two GMM techniques drastically improves the accuracy of the estimators if the independent variables are sufficiently serially correlated, which is the case in this example. Given the size of the sample (just 25 countries)[4], using a single GMM technique would have yielded seriously biased estimates.

The quality of the GMM estimate depends in particular on two factors: the assumption that the error term is not serially correlated; and the validity of the matrix of instruments. Arellano and Bond (1991) propose the following two tests:

Test 1 (Instruments):

Let Z be the matrix of instruments. Recall that for the regression to be correct, Z must not be correlated with disturbances. This assumption is evaluated using a Sargan test.

Test 2 (Serial correlation of residuals):

Given that the baseline equation has been first-differenced, the resulting residuals should be first-order serially correlated but not second-order serially correlated. AR(1) and AR(2) tests developed by Arellano and Bond (1991) are used to verify this point.

Lastly, Arellano and Bond (1991) and Blundell and Bond (1998) propose a two-step GMM estimator. The residuals of the first-step estimate are used to make a robust estimate of the heteroskedasticity of the variance-covariance matrix in the second step. However, the authors demonstrate that while the two-step estimator is far more accurate than the one-step estimator, the latter nonetheless provides a much more accurate estimate of standard deviations on small samples. The small size of the sample and the large number of instruments used could therefore cause us to strongly underestimate the standard deviations of the two-step GMM estimators.[5] We follow Calderon, Chong and Loayza (1999) and Beck and Levine (2002), and use the two-step estimator after assessing its significance in the first step.

Data sources

GDP, investment and employment data were taken from the OECD's Economic Outlook database. Data on ICT production came from the OECD's STAN database, while the World Information Technology Service Alliance's (WITSA) database (2002) supplied the figures for ICT spending. Data on hours worked were extracted from the Total Economy Database of the Groningen Growth and Development Centre. Capacity utilisation rates were taken from standardised national sources.

Findings

Overall findings

Table 10.1 sets out the results of the baseline equation estimates. The first column gives the estimate of the baseline equation with ICT production and spending (specification 1). The second column gives the estimate of the equation excluding ICT spending (specification 2), while the third column excludes ICT production (specification 3).

Table 10.1   Baseline equation with GMM

$$\Delta Y_{i,t} = a.\Delta Y_{i,t-1} + b.ITP_{i,t} + c.ITS_{i,t} + d.\Delta H_{i,t} + e.\Delta TE_{i,t} + g.INV_{i,t} + f.\Delta TUC_{i,t} + u_i + \eta_t + \varepsilon_{i.}$$

	Specification 1	Specification 2	Specification 3
Autoregressive term $\Delta Y(-1)$	0.248^{**}	0.326^{***}	0.253^{**}
GDP share of ICT production (ITP)	1.586	3.228^{***}	–
GDP share of ICT expenditures (ITS)	1.354	-	2.789^{**}
Change in hours worked (ΔH)	0.477^{***}	0.437^{***}	0.388^{***}
Change in employment rate (ΔTE)	-0.378^{*}	-0.332^{*}	-0.307^{*}
Investment ratio (INV)	0.116^{*}	0.119^{**}	0.101^{*}
Change in capacity utilisation rate (ΔTUC)	0.0010^{**}	0.0012^{**}	0.0015^{**}
Joint significance of ICT	0.009	–	–
Number of points: 149			
Number of countries: 25			

Notes:
Specification 1: baseline equation. Specification 2: excluding ITS. Specification 3: excluding ITP.
* indicates that the estimate is significant at 10 per cent, ** at 5 per cent and *** at 1 per cent. The Wald test gives the significance level needed to reject the null hypothesis that the two ICT variables are jointly zero.

Under the first specification, neither of the ICT variables is significant individually (there is an empirical correlation of 0.45 between them). However, by running a Wald test, the two variables are jointly significant at 1 per cent. Specifications 2 and 3 show that when ICT production and ICT expenditures are taken separately, they have a positive and significant influence on the growth rate of apparent labour productivity. These results only partially bear out those of Gust and Marquez (2002), who find ICT production and expenditures to be concurrently significant. The divergence in findings may stem from:

(1) the difference in estimation methods (GMM rather than OLS), or
(2) the difference in databases used (25 countries in this article, compared with 13 countries for Gust and Marquez, 2002).

Despite the difference with Gust and Marquez (2002), these findings confirm ICT's marked influence on changes in productivity. ICT spending has a strong impact on per capita productivity. Using specification 3, let us take the example of a country with an average ICT-expenditure-to-GDP ratio, i.e. 5.91 per cent; if we assume that at a given date this country devotes an additional 1 per cent of GDP to ICT spending, this will trigger an immediate increase of around 0.45 of a percentage point[6] in the growth rate of apparent labour productivity (compared with about 1 percentage point for Gust and Marquez, 2002). Of course, this is an unrefined interpretation, ceteris paribus, of the table's results. As Pilat and Lee (2001) rightly remind us, corresponding changes in other areas are required before the impact of higher ICT investment can feed through into productivity. Accordingly, caution must be exercised when interpreting the results of Table 10.1. Note, however, that a 1 per cent-of-GDP increase in ICT spending would be a large jump; in France, it would be equivalent to a rise of some 15 per cent in ICT expenditures. These results confirm the impact of ICT expenditure on productivity, an aspect already discussed by Oliner and Sichel (2000), and by Jorgenson and Stiroh (2000). Further, these findings square with those of Colecchia and Schreyer (2001), who conclude that the impact of capital deepening from ICT investment was responsible for the sharp surge in US productivity relative to the European and Japanese economies in the mid-1990s.

Similarly, a one-percentage-point increase in the ratio of ICT production to GDP has an immediate impact of around 0.7 of a percentage point on the productivity growth rate, compared with more than 1 percentage point for Gust and Marquez (2002). This result affirms the impact on per capita productivity of an increase in TFP in ICT-producing sectors. Studies such as Oliner and Sichel (2002) and Gordon (2000) have demonstrated the significance of this mechanism on US data. Gust and Marquez (2002) and this paper confirm it on an international sample.

Findings for the other variables:

- Employment rate changes consistently have a negative and significant effect on the productivity growth rate across all specifications. There is little variation in the coefficient between specifications. The sign of this relationship was expected: it supports the hypothesis of diminishing returns for the employment rate in the production function put forward by Gust and Marquez (2002). Similarly, changes in average working hours have a positive and significant influence on the labour productivity growth rate. This is a logical finding because the endogenous variable is per capita productivity and not hourly productivity: an increase in working time naturally raises the extra production of an additional worker. These results are consistent with Malinvaud's estimates (1973).
- Remarkably, the investment ratio has a positive impact on the productivity growth rate. This contradicts Gust and Marquez's estimates (2002), which reject the significance of this variable. There are problems attached to the investment ratio, however: ICT investment is included in both ICT spending and in the investment ratio, even though it accounts for a fraction of the

latter. Therefore, estimates similar to those of Table 10.1 were conducted but without the investment ratio. The results are practically unaltered.
- Changes in the capacity utilisation rate influence the productivity growth rate significantly and positively. Thus, the capacity utilisation rate significantly captures part of the business cycle. This result is consistent with the estimates of Guellec and de la Potterie (2001), who identify a linkage between the capacity utilisation rate and the TFP level.

Plainly, the list of independent variables used is not an exhaustive one. Since the main aim of this chapter is to test the significance of ICT, other variables were rejected:

- R&D expenditures are too closely correlated with ICT and so are not included among the significant determinants of per capita productivity. This partially supports findings obtained by Greenan, Mairesse and Topiol-Bensaid (2001) on French microeconomic data. These authors demonstrate that the impact on productivity of ICT is markedly higher than that of R&D expenditures. Note that Gust and Marquez (2002) also reject R&D expenditures (which are significant if ICT variables are excluded).
- Years of schooling and human capital are also too strongly correlated with ICT to significantly influence per capita productivity. This supports Caselli and Coleman (2001), who identify a positive linkage between the level of human capital and computer expenditures. Human capital thus appears to have an indirect impact on productivity via its effect on ICT spending. It would therefore be pointless to include both ICT expenditures and human capital in the baseline equation.
- The degree of employment protection (cf. Gust and Marquez, 2002; and Scarpetta and Tressel, 2002) is rejected for similar reasons. Gust and Marquez (2002) demonstrate that employment protection is a determinant of ICT expenditures and so indirectly affects per capita productivity.

Additional findings

An analysis to determine the sensitivity of the findings to a decomposition of ICT expenditures is conducted. The two main components of these series are telecommunications expenditures and computer expenditures, which are taken from the WITSA (2002). The same relationship as before is estimated, by testing alternately each of the components as an independent variable.

The key finding in Table 10.2 is that computer expenditures appear to have a greater effect than telecommunications expenditures on the growth rate of apparent labour productivity. Indeed, the coefficient estimator is not significant for the communication expenditures component. One possible explanation for this result is that communication spending definitely includes a greater volume effect than computer spending, but also a fairly variable price effect across countries.

Table 10.2   ICT decomposition

	Specification 1	Specification 2
Autoregressive term ΔY(-1)	0.333***	0.182**
X	-0.043	3.184**
Change in hours worked (ΔH)	0.362**	0.264***
Change in employment rate (ΔTE)	-0.246	-0.562**
Investment ratio (INV)	0.115*	0.094*
Change in the capacity utilisation rate ΔTUC)	0.0012**	0.0013***
Number of countries: 25		
Number of points: 149		

Notes:
Specification 1: X = telecommunications expenditures. Specification 2: X = computer expenditures.
* indicates that the estimate is significant at 10 per cent, ** at 5 per cent and *** at 1 per cent.

10.4   FACTORS DETERMINING THE LEVEL OF APPARENT LABOUR PRODUCTIVITY IN 2000

This second section rounds out the preceding short-term study with a long-term analysis of the determinants of apparent labour productivity levels in 2000. In order to permit a cross-country comparison of productivity levels, the ratio of GDP in purchasing power parity (PPP) to total employment is used. This raises major evaluation and methodological problems, discussed in the Appendix entitled 'Statistical Difficulties in Measuring Productivity' of Lecat (2004).

Given the relative inertia of the productivity levels being compared, determinants are selected from the structural indicators of economic performance, namely the levels of education, public infrastructure, financial depth and macroeconomic stability.

Baseline equation, Methodology and Data Sources

Baseline equation and methodology

The method used, an OLS regression on the productivity level of a given year, does not take account of the time dimension. Some of the variables used as determinants could in fact reflect the country's level of development (a simultaneity bias). To get round this problem, determinants are taken, where appropriate, as a long-run average and prior to 2000. The baseline equation is therefore:

$$\Pi_i = a.X_i + \varepsilon_i \qquad (10.5)$$

where $i=1,\ldots, N$, the number of countries; Πi, is GDP in USD PPP million divided by the total employment of country i in thousands. X_i denotes the vector of determinants for country i, while a is the vector of parameters.

This method sheds light on static not dynamic correlations: a positive correlation between the productivity variable and one of the determinants of productivity identified by the equation does not signify that an increase in the level of the determinant in a given country will mechanically drive up the productivity level. This correlation merely captures the differences in productivity between countries in 2000.

This method is applied to two different country groups. The first sample comprises 77 countries representing the world's main economic areas – Western Europe, North America, Asia, Eastern Europe, Africa and the Middle East – and different levels of development, from OECD member countries and developing countries to the transition economies and the least developed countries. The second group comprises a narrower sample of just 49 countries, allowing the inclusion of an ICT variable for which data are not available on the broader scale of the first sample.

Data sources

Data are taken from the World Bank's database of World Development Indicators, except data on total employment, which come from the International Labor Organisation's Laborsta database.

Findings

77-country sample[7], no ICT

The findings for the first group of countries, set out in Table 10.3 below, show that there is a positive correlation between the productivity level and public infrastructure, human capital, price stability and financial depth, while a negative correlation exists with the employment rate.

Table 10.3   Productivity levels in a broad country sample, excluding ICT

Dependent variable: GDP in USD PPP million divided by total employment in thousands (Π_i)

Independent variables	Unit	Coefficient	Significance
Public infrastructure			
Number of km of roads divided by surface area (RT)	Km/km² Average in 1990s	2.1	4.1%
Number of telephone lines per person (TEL)	Lines per person Average, 1960–2000	77.1	0.0%
Education			
Gross enrolment rate in primary education of a given age group[a] (PRIM)	As a % Average, 1970–1995	0.13	0.6%
Gross enrolment rate in tertiary education of a given age group[a] (TERT)	As a % Average, 1970–1999	0.22	3.6%
Macroeconomic variables			
Employment rate: total employment divided by total population[b] (TE)	As a % En 2000	-0.23	5.6%
GDP share of domestic credit to the private sector (CRD)	As a % Average, 1970–2000	0.13	0.4%
Standard deviation of the inflation rate (consumer prices)[c] (INFL)	In points Average, 1970–2000	-0.56	6.3%

Notes:
R^2 adjusted for the number of independent variables 82.4%.
[a] *Official age group varies across countries.*
[b] *In some countries, working age begins before 15 and ends after 65. As a result, the employment rate is calculated as a percentage of the entire population.*
[c] *The standard deviation is slightly more significant than the level of inflation.*

Public infrastructure, which is represented by the density of the road and telephone networks, is an especially significant determinant of the productivity level. Aschauer (1989) calls attention to the impact of the public capital stock on private sector TFP. He thus attributes the break in the pace of US productivity growth in the 1970s to the slowdown in public investment capital spending. The public infrastructure made available to private agents is necessary for a wide range of economic activities, and the productivity of private companies may depend on the quality of such infrastructure. To limit problems of simultaneity, telephone and road density levels are calculated as averages over periods that are made as long as possible. The existence of externalities related to public infrastructure is often contested, with critics pointing to the high income elasticity of demand of the main categories of infrastructure (cf. notably Englander and Gurney, 1994). Because variables that group countries by income level are used, the coefficient of the public infrastructure variables is reduced but nonetheless remains significant (see below). Telephone and road network densities do a particularly good job of explaining differences in productivity within the group of high- and upper-middle-income countries,[8] as the additional tests show.

The level of human capital is estimated by gross enrolment rates in primary, secondary and tertiary education. This ratio is calculated by the number of people enrolled in a given level of education, regardless of age, divided by the total number of people in the corresponding official age group. Lucas (1988) formulated the idea that human capital exhibits constant returns, not diminishing returns like other inputs, thereby placing education at the heart of the catch-up strategies of developing countries. In this chapter, enrolment rates in primary and tertiary education are significant determinants of the productivity level, with a particularly strong coefficient for tertiary education. By contrast, the enrolment rate in secondary education is not significant because of its collinearity with tertiary education (70.8 per cent correlation) and does not improve the regression's overall significance. The variables for teaching quality, i.e. the teacher/student ratio and the GDP share of education spending, do not strengthen the regression's significance, but a finer level of data is doubtless required.

A country's financial depth, measured by the GDP share of domestic credit to the private sector, also emerges as a significant determinant of labour productivity. The banking system helps to ensure that resources are efficiently allocated, by making it easier for the business community to finance projects, but also by selecting the most productive undertakings. Conversely, the market capitalisation of listed companies as a percentage of GDP is not significant. This may be because of the small role of equity markets in some high-productivity countries like Ireland, France and Italy, and because these markets have become international in scope, allowing companies to issue securities on foreign markets.

Turning to the indicators of macroeconomic stability, the volatility and level of inflation both have a negative effect on productivity. High price volatility raises the level of uncertainty in the economy and undermines the efficiency of the price system. A stable macroeconomic environment provides support for investment decisions, which can strengthen labour productivity by increasing the capital stock per employee. A poorly functioning price system prevents inputs from being channelled to the most productive opportunities. By contrast, a large current-account deficit does not have a significant impact on the productivity level. Some countries that are structurally in deficit are highly productive, like the United States and Ireland, while oil-exporting countries, such as Venezuela and Kuwait, exhibit low or average levels of productivity. Similarly, (official) exchange rate volatility does not have a significant effect, doubtless because of foreign exchange controls in certain countries.

The employment rate has a negative impact on the level of labour productivity. Here, the rate is computed as a percentage of total population because in many countries the working age extends outside the 15–65 age group.[9] A low employment rate indicates that only the most productive workers are involved in the production process, because of their skill level or their age; as the employment level rises, less productive workers are hired (Artus and Cette, 2004).

Unlike in the preceding section, it was not possible to test the impact of working time, because there were insufficient reliable data on all the countries in the sample.

Other determinants[10] are tested, but they prove to have insufficient explanatory power. R&D expenditures as a percentage of GDP do not improve the significance of the regression. This contrasts notably with the findings of Guellec and de la Potterie (2001) for OECD countries. First, there are gaps in the database, especially for developing countries, which account for a large section of the panel. Second, in these countries, where economic take-off relies on a phase of imitation rather than innovation, the R&D drive may also be of less significance.

The medium-term and long-term investment ratio is used as a proxy for the capital stock, with no significant results. Indeed, the investment ratio was especially high in former planned economies, even though the investments there proved to be unproductive.

An indicator of the size of the market to which companies have access was also taken into account. Some sectors may enjoy economies of scale associated with access to a larger market, either because of the size of the domestic market (estimated by national GDP divided by world GDP), or because of access to foreign markets (estimated by the economy's degree of openness). These two indicators do not have a significant effect: large countries like China, Russia and Brazil do not have high productivity levels; nor do countries, such as Nigeria, that display a high degree of openness because they export raw materials.

Lastly, the countries were sorted into groups by income.[11] Differences in the density of telephone and road networks do not explain differences in productivity in low- or lower-middle income countries. But they do explain differences in productivity for high- and upper-middle-income countries. Furthermore, these groupings qualify the importance of certain determinants and confirm the significance of others. Thus, the coefficients for enrolment rates in tertiary education, for inflation volatility and for the employment rate are impressively stable and significant across all specifications. By contrast, the coefficients for the public infrastructure variables are halved for the richest countries, while the enrolment rate for primary education and the financial depth indicator no longer appear significant.

49-country sample[12], with ICT spending

The second group of countries, like the first, represents the world's main geographical regions. Unlike in the first, though, half the countries in this sample are OECD members. Additional data on ICT spending were taken, as in the first section of the chapter, from the database published by the World Information Technology Service Alliance (2002).

The results of tests carried out on this second group of countries (see Table 10.4) reveal fewer significant variables: public infrastructure, human capital, and ICT spending have a significant and positive impact on the level of productivity, while financial depth and macroeconomic stability variables do not appear to be significant. As in the previous study, R&D spending, although positively correlated with the productivity level, does not have a significant effect in the regression.

As in the first part of the study, the average long-run densities of the road and telephone networks are used as indicators of the level of development of public infrastructure. And, as with the previous sample, when per capita income dummies are included, they notably explain differences in productivity between high-income and upper-middle-income countries. The coefficient of telephone network density is lower than in the previous equation: the marked difference between OECD countries and developing countries plays a smaller role than in the previous sample.

In terms of the level of education, the rate of enrolment in tertiary education is a significant determinant of labour productivity. The rates of primary and secondary enrolment were also tested, but the former failed to yield significant results and the latter is closely correlated with tertiary rates of enrolment (correlation of 67.7 per cent). It might be expected that the difference in productivity would occur at the tertiary level in developed countries, given the high and similar rates of primary and secondary enrolment. In their study of OECD countries, Englander and Gurney (1994) also estimate that productivity gains of 0.6 point per year could be traced back to a higher rate of enrolment in secondary education.

Average ICT spending between 1992–2000 was used as a proxy for the contribution made by ICT. This is a more satisfactory variable than a snapshot of the level of spending in 2000 because it suggests that it is the accumulation of these expenditures over a given period that may have a positive effect on productivity. In addition, this average variable yields more significant results than the snapshot variable.

Table 10.4 Productivity levels in a narrow sample of countries, including ICT

Dependent variable: GDP in USD PPP million divided by total employment in thousands			
Independent variables	**Unit**	**Coefficient**	**Significance**
Public infrastructure			
Density of road network (number of km of roads divided by surface area) (RT)	Km/km² Average, 1990s	4.2	0.3%
Density of telephone network (number of telephone lines per person) (TEL)	Lines per person Average, 1960–2000	46.9	0.1%
Education			
Gross enrolment rate in tertiary education for a given age group (TERT)	As a % Average, 1970–1999	0.43	0.1%
ICT			
ICT spending (ITS)	As a % of GDP Average, 1992–2000	200	0.2%

Note: R^2 adjusted for the number of independent variables = 78.9%.

Other variables were tested but did not improve the specification. R&D spending displays strong collinearity with other independent variables, exhibiting a 69.7 per cent correlation with telephone network density and 63.5 per cent correlation with enrolment in tertiary education. In addition, compared with the results ultimately provided by the selected specification, regressions based on R&D or on the number of scientists and engineers per million people explain a smaller part of the differences in productivity between the sample countries (adjusted R^2 of 64 per cent instead of 79 per cent). This is consistent with the microeconomic results of Greenan, Mairesse and Topiol-Bensaid (2001). They found that ICT and R&D had a combined effect on business productivity but that this was smaller than the sum of the individual impacts of the two variables, offering clear evidence of duplication between R&D and other independent variables. Furthermore, R&D appears to have a weaker impact than ICT, providing grounds to prefer the latter as an independent variable.

The share of services in value added emerges as a significant factor. However, it is difficult to break down the contribution made to growth in services between increases in income (services regarded as superior goods) and other factors, such as more intensive use of ICT on average by the services sector. The share of credit to the private sector does not appear to have a significant effect. Indeed, in the case of developed countries, it acts more as an indicator of debt levels than of the sophistication of the financial system. The indicators of macroeconomic stability do not yield significant results. As regards inflation, the difference in findings stems from the lower variance of the second sample: while countries that have experienced hyperinflation, like Argentina, Chile and Poland, have lower productivity levels than countries with moderate inflation, the difference within the smaller sample is less marked than in the broad sample. That said, in their study of OECD member countries, Englander and Gurney (1994) estimated that 10 additional points of inflation took 0.6 of a point per year off productivity gains.

As for the first sample, the countries are grouped by income, with similar results road density is the only public infrastructure variable to have a significant impact; the ICT coefficient is greatly reduced and is no longer significant.

Several key findings emerge from this study, which focuses on the determinants of apparent labour productivity and the impact on productivity of information and communication technologies (ICT):

- An initial analysis of the 1990s demonstrates that the GDP share of ICT spending and the GDP share of ICT production may have a separate and positive impact on the productivity growth rate. Of the components of ICT spending, the computer sector appears to have a far more influential role than the telecommunications sector. The positive and significant role played by ICT is confirmed in an examination of productivity levels.
- A negative association between apparent labour productivity and the employment rate is found, linked to the concentration of employment on the most productive members of the workforce. This result holds for both analyses, i.e. of levels and of growth rates. The analysis of growth rates also reveals a positive relationship between hours worked and productivity.
- A long-term analysis of productivity levels demonstrates the positive impact of public infrastructure in a 77-country and a 49-country sample. The level of education is also shown to have a positive impact in both samples. Meanwhile, inflation volatility and the depth of the banking system have a positive impact in the 77-country sample only.

This analysis confirms the role of the traditional determinants of productivity, some of which, such as public infrastructure, are still disputed. Until now, ICT have been examined as part of growth decomposition analyses (Oliner and Sichel, 2002, for example) or across a small number of countries (13 countries in Gust and Marquez, 2002). In this estimate on a panel of 25 industrialised countries and using the generalised method of moments, ICT appear to have played a significant role in labour productivity trends in the 1990s.

These findings offer some explanation as to why Europe ceased to narrow the productivity gap with the United States in the 1990s: the extensive use of ICT in the United States is one reason; the rise in employment rates in European countries is another.

NOTES

1. Bart van Ark, Robert Inklaar and Robert McGuckin, 2002.
2. McKinsey Global Institute (2002).
3. ICT spending by businesses, which are directly responsible for the productive process, is unlikely to have the same effect as ICT spending by households, which merely participate in the process. However, the data used here do not allow us to distinguish between the two categories. Furthermore, household expenditures also have an effect on productivity through increased human capital resulting from the use of IT at home. As this paper is exploring macroeconomic issues, and since there are no data allowing us to separate the impact of household expenditures from businesses expenditures, household ICT spending cannot be entirely excluded from the determinants of productivity.
4. Australia, Austria, Belgium, Canada, Czech Republic, Denmark, Finland, France, Germany, Greece, Hungary, Ireland, Italy, Japan, Mexico, Netherlands, Norway, Poland, Portugal, Slovakia, South Korea, Spain, Sweden, United Kingdom, United States.
5. The same problem affects the Sargan test and the residual serial correlation test.
6. Recall that the ratio of ICT expenditure to GDP is expressed logarithmically in the baseline equation.
7. Argentina, Armenia, Australia, Austria, Belarus, Belgium, Brazil, Bulgaria, Canada, Chile, China, Cyprus, Colombia, Costa Rica, Croatia, Czech Republic, Denmark, Egypt, El Salvador, Estonia, Fiji, Finland, France, Germany, Greece, Guatemala, Hungary, Iceland, India, Indonesia, Iran, Ireland, Israel, Italy, Jamaica, Japan, Kazakhstan, Kyrgyzstan, Kuwait, Lithuania, Macedonia, Madagascar, Malaysia, Malta, Mauritius, Mexico, Moldavia, Mongolia, Netherlands, New Zealand, Nigeria, Norway, Panama, Peru, Philippines, Poland, Portugal, Romania, Russia, Singapore, Slovakia, Slovenia, South Africa, South Korea, Spain, Sri Lanka, Sweden, Switzerland, Thailand, Trinidad and Tobago, Tunisia, Turkey, Uganda, Ukraine, United Kingdom, United States, Venezuela.
8. 10 years for road density, 40 years for telephone line density.
9. However, the employment rate computed for the 15-65 age group is also significant.
10. Some indicators used in the literature to capture cross-country differences in productivity on the basis of differences in regulatory levels are not available on a sufficiently large scale to be included here. This is the case notably for the Employment Protection Legislation (EPL) and Product Market Regulation (PMR) indicators used by Scarpetta and Tressel (2002).
11. Again using the World Bank's classification based on average per capita income.
12. Argentina, Australia, Austria, Belgium, Brazil, Bulgaria, Canada, Chile, China, Colombia, Costa Rica, Czech Republic, Denmark, Egypt, El Salvador, Finland, France, Germany, Greece, Hungary, India, Indonesia, Iran, Ireland, Israel, Italy, Japan, Malaysia, Mexico, Netherlands, New Zealand, Norway, Philippines, Poland, Portugal, Romania, Russia, Singapore, Slovakia, Slovenia, South Africa, South Korea, Spain, Sweden, Switzerland, Thailand, Turkey, United Kingdom, United States, Venezuela.

REFERENCES

Alonso-Borrego, C. and M. Arellano (1999), 'Symmetrically normalized instrumental-variable estimation using panel data', *Journal of Business and Economic Statistics*, **17**, 36–49.

Arellano M. and S. Bond (1991), 'Some tests of specification for panel data: Monte Carlo evidence and an application to employment equations', *Review of Economic Studies*, **58**, 277–297.

Arellano, M. and O. Bover (1995), 'Another look at the instrumental-variable estimation of error-components models', *Journal of Econometrics*, **68**, 29–52.

Ark, B. van, R. Inklaar and R. McGuckin (2002) 'Changing Gear, Productivity, ICT and Services Industries: Europe and the United States', *Research Memorandum*, GD-60, Groningen Growth and Development Centre.

Artus, P. and G. Cette (2004), 'Productivité, croissance et emploi', Rapport du Conseil d'analyse économique, 2003, No. 48, *La Documentation Française*, Paris.

Aschauer, D. (1989), 'Is public expenditure productive?', *Journal of Monetary Economics*, **23**, 177–200.

Beck, T. and R. Levine (2002), 'Stock markets, banks, and growth: panel evidence', *NBER Working Papers,* 9082, Cambridge, Massachusetts.

Blundell, R. and S. Bond (1998), 'Initial conditions and moment restrictions in dynamic panel data models', *Journal of Econometrics*, **87**, 115–143.

Calderon, C., A. Chong and N. Loayza (1999), 'Determinants of current account deficits in developing countries', *World Bank Research Policy Working Paper,* 2398, Washington.

Caselli, F. and W.J. Coleman (2001), 'Cross-country technology diffusion: the case of computers', *NBER Working Paper*, 8130, Cambridge, Massachusetts.

Colecchia, A. and P. Schreyer (2001), 'ICT investment and economic growth in the 1990s: is the United States a unique case? A comparative study of nine OECD countries', *OECD Directorate for Science, Technology, and Industry Working Paper, 7*, Paris.

Englander, A.S. and A. Gurney (1994), 'La productivité dans la zone de l'OCDE: les déterminants à moyen terme', *Revue économique de l'OCDE, 22*, Spring 1994.

Gordon, R. (2000), 'Does the new economy measure up to the great inventions of the past?', *Journal of Economic Perspectives*, **14**, 49–74.

Greenan, N., J. Mairesse and A. Topiol-Bensaid (2001), 'Information technology and research and development impacts on productivity and skills: looking for correlation on French firm level data', *NBER Working Paper*, 8075, Cambridge, Massachusetts..

Guellec, D. and B. de la Potterie (2001), 'Recherche-développement et croissance de la productivité: analyse des données d'un panel de 16 pays de l'OCDE', *Revue économique de l'OCDE*, **33**, 2001/II, pp. 111–136.

Gust, C. and J. Marquez (2002), 'International comparisons of productivity growth: the role of information technology and regulatory practices', *International Finance Discussion Papers*, 727, Board of Governors of the Federal Reserve System, New York.

Holtz-Eakin, D., W. Newey and H.S. Rosen (1988), 'Estimating vector autoregression with panel data', *Econometrica*, **56**, 1371–1396.

Jorgenson, D.W. and K.J. Stiroh (2000), 'Raising the speed limit: US economic growth in the information age', *Brookings Papers on Economic Activity*, **2**.

Lecat, R. (2004), 'Labour Productivity in the Major Industrialised Countries: the End of the Catch-up Process with the United States?', *Bulletin de la Banque de France*, 121, Paris.

Lucas, R.E. (1988), 'On the mechanics of economic development', *Journal of Monetary Economics*, **22**, 3–42.

Malinvaud, E. (1973), 'Une explication de l'évolution de la productivité horaire du travail', *Economie et statistique*, **48**.

McKinsey Global Institute (2002), *Dynamiser la productivité en France et en Allemagne*. Paris

Oliner, S.D. and D.E. Sichel (2000), 'The resurgence of growth in the late 1990s: is information technology the story?', *Journal of Economic Perspectives*, **14** (4), 3–22.

Oliner, S.D., and D.E. Sichel (2002), 'Information technology and productivity: where are we now and where are we going?', Federal Reserve Board, New York.

Pilat, D. and F.C. Lee (2001), 'Productivity growth in ICT-producing and ICT-using industries: a source of growth differentials in the OECD?', *STI Working Paper*, 2001/4, OECD, Paris.

Scarpetta. S. and T. Tressel (2002), 'Productivity and convergence in a panel of OECD industries: do regulations and institutions matter?', *Economics Department Working Papers*, 342, OECD, Paris.

World Information Technology Service Alliance (2002), *Digital Planet 2002: the global information economy,* Arlington.

11. Labour Quality and Skill Biased Technological Change in France

Johanna Melka and Laurence Nayman

11.1 SUMMARY

New interest for the Skill Bias Technological Change hypothesis (SBTC) has been refueled in the wake of ICT capital deepening in the economy. The shift in the share of more educated workers has been explored for France over the 1982–2001 period.

It was first shown that differentiating supply and demand changes across different categories of labour mattered on account of important composition effects retraced in the labour quality index. Women and younger educated workers and also, fitting the demographic structure change, the 35–54 age bracket, have increased their hours worked over the 1995–2001 period.

The analysis of demand favouring college educated labour across sectors brings also some insight into the debate about the factor/sector bias of SBTC. Demand for college educated workers has, indeed, mainly increased in sectors already intensive in skilled labour and in ICT investment. This in turn suggests that the sector bias of technological change has driven up the share of college educated labour.

The econometric analysis provides evidence of SBTC over the 1990–2001 period. Across education types, ICT capital accumulation and the R&D stock impact favourably the share of college educated labour. Sectorwise, the impact of SBTC is stronger in the non producing sector over the 1990–95 period. In contrast, the ICT producer sector experienced a large SBTC effect over the 1996–2001 years.

11.2 BACKGROUND AND MOTIVATIONS

How to explain the increasing share of skilled labour relative to unskilled labour is a question that has regained interest with the deepening of ICT capital in total economy over the '80s in the United States and over the '90s in Europe.

The skill upgrading of labour input, associated with a rise in the relative wages of skilled workers, was paid much attention since the '70s in the changing context of international trade. First, the low-skill contents of imported products were found to compete with unskilled labour in the developed countries and cause a skill bias (Wood, 1995; Goux and Maurin, 2000). Further, recent literature has focused more specifically on outsourcing (imported intermediate inputs) as a major explanation of wage inequality. Feenstra and Hanson (2001) for example assess that outsourcing can account for half or more of the observed skill upgrading.

Besides international trade and also institutional-type factors as wagesetting practices and norms that impact the wage gap (DiNardo, Fortin and Lemieux, 1996), the other candidates that have emerged as a potential explanation for the skill-bias are technological and organisational changes.

As technology is complementary to skills, a technological change embodied in capital together with a changing organisational environment will increase the demand for skilled labour. The skill premium, defined as the relative wages ratio, then in turn increases. Numerous studies have given support for the skill biased technological (and/or organisational) change (SBTC) hypothesis linked to ICT in the United States and also in European countries (Autor, Katz and Krueger,1998; Caroli and van Reenen, 2001; Haskel and Heden, 1999; Greenan et al., 2001; O'Mahony et al., 2003; Piva et al., 2003). Some have done this by using the plain model of supply of and demand for skilled relative to unskilled labour devised by Katz and Murphy (1992), which fails however to explain the slowdown of the skill premium in the United States over the '90s (Beaudry and Green, 2002).

Further, an opposite view to the labour-augmenting aspect of SBTC is its sector bias. Haskel and Slaughter (2002), for example point out that it is the sector bias of SBTC that determines the change in relative factor prices and not the SBTC's factor bias. They find that in a multi-sector framework, SBTC is concentrated in skill-intensive sectors.

Card and DiNardo (2002) question SBTC on the account of two competing approaches: the ICT capital and high skills complementarity and the skill price rise across all dimensions of skills. The first version fails to explain why in spite of ICT capital deepening acceleration, the wage gap in the United States was only persistent from 1982 to 1986, and the second version of SBTC cannot explain why the returns to education are concentrated among younger workers or why the gender gap has been closing.

This chapter aims at checking if SBTC played a role in France over the period 1982–2001.

Section 11.3 will stress on descriptive statistics linked to gender, age brackets and skills.

As composition effects in supply and demand across skills may shift out the skill premium and counterbalance the SBTC's effect, it seems necessary to examine supply and demand by gender and age brackets across skills.

Firstly, the labour quality index, measuring the growth rate of efficient hours worked relative to the growth rate of non weighted hours, is a useful indicator as it globalises trends in supply and demand across gender, age brackets and education categories.

Secondly, to give an insight into demand and supply shifts in labour quality changes, some more detailed indicators are displayed. The supply and demand effects are further assessed by using the framework developed by Katz and Murphy (1992), Autor et al. (1998).

Thirdly, a shift-share analysis is carried out. It breaks into two components: the 'between' effect and the 'within' effect. If the former prevails, studies conclude to a skill bias induced by international trade or to a sectoral supply shock (i.e. the defence sector in the United States); if the latter is larger, then the SBTC is seen as the relevant explanation.

In section 11.4, the econometric analysis provides evidence of SBTC over the 1990–2001 period. ICT capital accumulation and the R&D stock impact favourably the share of college educated labour. Sectorwise, SBTC is very positive in the ICT non producing sector over 1990–95, whereas the impact is boosted in the ICT producing sector over the 1996–2001 years. Moreover, the trade explanation is not validated, empirically, over the nineties.

11.3   DESCRIPTIVE STATISTICS

Data and Notions

The data for hours and compensation are mainly from two main databases: the Déclarations Annuelles de Données Sociales (DADS) from the INSEE, a sample based on the forms filled in by employers and the Labour Force surveys (LFS) for France from 1982 to 2001.

Ratios by gender, age, education are calculated in the LFS and then applied to the DADS. The merged database is then controlled for National Accounts totals. Total hours and compensation entail the self-employed workers. Moreover, compensation includes the gross wage and the employers' contributions (provided by INSEE).

The skills considered in this chapter are skills by education and not by occupations.

The Labour Quality Index

ICT can be assumed to impact labour categories differently, as some studies using detailed surveys on ICT use have shown that younger and educated people are more ICT-friendly than other labour categories. The skill bias may then be of different magnitude across education categories.

The labour quality index is mostly interesting as it synthesises trends in supply and demand across gender, age brackets and education categories and can be viewed as a proxy for the productivity effort of each labour category (Table 11.1). French labour quality is compared to the US in order to stress differences between both countries.

Table 11.1   Contributions to labour quality, average annual changes

	Quality	Age	Gender	Education
1982–2001				
United States	0.46	0.24	-0.08	0.33
France	0.87	0.18	-0.02	0.71
1982–1990				
United States	0.49	0.26	-0.12	0.40
France	1.13	0.44	0.00	0.70
1990–1995				
United States	0.55	0.25	-0.01	0.27
France	0.84	0.26	-0.06	0.70
1995–2001				
United States	0.36	0.21	-0.08	0.29
France	0.54	-0.22	-0.02	0.72

Note: The labour quality index equals growth rate of hours times the compensation share of labour category i in total compensation. Quality sums on the different contributions of age, gender, education and interactions not shown here.

$$Q = \sum_i H_i * 0.5 * \left[\frac{(wL)_{i,t-1}}{(wL)_{.,t-1}} + \frac{(wL)_{i,t}}{(wL)_{.,t}} \right] - \dot{H} \, .$$

Source: US: Harvard, CEPII, authors' calculations; France: INSEE, DADS, LFS, CEPII, authors' calculations.

Following the works of Jorgenson et al. (1987), the labour quality is measured by the difference between labour services and the growth rate of hours worked. Labour services are measured by the growth rate of total hours worked by each individual labour category weighted by their compensation share in total labour compensation. Each component is weighted by its marginal product under the neo-classical hypothesis according to which labour is compensated at its marginal productivity.

The contribution of education to labour quality in the US decreases in the '90s relative to the '80s, whereas in France, it increases strongly over the whole period. Table 11.2 exhibits statistics related to the growth rate of hours worked by education type and age bracket. While the upper education categories (down to baccalaureate) see an increase in their hours worked over the whole period, the hours worked by the less educated in contrast are undercut. Had the growth rate of hours been calculated across occupations, an increase in hours would have appeared in the second half of the nineties. It is worth mentioning that the qualification of the unskilled improves, as the share of unskilled workers with for instance a baccalaureate increases from 2 per cent in 1982 to 10 per cent in 2001 and the share of unskilled workers with no diploma tumbles down from about 75 per cent in 1982 to 46 per cent in 2001.[1]

By gender, women have raised their labour supply dramatically in the US over the '80s (Table 11.1). In France, no inroad of this magnitude is observed. By age bracket, the contribution of the youngest and the oldest workers goes up in the US in the '90s relative to the '80s. In France, over the 1990–95 period, the sharper decrease in hours relative to labour services calculated on age explains why the age contribution to labour quality remains positive. In the 1995–2001 years, increased hours of the youngest and of the 35–54 age bracket hardly balance a sharp decrease in the hours worked by the oldest. This translates into a very negative contribution of age in the second half of the '90s, all the more as non weighted hours increased over this period (Table 11.2).

Table 11.2   Growth rate of hours worked by education type and age bracket, per year, in %

	1982–01	1982–90	1990–95	1995–01
Tertiary+4	4.8	5.7	3.4	4.7
Tertiary+2	4.0	4.0	4.4	3.7
Baccalaureate	2.1	1.9	0.0	4.0
Mid-high school	0.3	1.1	0.3	-0.6
Low vocational	-0.2	0.6	-1.5	-0.1
No diploma	-3.8	-3.2	-4.7	-3.7
<25	-2.9	-7.1	-7.5	7.2
25–34	-0.5	-0.1	-1.1	-0.5
35–54	1.3	2.1	1.1	0.4
>54	-1.7	0.6	-3.5	-3.4

Source: LFS and DADS, National Account,; CEPII, authors' calculations.

Interestingly, in spite of a growing integration of the youngest in employment (hours), their share in compensation hardly moves up over the '90s. On the contrary, the 35–54 age bracket compensation share swells up to 59 per cent over 1995–2001 (Table 11.3). These evolutions reflect in part what occurs on the labour supply side.

Table 11.3 Breakdown of total compensation by education type and age bracket, in %

	1982–01	1982–90	1990–95	1995–01
Education				
Tertiary+4	13	10	14	16
Tertiary+2	10	7	11	14
Baccalaureate	13	13	14	14
Mid-high school	29	28	30	29
Low vocational	7	7	7	7
No diploma	27	34	27	20
TOTAL	100	100	100	100
Age bracket				
<25	7	9	6	5
25–34	29	30	29	27
35–54	55	52	56	59
>54	9	9	9	8
TOTAL	100	100	100	100

Source: LFS and DADS, National Accounts, CEPII, authors' calculations.

Labour Supply and Demand Shifts

Hours and the wage bill

A closer look at supply and demand shifts in the French economy teaches us that over the '90s the population of tertiary educated people aged 25–34 has attained 34 per cent of the total age group, with the share of women outstripping the men's share (OECD: Education at a glance). On the demand side, the same statistics but in hours worked indicate that the ratio of tertiary educated people aged 25–34 reaches 38 per cent. The total intensity indicator, dividing the demand into the supply share, amounts to 111 per cent and even 127 per cent for women in 2001, pointing to a higher concentration of education in labour than in population. This intensity was a bit greater in the first half of the '90s.

The stylised facts about the participation and employment rates of women, the youngest and oldest workers in France are well-known. The participation rate of women has increased a lot over the 1982–2001 period (OECD: Employment Outlook). The share of the youngest (24.3 per cent in 2001) and the oldest (36.5 per cent in 2001) in employment is very weak relative to the United States (57.7 per cent and 58.6 per cent respectively) or to the EU average at least for the young (40.8 per cent and 39.3 per cent respectively). The still high unemployment rate, though declining at the very end of the period, has left France with an oversupply of young and educated labour. It has been argued that the lack of flexibility in the French labour market involved an adjustment on quantities. This in turn pushes wages down in downturns.

To summarise, demand seems to increase for women, younger and educated workers. If demand exceeds supply, then the hourly wages of these categories should in turn increase. On the contrary, non-educated workers should see their hourly wages decrease as supply of labour for this category is larger than demand. Also, the 35–54 years old supply of labour seems to go up but it has not been translated yet into a lower share of their wages in the wage bill over the recent period.

Hourly compensation

The skill premium, the hourly compensation of college educated labour to non college educated, should rise in the wake of the massive introduction of a new technology such as ICT entailing an increased demand for educated labour. But across education, the demand for gender or age categories may increase for other reasons than SBTC. For example, firms can hire younger women taking advantage of historically lower wages relative to men unrelated to productivity differences.

Figures 11.1 and 11.2 provide evidence for such shifts within the education criterion. The wage gap between men and women still amounts to more than 20 per cent in France over the last period (Figure 11.1). This suggests that firms fancy different career perspectives for women, as they anticipate bumps in women's careers due to child raising, etc. Further, the wage gap for highly educated women relative to men is larger than for women in the lower education levels. Less flexible hours worked by high educated women would keep them on a lower career track than men, explaining the magnitude of the wage gap between highly educated women and men. By contrast, the less educated women experience about the same career progress as men.[2]

By age bracket, the age-weighted skill premium rise is steady throughout the period and stiffer in the second part of the '90s (Figure 11.2). However, composition effects may be linked to economic fluctuations.

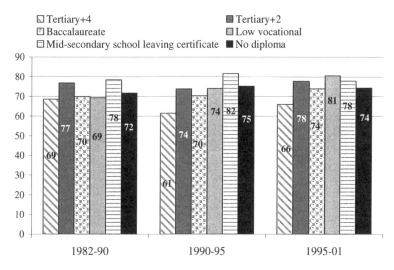

Note: Hourly compensation of men:100.

Source: LFS and National Accounts, CEPII, authors' calculations.

Figure 11.1 Hourly compensation gap between women and men according to education type

Over the first half of the '90s, a period of slack growth, the demand for the youngest and the oldest has dramatically decelerated, weakening even more their share in total employment. This is in line with the disaffection of employers with these categories in sluggish times, when employers gauged wages earned by these categories too high relative to their productivity level. Then, those in search of a job could only find one at the price of a weaker entry wage. These age brackets (below 25 and above 54 years old) are small in total hours worked and compensation and do not impact much the weighted total.

Over the 1995–2001 period, the 25–34 years old bracket and the youngest are the most involved, pointing to a sustained demand effect for these categories of workers. Although the wage premium of the youngest has increased a lot over this period, this has not translated into the improvement of their compensation share as the growth in compensation of the better paid 35–54 years old has enlarged total compensation.

In France, as the education distribution is more splayed out than in the United States, the skill premium of the college educated was computed against workers with no diploma. The skill premium rise is then much

stronger for younger educated people than for their elders across all categories of education over the 1995–2001 period.

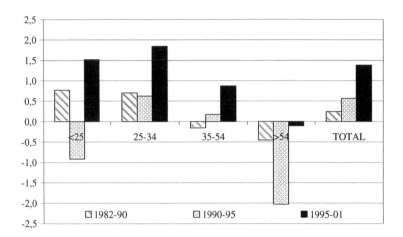

*Note: College: tertiary education (>bac+2); non college: high school and below. Total is
weighted by the share of hours worked by each age bracket in total hours.*

Source: LFS and National Accounts, CEPII, authors' calculations.

*Figure 11.2   Average annual changes in hourly compensation of college/non
college educated, by age bracket, in %*

Relative education supply and demand shifts

To synthesise further the education supply and demand for total economy, the
model used by Katz and Murphy (1992) and Autor et al. (1998) is used. The
following equation derived from a CES function, is calculated:

$$\Delta \ln D_t = \Delta \ln(W_{ct} / W_{nct}) + (\sigma - 1)\Delta \ln(w_{ct} / w_{nct}).$$

With σ the aggregate elasticity of substitution between college and non
college workers, D the demand for college educated relative to non college
educated workers, W total compensation, w the hourly compensation, the subscripts t, c, and nc stand for time, college and non college workers.

Both studies retain, as a preferred estimate, an elasticity of substitution of
1.4. Results are displayed in Table 11.5. The wage premium amounts to 0.31
per cent on average per year over the 1982–2001 period. 40 per cent of this
increase being kept due to the elasticity of substitution, this results into a

lower skill premium (0.12 per cent). The wage premium rise is steady and reaches 0.26 per cent in the '80s, 0.30 per cent over 1990–95 and 0.38 per cent over 1995–2001.

The total demand effect favouring college educated labour is the sum of the change in the relative wage bill and the change in the wage premium[3] times the elasticity of substitution. The demand curve for college educated labour shifts on account of technological change, relative product price changes, increased outsourcing processes, etc. Supply, here in this model, is the change in relative hours of the college educated workers.

Demand is greater than the supply effect in France over the whole period. It outstrips the supply effect chiefly over the '80s (4.66 per cent) just as in the US (4.60 per cent).

Demand favouring college educated labour can be split up into sectoral demand schemes. The sectoral breakdown, i.e. the producer sector, the user sector and other industries, stems from the prediction that college educated workers will be attracted in those sectors that are intensive in ICT investment.[4] The overall relative demand over the 80s is shifted by the other industries' demand change for college educated labour (particularly in the health and government services, the wholesale trade, the plastics and rubber industry and textiles). The shift in global demand favouring college educated labour between 1990 and 1995 was towed by the user sector. Since 1995, demand is fully due to the ICT producer sector's contribution. Demand exceeds supply by about 4 points in the producer sector over 1995–2001. The ICT boom has generated increased output and employment in this sector. Moreover, the year 2000 bug has played a major role in these trends. Helped by a declining supply change over time, demand in the user sector ranks first over the '90s, at a time of greater ICT diffusion. In the ICT user sector as in other industries, demand has exceeded supply by less than 0.1 per cent over 1995–2001 in spite of growth acceleration.

Shift-share Analysis

Berman, Bound and Griliches (1994) have assessed the impact of the skill bias technological change by using the shift-share method. It allows the share of college educated hours (compensation) to be decomposed into two effects: the 'between' and the 'within' effect. The former relates to inter-industry labour shifts and the latter to intra-industry labour changes for college educated workers. The 'between' effect coincides with international trade changes or with a sectoral shock meaning that college educated labour is attracted to (and unskilled labour decreases in) some specific sectors. The 'within' effect indicates an increase in skilled labour in all sectors as a result of the diffusion of technologies such ICT or the increase in R&D. It could also be interpreted as the occurrence of more outsourcing transactions between firms within a sector (Feenstra and Hanson, 2001).

The initial formula is the following:

$$\Delta S_{DIP} = \underbrace{\sum_i \Delta \frac{H_i}{H} * \overline{S}_{DIP,i}}_{between} + \underbrace{\sum_i \Delta S_{DIP,i} * \frac{\overline{H}_i}{H}}_{within} \tag{11.1}$$

S_{DIP} = proportion of hours worked (compensation) by college educated workers in total hours (compensation), $S_{DIP,i}$ = proportion of sector hours worked (compensation) by college educated workers in total sector hours (compensation), H = total hours worked, H_i =hours worked in industry i, the long dash overtopping the variables indicates a mean over the whole period and relates to a change between end and initial dates of the period. This breakdown can be performed on hours and also on compensation. In the alternate equation, W stands for compensation.

The above equation is further decomposed into sectors in order to obtain both effects in the ICT producer, ICT user and in the other industries:

$$\Delta S_{DIP} = \underbrace{\sum_{p=1}^{P} \Delta \frac{H_p}{H} * (\overline{S}_{DIP,p}) + \sum_{u,u \neq p} \Delta \frac{H_u}{H} * (\overline{S}_{DIP,u}) + \sum_{k,k \neq j \neq p} \Delta \frac{H_k}{H} * (\overline{S}_{DIP,k})}_{between}$$

$$+ \underbrace{\sum_{p=1}^{P} \Delta S_{DIP,p} * \frac{\overline{H}_p}{H} + \sum_{u,u \neq p} \Delta S_{DIP,u} * \frac{\overline{H}_u}{H} + \sum_{k,k \neq j \neq p} \Delta S_{DIP,k} * \frac{\overline{H}_k}{H}}_{within} \tag{11.2}$$

with p the ICT producer sector, u the ICT user sector, k the other industries.

Table 11.4   *Changes in the share of hours worked by college educated (tertiary education)*

% points	1982–01	1982–90	1990–95	1995–01
(1) **Between**:	**0.34**	**0.06**	**0.05**	**0.23**
ICT producer sector	0.13	-0.01	-0.01	0.15
ICT user sector	1.09	0.35	0.19	0.55
Other industries	-0.88	-0.27	-0.13	-0.48
(2) **Within**:	**13.39**	**3.88**	**4.56**	**4.95**
ICT producer sector	1.17	0.31	0.26	0.60
ICT user sector	4.73	1.81	1.33	1.60
Other industries	7.48	1.76	2.97	2.75
(3) = (1) + (2) Total effect (%)	**13.73**	**3.95**	**4.61**	**5.17**

Note: With the notations indicated in the text. The total change in the share of college educated in total hours between 2001 and 1982 is the share in 2001 minus the share in 1982. The average on a variable is the average of its share at the final date and its share at the initial date ($0.5*(share_{t-n}+share_t)$).

Sources: LFS and National Accounts, CEPII, authors' calculations.

The global effect results from the sum of different sub-periods as it is also summed over the different sectors. Both effects can also be added up. Sum in columns and lines (Table 11.3 and 11.4).

Over 1982–2001, the total 'between' effect amounts to 0.34 for hours (0.65 for compensation) whereas the 'within' effect indicates a well above change: 13.39 (18.56 for compensation). This 'within' effect increases throughout the period. Surprisingly, the 'between' effect contribution to the share of college hours, although of a small size, increases too chiefly in the user sector. Computed on compensation, the 'between' contribution of the producer sector is the highest, indicating a strong increase in the total compensation of this sector for skilled labour.

The 'within' effect ratio to the change in the share of wages earned by the college educated can be allocated to the relative wage bill in order to highlight the 'within' component of demand. It thus measures the impact of SBTC on the demand shift towards more educated workers. When the wage premium and the relative wage bill in its 'within' component are added, it results in the 'within' component of demand (Table 11.5, part A).

The contribution of sectors to the 'within' effect depends on the magnitude of the share of each sector in total hours or compensation. Table 11.6 displays these shares. For example, the ICT producer sector represents only 3.6 per cent and 5.6 per cent in total hours and compensation respectively over the 1995–2001 period. When the change in the sector share of skilled hours is weighed by the sector's share in the 'within' effect, the contribution of this sector is bound to be tiny. On the reverse, the contribution of other industries is likely to be large for the same reasons.

Table 11.5   Relative demand favouring college graduates and supply shifts (college graduates/non college)

A. Total Economy

	Relative wage bill			Wage pre-mium*0.4	Supply	Demand
	Total (a)	*between*	*within*	(b)		(a+b)
1982–01	5.02	0.17	4.85	0.12	4.71	5.14
1982–90	4.55	0.12	4.43	0.11	4.29	4.66
1990–95	5.60	0.05	5.54	0.12	5.30	5.72
1995–01	5.16	0.31	4.85	0.15	4.78	5.31

B. ICT producer sector

	Relative wage bill	Wage premium*0.4	Supply	Demand
1982–01	8.56	-0.16	8.97	8.40
1982–90	6.72	-0.05	6.84	6.67
1990–95	4.02	-1.65	8.15	2.37
1995–01	15.08	0.96	12.67	16.04

C. ICT user sector

	Relative wage bill	Wage premium*0.4	Supply	Demand
1982–01	5.73	-0.13	6.05	5.59
1982–90	6.01	-0.51	7.28	5.51
1990–95	6.13	0.31	5.35	6.44
1995–01	5.01	0.01	4.99	5.02

D. Other industries:

	Relative wage bill	Wage premium*0.4	Supply	Demand
1982–01	4.19	0.15	3.80	4.34
1982–90	3.57	0.24	2.98	3.81
1990–95	5.46	0.18	5.01	5.63
1995–01	3.95	0.02	3.90	3.97

Notes:
ICT producer = NACE 30, 32, 64, 72, ICT user = NACE 22, 24, 29, 31, 33,35, 40-41, 65, 66, 67, 71, 73, 74, 90-95

$$\Delta \ln D_t = \underbrace{\Delta \ln \left([w_h * N_h] / [w_u * N_u] \right)}_{a} + \underbrace{(\sigma - 1) * \Delta \ln (w_h / w_u)}_{b}$$

w: hourly compensation; N: employment; : elasticity of substitution; ln: growth rate. Supply is the growth rate of hours worked by skilled relative to unskilled labour.
College graduates: tertiary education; non skilled: baccalaureate, vocational upper secondary education, lower secondary education and below.

Source: LFS and National Accounts, CEPII, authors' calculations.

Table 11.6   Change in the share of college educated (tertiary education) compensation

In % points	1982–01	1982–90	1990–95	1995–01
(1) Between:	**0.65**	**0.18**	**0.06**	**0.42**
ICT producer sector	1.02	0.13	0.07	0.82
ICT user sector	1.37	0.73	0.15	0.49
Other industries	-1.74	-0.69	-0.17	-0.89
(2) Within:	**18.56**	**6.31**	**5.68**	**6.57**
ICT producer sector	1.85	0.48	0.22	1.15
ICT user sector	6.55	2.51	1.94	2.10
Other industries	10.16	3.33	3.51	3.32
(3) = (1) + (2) Total effect (%)	**19.21**	**6.49**	**5.73**	**6.99**

Sources: LFS and National Accounts, CEPII, authors' calculations.

Tables 11.7 and 11.8 then report the absolute change in the share of college educated workers hours and compensation. The ICT producer sector displays the highest change, as it is a very intensive sector in skilled labour. The intensity in college educated workers in the producer sector relative to the total economy has kept, indeed, on increasing to reach 183 per cent in 2001.

Table 11.7   Absolute changes in the college educated hours share by sector

In % points	1982–01	1982–90	1990–95	1995–01
Total economy:	**13.7**	**3.9**	**4.6**	**5.2**
ICT producer sector	33.7	9.2	7.7	16.8
ICT user sector	19.3	7.8	5.4	6.2
Other industries	10.43	2.4	4.1	3.9

Note: Changes in the share of college educated workers in sector total hours. The total economy change is weighted by the share of sectors in the economy.

Sources: LFS and National Accounts, CEPII, authors' calculations.

The change in the college educated workers share in the user sector is close enough to the other industries' share, mainly over the last period. This could be misleading, as it could be concluded that nothing happened in the user sector. As a matter of fact, demand for skilled labour in this sector occurred chiefly in the eighties. The intensity in college educated workers in the user sector relative to the total economy increased from 103 per cent to 129 per cent in 1991 and then increased again from 1997 on, to stabilise to 122 per cent in 2001. By contrast, in the other industries, this intensity has decreased down to 0.87 per cent in 2001.

Table 11.8   Absolute changes in the college educated compensation share by sector

In % points	1982–01	1982–90	1990–95	1995–01
Total economy:	**19.2**	**6.5**	**5.7**	**7.0**
ICT producer sector	36.4	11.0	4.7	20.7
ICT user sector	23.2	9.3	6.8	7.2
Other industries	15.2	4.9	5.3	5.1

Note: Changes in the share of college educated workers in sector total compensation. The total economy change is weighted by the share of sectors in the economy.

Source: LFS and National Accounts, CEPII, authors' calculations.

ICT expansion over the second half of the 90s has mainly brought about a boom in the producer sector, and hardly any change in the user sector. This can also be related to the flexibility degree and turnover rate (entry rate) in both sectors. Firms in the user sector have trained those in tenure to use ICT, whereas in the producer sector, the entry rate of firms and employees is very high, enticing a match between ICT capital deepening and the observed higher demand for college educated labour over 1995–2001.

To end this first section, it can be concluded that younger and educated workers benefit from the demand shifts in hours worked. It then impacts labour quality as wages of a category are representative of the productivity of this category. The skill premium rise concerns the youngest college educated workers and also to a lesser extent the 25–54 years old bracket that is the largest represented cohort.

Results of supply and demand shifts favouring the college educated workers show that, sectorwise, demand outstrips supply in the producer sector over the 80s. Furthermore, the 'within' component was chiefly driven up by the producer sector over the 1995–2001 period. Obviously, ICT investment deepening has chiefly impacted the change in the share of college educated workers in the producer sector.

However, demand for college educated workers has chiefly taken place in sectors already intensive in college educated labour. This relates to the debate of SBTC in terms of its factor bias versus its sector bias. Probably, both effects play a role in explaining skill upgrading in hours and compensation.

These differentiated trends should shed light on the econometric analysis exploring further the link between the rise in compensation of the skilled and SBTC.

11.4   DEMAND FOR COLLEGE EDUCATED WORKERS: DEMAND FROM TECHNOLOGICAL CHANGE

Two major results can be drawn from the preceding sections. Firstly, the descriptive analysis shows that the labour force composition in France has changed favouring college educated employment. The share of hours worked by tertiary +4 and tertiary +2 educated workers has strongly increased over 10 years,[5] this phenomenon being associated with an increase in their wage bill.[6] Secondly, the shift share analysis shows that the college educated workers' share increase has occurred in all sectors.

The goal, in this last section, is to show, empirically, that technical change explains this demand increase for high skilled workers (tertiary +4 and tertiary +2 educated workers).

Theoretical Framework

The objective in this study is to validate the hypothesis of skill biased technological change. Have R&D stock and ICT capital accumulation contributed to the employment of college educated workers? Has the share of their compensation increased?

Given n types of labour ($j = 1, \ldots, n$) and m environmental variables ($k = 1, \ldots, m$), the total labour cost of industry i can be expressed as:

$$TLC_i = f\left[w_{ij}, K_i, Y_i, Z_{ik}\right] \tag{11.3}$$

where:
w_{ij} : vector of wages of n categories of workers
K_i : real capital stock of industry i
Y_i : real value added of industry i
Z_{ik} : vector of m environmental variables
or, in translog form (suppressing the i subscript):

$$\ln TLC = \alpha_0 + \sum_{j=1}^{n} \alpha_j \ln w_j + \alpha_Y \ln Y + \alpha_k \ln K + \frac{1}{2} \sum_{j=1k=1}^{n} \sum \alpha_{jk} \ln w_j \ln w_k + \sum_{j=1}^{n} \alpha_{jk} \ln w_j \ln K \tag{11.4}$$
$$+ \sum_{j=1}^{n} \alpha_j \ln w_j \ln Y + \frac{1}{2} \alpha_{YY} (\ln Y)^2 + \frac{1}{2} \alpha_{KK} (\ln K)^2 + \phi(w, K, Y, Z)$$

where:

$$\phi(w, K, Y, Z) = \sum_{k=1}^{m} \delta_k Z_k + \sum_{k=1j=1}^{m} \sum^{n} \lambda_{kj} \ln(w_j) Z_k + \sum_{k=1}^{m} \zeta_k \ln(Y) Z_k + \sum_{k=1}^{m} \psi_k \ln(K) Z_k + \frac{1}{2} \sum_{k=1}^{m} \gamma_k (Z_k)^2$$

It can be shown that cost minimisation by producers requires that the share of each type of labour in total labour costs be equated with the first partial derivative of the cost function, with respect to that type of labour's wage:

$$S_j = \frac{\partial \ln TLC}{\partial \ln w_j} \text{ with } S_j \text{ the share of labour type } j \text{ in total labour cost.}$$

Assuming only two types of labour, college educated and non college educated ($j = h$, l) – receiving wages equal to and respectively – and only one environmental variable – an index of the stock of technology denoted TECH, yields the following equation for the share of high skilled labour in the total labour cost of industry i:

$$S_h = \alpha_h + \alpha_{hY} \ln Y + \alpha_{hK} \ln K + \alpha_{hh} \ln w_h + \alpha_{hl} \ln w_l + \lambda_{hh} TECH \quad (11.5)$$

Note that the derivation of the above equation assumes that the parameters of the cost function are symmetric, that is:

Assuming homogeneity of degree one in prices implies that :

$$S_h = \alpha_h + \alpha_{hY} \ln Y + \alpha_{hK} \ln K + \alpha_{hh} \ln\left(\frac{w_h}{w_l}\right) + \lambda_{hh} TECH \quad (11.6)$$

Assuming that the returns to scale are constant implies that equation (11.6) can be written as:

$$S_h = \alpha_h + \alpha_{hY} \ln\left(\frac{K}{Y}\right) + \alpha_{hh} \ln\left(\frac{w_h}{w_l}\right) + \lambda_{hh} TECH \quad (11.7)$$

In this study, it was chosen to break down the capital stock (K) in ICT capital ($KICT$) and non ICT equipment capital ($KNICT$). The technological variable is represented by the R&D stock (RD).

Econometric Results

In order to take into account structural differences between sectors, the model is estimated using the panel methodology with fixed effects.

The model is as follows:

$$S_{i,t} = \alpha_i + \beta_1 \ln \frac{KICT_{i,t}}{Y_{i,t}} + \beta_2 \ln \frac{KNICT_{i,t}}{Y_{i,t}} + \beta_3 \frac{RD_{i,t}}{Y_{i,t}} + \beta_4 \ln \frac{w_{i,t}^h}{w_{i,t}^l} + \varepsilon_{i,t} \quad (11.8)$$

where:

i: industry

t: time

S: share of high skilled workers wage bill

KICT: ICT real capital stock (calculated using the perpetual inventory method)

KNICT: non ICT equipment real capital stock

Y: real value added

RD: R&D stock (calculated with the PIM method)

$w_{i,t}^{h}$ / $w_{i,t}^{l}$: ratio of hourly wage of college educated workers to hourly wage of non college educated workers.

Data

ICT and non ICT capital stock are constructed with the Perpetual Inventory Methodology (PIM) using investment series from INSEE. Hours worked and compensation[7] by category of education (postgraduates, university or higher vocational degree, 'A' level, low vocational school degree, mid-secondary school leaving certificate, no certificate or almost none) are extracted from the DADS database and the Labour Force Surveys from INSEE. The college educated workers have Master and bachelor degrees (above baccalaureate plus 2 years in college). The non college educated workers are the other skill categories.

The value added series are extracted from the National Accounts (INSEE). All these series are available from 1990 to 2001 for 37 industries. The R&D stock is constructed using the RDSMAN indicator extracted from the STAN database, from 1990 to 2000 for the manufacturing industries.

Methodology

Equation (11.8) is estimated by the Generalised Least Squares methodology in panel. Moreover, the relative wage variable is excluded from the regression. Indeed, this variable is used in the dependent variable construction. One commonly encountered solution in the literature is to introduce time dummies instead of the relative wage terms. These dummies represent macroeconomic shocks and missing variables.

The model is estimated from 1990 to 2001 and for two sub-periods: 1990–95 and 1996–2001 in order to test the stability of coefficients.

To begin with, in order to determine if fixed effects have to be introduced in the regression, a Fisher test is implemented. Moreover, a Hausman test is performed (which determines if random effects are preferred to fixed effects) and concludes that the fixed effects model is preferred over the random effects. Introducing fixed effects reflects structural differences between industries.

The estimation results (Table 11.9), significant at the 1 per cent level, support the SBTC thesis. Technological progress, represented by the R&D

stock and ICT capital stock, has a positive effect on the college educated wage bill share.

In contrast, non ICT equipment capital has a negative effect on the college educated wage bill share. This result (significant at the 1 per cent level) indicates that investment in ICT or non ICT equipment will not have the same impact. In the first case, the wage bill share of college educated workers is likely to increase, whereas in the second case, the relative non college educated share is due to increase.

Table 11.9   College educated wage bill share, 1990–2001

Explanatory variables	
Fixed effects	α
ln(RD/Y)	0.02*
	(0.009)
ln(KICT/Y)	0.06**
	(0.01)
ln(KNICT/Y)	-0.12**
	(0.02)
R^2	0.95
F	373
N	256

Notes:
*Heteroskedasticity-consistent standard errors are in parentheses **: significant at the 1 per cent level, *: significant at the 5 per cent level.*
KICT: ICT real capital stock; KNICT: non ICT equipment real capital stock; Y: real value added; RD: R&D stock. The regression includes a full set of time dummies.

Source: INSEE, DADS, Labour Force Survey and National Accounts, STAN, CEPII, authors' calculations.

Introducing fixed effects in the regression illustrates structural differences between industries (organisational change). Nevertheless, fixed effects may reflect error measures, or missing variables. Consequently, interpreting fixed effects is not easy. Estimation results show that the college educated wage bill share is higher ceteris paribus in some ICT producer and ICT user industries: office accounting and computing machinery, business activities, education, health and social services, printing and publishing. In the office accounting and computing machinery industry, the share of higher college educated wage bill is the highest.

Moreover, leaning on statistics in the preceding section, it can be suspected that the impact of technological change on the college educated wage bill share should be stronger in the ICT producer sector. Indeed, Haskel and Slaughter (2002) showed that the stronger technical change in industry, the higher the wage bill share for high skilled workers. In order to show that

SBTC is stronger in ICT producing industries, a simplified version of the model is estimated introducing a dummy for ICT producer industries: [8]

$$S_{i,t} = \alpha_i + \beta_1 \ln\left(\frac{KICT_{i,t}}{Y}\right)d + \beta_2 \ln\left(\frac{KICT_{i,t}}{Y}\right)(1-d) + \beta_3 \ln\left(\frac{KNICT_{i,t}}{Y}\right) + \beta_4 \ln\left(\frac{w_{i,t}^s}{w_{i,t}^l}\right) + \varepsilon_{i,t}$$

where: $d = 1$ for the ICT producer sector, 0 otherwise;

As in the preceding estimation, the hourly relative wage is proxied by time dummies.

In this regression, performed over the whole sectors (36 sectors), the R&D stock variable is not introduced because it is only defined for the manufacturing sector. Had we done so, data on services in the ICT producer sector would not have been taken into account (computer services, telecommunications).

Results (Table 11.10) confirm that the ICT capital stock impact on the college educated wage bill share is higher in ICT producer industries than in other industries.[9] The skill biased technological change is four times as important in ICT producer industries as in other industries.

Table 11.10   College educated wage bill share in the ICT producer sector and in other industries

		1990–2001	1990–95	1996–01
	ln(KICT/Y)	0.03**	0.16**	0.01**
(1)		(0.07)	(0.01)	(0.002)
	ln(KNICT/Y)	-0.05	-0.20**	-0.17**
		(0.014)	(0.02)	(0.001)
	R^2	0.94	0.95	0.99
	N	432	216	216
	ln(KICT/Y)d	0.12**	0.03	0.13**
		(0.025)	(0.06)	(0.02)
	ln(KICT/Y)(1-d)	0.03**	0.17**	0.01**
(2)		(0.007)	(0.01)	(0.002)
	ln(KNICT/Y)	-0.07**	-0.18**	-0.17**
		(0.0129)	(0.02)	(0.01)
	R^2	0.96	0.95	0.99
	N	432	216	216

Notes:
*Heteroskedasticity-consistent standard errors are in parentheses **: significant at 1 per cent level.*
KTIC: ICT real capital stock; KNICT: non ICT equipment real capital stock; Y: real value added. Time dummies are introduced in the regressions.

Source: INSEE, DADS, Labour Force Survey and National Accounts, STAN, CEPII, authors' calculations.

In order to analyse if the magnitude of the technology impact on the college educated wage bill share is the same over time, the impact of ICT is estimated from 1990 to 1995 and from 1996 to 2001. The estimation results (Table 11.10, regression (1)) indicate the capital stock impact on the college educated wage bill share is higher over the 1990–95 than in the 1996–2001 period. Nevertheless, the analysis isolating the ICT producer sector from the other ones tones down this result (regression (2)). Over the 1990–95 period, the ICT capital accumulation involves an increase in the college educated wage bill share in the other industries. In the ICT producer sector, the impact is insignificant. On the contrary, over the 1995–2001 period, the ICT stock impact is much stronger in the ICT producer sector than in other industries.

Estimation by Education Category

The descriptive analysis in the first section shows a large increase in hours worked and in the wage bill share of college educated workers. Over the 1990–2001 period, the annual average growth rate of hours worked by tertiary +4 and tertiary +2 educated workers are respectively 4.1 per cent and 4.04 per cent per year (against 2.2 per cent for workers with a baccalaureate and -1.6 per cent for the other non college educated workers). Their wage bill increased, over 1990–2001, by 6.8 per cent and 7.2 per cent per year respectively (against 3.8 per cent for workers with a baccalaureate and 1.8 per cent for the other non college educated workers). However, between 1990–95 and 1995–2001 a slowdown in the annual average growth rate of the college educated hourly wage is observed whereas the wage bill and the hourly relative wage growth rate of workers with a baccalaureate has strongly increased.

In order to analyse the contribution of technology to changes in the wage bill composition, the wage bill is estimated by education category.

The results by education category (Table 11.11) show a difference between ICT producer and non ICT producer sectors. In the former, the ICT capital stock has a significant and very strong impact on the wage bill share of baccalaureate educated workers. The relationship between the wage bill share and technological change is even higher for this education category than for tertiary +4 workers. On the contrary, in the other industries, the ICT capital stock has a stronger impact on tertiary +2 than on other type of workers.

A complementary explanation to the increase in skilled wage bill share is international trade. In order to estimate the trade impact on skilled wage bill share, imports and exports variables are introduced in the regression.

Table 11.11   Wage bill shares by education category, 1990–2001

	Tertiary +4	Tertiary +2	Bacc.	Low voca- tional	mid- secondary	No diploma
ln(KICT/Y)*d	0.02	0.03**	0.08**	0.005	-0.009	-0.01
	(0.02)	(0.01)	(0.006)	(0.008)	(0.009)	(0.01)
ln(KICT/Y)*(1-d)	0.006**	0.03**	0.01**	-0.002	-0.002**	-0.06**
	(0.0008)	(0.001)	(0.001)	(0.002)	(0.0004)	(0.002)
ln(KNICT/Y)	-0.03**	-0.03**	-0.03**	0.03**	0.01**	0.05**
	(0.006)	(0.004)	(0.003)	(0.004)	(0.002)	(0.005)
R^2	0.90	0.96	0.94	0.99	0.92	0.97
N	432	432	432	432	432	432

Notes:
*Heteroskedasticity-consistent standard errors are in parentheses **: significant at the 1 per cent level, *: significant at the 5 per cent level.*
KICT: ICT real capital stock; KNICT: non ICT equipment real capital stock; Y: real value added. The regression includes a full set of time dummies.

Source: INSEE, DADS, Labour Force Survey and National Accounts, STAN, CEPII, authors' calculations.

Trade Augmented Model

Imports and exports as a share of value added are included separately in the specification (in Table 11.12). Trade variables are extracted from the STAN database (OECD) and are available for the manufacturing industry from 1990 to 2001. Thus, in order to estimate the impact of trade on college educated wage bill share, the analysis is implemented on the manufacturing sector. Then the R&D stock, also available in these industries, is introduced in this estimation.

Results from this model provide little support for the trade explanation for the college educated wage bill share increase. The import and export coefficients are insignificant in all cases.

Table 11.12   International trade and college education wage bill share,
*   1990–2001*

Explanatory variables	
Fixed effects	
ln(RD/Y)	0.04**
	(0.008)
ln(KICT/Y)	0.06**
	(0.009)
ln(KNICT/Y)	-0.12**
	(0.02)
ln(IMP/Yv)	0.02
	(0.01)
ln(EXP/Yv)	0.01
	(0.02)
R^2	0.91
F	93
N	207

Notes:
*Heteroskedasticity-consistent standard errors are in parentheses **: significant at the 1%*
*level, *: significant at the 5% level.*
KTIC: ICT real capital stock; KNICT: non ICT equipment real capital stock; Y: real value
added, RD: R&D stock, Yv: current value added; IMP: imports, EXP: exports. The regression
includes a full set of time dummies.

Source: INSEE, DADS, Labour Force Survey and National Accounts, STAN, CEPII, authors'
calculations.

11.5   CONCLUDING REMARKS

Skill biased technological change has been studied for France, over the
1982–2001 period in the first section and the 1990–2001 period in the second section.

It was first shown that differentiating supply and demand changes across
different categories of labour mattered on account of important composition effects.

Labour quality then exemplifies these trends across labour categories.
Women, younger and better educated workers increase their hours. The labour quality index increases with education but decreases with age and gender over 1995–2001. Younger workers, even if better educated than their
elders, must be trained and acquire experience before their efforts translate
into higher productivity growth. Women take over executive positions more
often but in lesser proportion than men, allowing for wage differences.

Turning to demand favouring the more educated across sectors, the producer sector explains a great deal of demand over the 1995–2001 period. This is confirmed by the shift-share analysis. The much greater 'within' component indicates that the demand for high educated workers has occurred in all sectors and when broken down across sectors, the skilled labour share in the producer sector displays the greatest increase. It is then suspected that ICT is a good candidate to explain the demand shift towards more educated labour. However, this demand shift occurs in sectors already intensive in skilled labour, also suggesting a sector bias of SBTC.

The econometric analysis shows in turn that ICT and the R&D stock impact greatly the relative share of college educated labour. Nevertheless, this impact is stronger on the wage bill of workers holding a baccalaureate in the producer sector and on that of workers holding a Bachelor of Arts equivalent in the other industries over the 1990–2001 period.

Sectorwise, the strong impact of technological change over the 1990–2001 period must be differentiated over time. In ICT producer industries, the impact is very positive over the 1996–2001 period whereas for the other industries it is stronger over 1990–95.

Moreover, the explanation according to which international trade brings about a decrease in the share of unskilled labour does not seem to hold over the nineties. However, allowing for the changing nature of the international trade environment, with growing outsourcing transactions, it would be interesting to add an outsourcing variable to complete the analytical framework.

APPENDIX

Data

Detailed data on employment, hours worked and labour compensation by type come from two sources: the DADS and the labour force surveys. The Déclarations Annuelles de Données Sociales (DADS) is a form filled in by employers that covers 15 million people. Till 1992, one wage-earner out of 25 was included in the sample operated by the INSEE. After 1992, the database is exhaustive. A break in the series occurs in 1993. Hours worked before 1993 have been deduced from the wages duration provided in the DADS. Series for years 1981, 1983 and 1990 that are not available in the DADS have been interpolated and the years 1999 and 2000 extrapolated forward thanks to the labour force surveys.

A second source has been used in order to get skills by education: the labour force surveys that cover households. The poll rate of this survey amounts to 1/300. As wages are not available before 1982, the period under review spans 1982–2001 in that database. The database has been wiped out in order to fit in the same field definition as the DADS. Ratios are calculated on the distribution of total hours and wages on gender, age and degrees relative to total hours and wages summed on gender and age. These ratios are then applied to the DADS. database. We mean to keep the highest consistency by maintaining a common distribution by gender and age (the one of the DADS).

After integrating degrees in the DADS, ratios are calculated on gender, age and degrees by year and then applied to the series of hours worked and labour compensation found in the national accounts in order to remain consistent with the growth accounting framework. The series used are total employment times average hours. For the year 2000, hours worked were estimated with the labour force surveys figures. Underlying this extrapolation is that average hours have decreased by a rate of 3 per cent due to the extension of the 35-hour week in France.

In the final database, we have chosen to separate out three categories: gender, age and degrees. Gender regroups two (men, women), and age gathers four (<25 years old, 25–34, 35–54, >54) characteristics. Age brackets have been set in order to be comparable with the results obtained by Jorgenson in the framework of the KLEMS project.

By integrating degrees in the DADS, we include six extra dimensions: postgraduates (A level + 4 years), university or high vocational degree (A level + 2), A level (high school or vocational), low vocational school degree (CAP, BEP or equivalent), mid-secondary school leaving certificate (BEPC), no degree or almost none (CEP). The quality of labour when calculated with gender, age and degrees entails 48 (2*4*6) categories.

NOTES

1. Chardon Olivier (2001) 'Les transformations de l'emploi non qualifié depuis vingt ans' INSEE Première, n°796, juillet.
2. An extensive literature exists on the gender gap and on the discrimination in women's wages: see for example Baldwin et al. (2001).
3. Here, the total wage bill refers to total compensation and the wage premium is the compensation premium.
4. The industries in the ICT user sector have been identified by calculating the ICT investment intensity in each industry (share of ICT investment in total investment of the industry compared to the share of ICT investment in investment of total economy).
5. The share of hours worked by tertiary +4 and tertiary +2 ('skilled workers') increased from 17 per cent to 28 per cent between 1990 and 2001.
6. The wage bill share of tertiary +4 and tertiary +2 educated workers increased from 26 per cent to 38 per cent between 1990 and 2001.
7. Wage bill will stand for total compensation and wage for the hourly compensation in the rest of the paper.
8. Industries 30, 32 and 64, 71-74 in the ISIC Rev.3 classification.
9. The Fisher test rejects the null hypothesis of coefficients equality at the 1 per cent level.

BIBLIOGRAPHY

Autor, D.H., L.F. Katz and A. B. Krueger (1998), 'Computing Inequality: Have Computers Changed the Labour Market', *Quarterly Journal of Economics*, **13** (4), 1169–1214.

Balwin, M.L., R.J. Butter, W.G. Johnson (2001), 'A Hierarchical Theory of Occupational Segregation and Wage Discrimination', *Economic Inquiry*, **39** (1), pp. 94–110.

Beaudry, P. and D.A. Green (2002), 'Change in the US Wages 1976–2000: Ongoing Skill Bias or Main Technological Change?', *NBER Working Paper*, 8787.

Berman, E., J. Bound and Z. Griliches (1994), 'Changes in the Demand for Skilled Labour within US Manufacturing: Evidence from the Annual Survey of Manufactures', *Quarterly Journal of Economics*, **109** (2), 367–397.

Berman, E., J. Bound and S. Machin (1998), 'Implications of Skill-Biased Technological Change: International Evidence', *Quarterly Journal of Economics*, **113** (4), 1245–1280.

Card, D. (1996), 'The Effects of Unions on the Structure of Wages: a Longitudinal Analysis', *Econometrica*, **64** (4).

Card, D. and J.E. DiNardo (2002), 'Skill Biased Technological Change and Rising Wage Inequality: Some Problems and Puzzles', *NBER Working Paper*, 8769.

Caroli, E. and J. van Reenen (2001), 'Skill Biased Organizational Change? Evidence from a panel of British and French Establishments', *Quarterly Journal of Economics*, **116**, 1449-1492.

Chennels, L. and J. Van Reenen (1999), 'Has Technology Hurt Less Skilled Workers?', *The Institute for Fiscal Studies Working Paper*, 99/27.

Chun, H. (2003), 'Information Technology and the Demand for Educated Workers: Disentangling the Impacts of Adoption Versus Use', *The Review of Economics and Statistics*, **85** (1).

DiNardo, J.E., N. Fortin and T. Lemieux (1996), 'Labor Market Institutions and the Distribution of Wages, 1973–1992: A Semi-Parametric Approach', *Econometrica*, **64** (5).

Dunne, T., L. Foster, J. Haltiwanger and K. Troske (2000), 'Wage and Productivity Dispersion in US Manufacturing: the Role of Computer Investment', *NBER Working Paper*, 7465.

Feenstra, R.C. and G.H. Hanson (2001), 'Global Production Sharing and Rising Inequality: a Survey of Trade and Wages', *NBER Working Paper*, 8372.

Goux, D. and E. Maurin (2000), 'The Decline in Demand for Unskilled Labour: An Empirical Analysis Method and its Application to France', *The Review of Economics and Statistics*, **82** (4), 596–607.

Green, F., A. Felstcad and D. Gallie (2000), 'Computers Are Even More Important Than You Thought: An Analysis of The Changing Skill-Intensity of Jobs', *Centre for Economic Performance, Discussion Paper*, 439.

Greenan, N., J. Mairesse and A. Topiol-Bensaid (2001), 'Information Technology and Research and Development Impacts in Productivity and Skills: Looking for Correlations on French Firm Level Data', *NBER Working Paper*, 8075.

Haskel, J.E., and Heden, Y., (1999), 'Computers and the Demand for Skilled Labour: Industry and Establishment Panel Evidence for the UK', *Economic Journal*, Volume 109, No 454, pp. C68-C79

Haskel, J.E. and M.J. Slaughter (2002), 'Does the Sector Bias of Skill-Biased Technical Change Explain Changing Skill Premia?', *European Economic Review*, **46**, 1757–1783.

Ho, M.S. and D.W. Jorgenson (1999), 'The Quality of the US Work Force, 1948–95', mimeo, Harvard University.

Jorgenson, D.W., F.M. Gollop and B. Fraumeni (1987), *Productivity and US Economic Growth*, Contributions to Economic Analysis, Elsevier, North Holland.

Katz, Lawrence F & Murphy, Kevin M, 1992. "Changes in Relative Wages, 1963-1987: Supply and Demand Factors," *The Quarterly Journal of Economics*, MIT Press, vol. 107(1), pages 35–78, February.

Machin, S. and J. Van Reenen (1998), 'Technology and Changes in Skill Structure: Evidence from Seven OECD Countries', *Quarterly Journal of Economics*, **113** (4), 1215–1244.

Melka, J., L. Nayman, S. Zignago and N. Mulder (2003), 'Skills, Technology and Growth,: Is ICT the Key to Success? Part I: An Analysis of ICT Impact on French Growth', *CEPII Working Paper*, 4.

OECD, 'Education at a glance', www.oecd.org.

OECD, 'Employment Outlook', www.oecd.org.

O'Mahony, M., C. Robinson and M. Vecchi (2003), 'The Impact of ICT on the Demand for Skilled Labour: a Cross-Country Comparison', mimeo.

Piva, M., E. Santarelli and M. Vivarelli (2003), 'The Skill Bias Effect of Technological and Organisational Change: Evidence and Policy Implications', *ZA Discussion Paper*, 934.

Savvidou, E. (2003), 'The Relationship between Skilled Labor and Technical Change', mimeo.

Sorrentino, C. and J. Moy (2002), 'US Labor Market Performance in International Perspective', *Monthly Labor Review*, **125**.

Wood, A. (1995), 'How Trade Hurt Unskilled Workers?', *The Journal of Economic Perspectives*, **9** (3), 57–80.

Index